Letters and Lives of the Tennyson Women

Letters and Lives of the Tennyson Women

Marion Sherwood and Rosalind Boyce

BLOOMSBURY ACADEMIC
LONDON • NEW YORK • OXFORD • NEW DELHI • SYDNEY

BLOOMSBURY ACADEMIC
Bloomsbury Publishing Plc, 50 Bedford Square, London, WC1B 3DP, UK
Bloomsbury Publishing Inc, 1385 Broadway, New York, NY 10018, USA
Bloomsbury Publishing Ireland, 29 Earlsfort Terrace, Dublin 2, D02 AY28, Ireland

BLOOMSBURY, BLOOMSBURY ACADEMIC and the Diana logo are trademarks of
Bloomsbury Publishing Plc

First published in Great Britain 2023
Paperback edition published 2025

Copyright © Marion Sherwood and Rosalind Boyce, 2023, 2025

Marion Sherwood and Rosalind Boyce have asserted their right under the Copyright,
Designs and Patents Act, 1988, to be identified as Authors of this work.

For legal purposes the Acknowledgements on p. xiii constitute an extension
of this copyright page.

Cover image: Top left: Mary Turner Tennyson (1753–1825). Top right: Frances Mary Hutton
Tennyson (1787–1878) (Mary Turner Tennyson's daughter-in-law.) Bottom right: Elizabeth
Tennyson Russell (1776–1865) (Mary Turner Tennyson's elder daughter). Bottom left: Mary
Tennyson Bourne (1777–1864) (Mary Turner Tennyson's younger daughter). Photos courtesy
of the Tennyson d'Eyncourt family, copyright of Frances Tennyson d'Eyncourt.

All rights reserved. No part of this publication may be: i) reproduced or transmitted in any form,
electronic or mechanical, including photocopying, recording or by means of any information storage
or retrieval system without prior permission in writing from the publishers; or ii) used or reproduced
in any way for the training, development or operation of artificial intelligence (AI) technologies,
including generative AI technologies. The rights holders expressly reserve this publication from the
text and data mining exception as per Article 4(3) of the Digital Single Market Directive (EU) 2019/790.

Bloomsbury Publishing Plc does not have any control over, or responsibility for, any
third-party websites referred to or in this book. All internet addresses given in this
book were correct at the time of going to press. The author and publisher regret any
inconvenience caused if addresses have changed or sites have ceased to exist, but can
accept no responsibility for any such changes.

A catalogue record for this book is available from the British Library.

A catalog record for this book is available from the Library of Congress.

Library of Congress Cataloging-in-Publication Data

Names: Sherwood, Marion, author. | Boyce, Rosalind, author.
Title: Letters and lives of the Tennyson women / Marion Sherwood and Rosalind Boyce.
Description: London ; New York, NY : Bloomsbury Academic, 2023. |
Includes bibliographical references and index. | Summary: "Contradicting common perception of them as
mere footnotes in Tennyson's career, this book examines the influence of his strong-minded female forebears
on the young poet and reveals that the women in Tennyson's family circle were prolific and engaging correspondents.
Their letters, preserved in archives in Lincoln and for the most part unpublished, cast a unique light on the Tennyson family's
interrelationships and the times in which they lived. Focusing on the letters and lives of four Tennyson women - the poet's
paternal grandmother, Mary Tennyson (1753–1825), her daughters Elizabeth Russell (1776–1865) and Mary Bourne
(1777–1864), and her daughter-in-law Frances Tennyson, later Tennyson d'Eyncourt (1787–1878) - this book includes
extensive and annotated extracts from the women's letters, linked by narrative passages providing context
and continuity. The case studies cover six decades, from the marriage of Mary Turner and George Tennyson in 1775 to
the death of George Tennyson in 1835, with brief Afterwords touching on the women's final years"– Provided by publisher.
Identifiers: LCCN 2022031268 | ISBN 9781350360563 (paperback) |
ISBN 9781350168244 (hardback) | ISBN 9781350168251 (ebook) |
ISBN 9781350168268 (epub) | ISBN 9781350168275
Subjects: LCSH: Tennyson, Alfred Tennyson, Baron, 1809–1892–Correspondence. |
Tennyson, Alfred Tennyson, Baron, 1809–1892–Family. | Poets,
English–19th century–Family relationships. | LCGFT: Personal correspondence.
Classification: LCC PR5581 .A4 2023 | DDC 821/.8 [B]–dc23/eng/20220926
LC record available at https://lccn.loc.gov/2022031268

ISBN: HB: 978-1-3501-6824-4
PB: 978-1-3503-6056-3
ePDF: 978-1-3501-6825-1
eBook: 978-1-3501-6826-8

Typeset by Newgen KnowledgeWorks Pvt. Ltd., Chennai, India

For product safety related questions contact productsafety@bloomsbury.com.

To find out more about our authors and books visit www.bloomsbury.com
and sign up for our newsletters.

Contents

List of Figures	vi
Timeline	vii
Tennyson Family Tree	xii
Acknowledgements	xiii
Preface	xiv
Introduction: Touching the past	1
1 'When I receive your letters I feel that inward Joy unspeakable': Mary Turner Tennyson's letters to her mother, 1775 to 1804	13
2 'The tenderest and best of Husbands': Mary Turner Tennyson and George Tennyson, 1775 to 1825	47
3 'Star of the North': Elizabeth Tennyson Russell, 1776 to 1865	75
4 Mother and sons: Mary Turner Tennyson, George Clayton Tennyson and Charles Tennyson, 1778 to 1825	113
5 'A delicate, pretty girl': Frances Mary Hutton Tennyson, 1787 to 1878	139
6 'Your truly affectionate Old Aunt Bourne': Mary Tennyson Bourne, 1777 to 1864	171
Conclusion: 'The noble letters of the dead'	207
Bibliography	211
Index	221

Figures

1	Mary Turner Tennyson to Mary Turner [28.08.1775 Tenn 2/5/18]	15
2	Mary Turner Tennyson to George Tennyson [February 1804 TdE/H/62/2]	56
3A/3B	Elizabeth Tennyson Russell to Charles Tennyson [August/September 1825 4TdE/H/33L]	107
4	Frances Mary Hutton Tennyson to Mary Hutton [15.09.1814 4TdE/H/6/59]	158
5	Mary Tennyson Bourne to Sarah Cooper [13.06.1816 4TdE/H/55/35]	188

Timeline

1750	George Tennyson born in Hedon, son of Elizabeth, née Clayton, and Michael Tennyson
	Early education at Betsey Dales's Dame School; meets lifelong friend William Gray
1753	Mary Turner born in Caistor, daughter of Mary, née Davis, and John Turner
1754	George's sister, Ann Tennyson, born in Hedon
1755	Elizabeth Clayton Tennyson dies
c. 1770	George apprenticed to William Iveson at Hedon
1773	George admitted as an attorney
1774	George sets up law practice in Market Rasen
1775	Mary Turner and George Tennyson marry at Caistor Parish Church on 22 June; move to Queen Street, Market Rasen
1776	Mary and George's daughter Elizabeth baptized at Market Rasen on 18 April
1777	Mary and George's daughter Mary (young Mary) baptized at Market Rasen on 4 May
1778	Mary and George's son George Clayton baptized at Market Rasen on 10 December
1778/79	Young Mary to maternal grandmother, Mary Turner, in Caistor
1779	Tennysons move to King Street, Market Rasen, in May
1780	Young Mary to remain with maternal grandmother in Caistor
1783	George Clayton with paternal grandfather in Hedon
	George buys half of Beacons Manor estate at Tealby
1784	John Turner, senior, Mary's father, buried at Caistor on 13 April
	Mary and George's son Charles baptized at Market Rasen on 20 July
1787	George Clayton to St Peter's School, York, in June
	Frances Mary Hutton born on 22 September
	George buys remaining half of Beacons Manor estate at Tealby
1788	Elizabeth at boarding school by January
	Young Mary taken back to Market Rasen from Caistor in April; joins Elizabeth at school
	George's sister, Ann Tennyson, marries William Raines

1789	Frances's father, John Hutton, dies
1793	Charles joins George Clayton at St Peter's School, York
	Tennysons living at Deloraine Court, Lincoln
1796	Michael Tennyson dies in Hedon on 6 October
	George Clayton to St John's College, Cambridge, on 8 October
1798	Elizabeth marries Matthew Russell at Church of St Mary Magdalene, Lincoln, on 23 January
	Tennysons move to Clayton House, Grimsby, in May
	Elizabeth and Matthew's son William born on 9 November; baptized at York on 10 November
	Charles moves to Louth Grammar School
c. 1798	Mary and George's brother-in-law, William Raines, dies
c. 1800	George's portrait painted by Thomas Lawrence
1801	John Bourne marries Mary Mather at Dalby on 16 March
	George Clayton ordained deacon in May
	Charles to St John's College, Cambridge, on 6 July
	Tennysons move to Tealby Lodge, Tealby; later renamed Bayons Manor
1802	Matthew Russell becomes MP for Saltash – until February 1807
	John and Mary Mather Bourne's daughter, Mary, baptized on 30 August
	George Clayton ordained priest on 19 December
1803	Young Mary living with maternal grandmother, Mary Turner, by April
	Mary Mather Bourne dies; buried at Dalby on 24 May
1804	Mary Turner dies; buried at Caistor on 24 February
1805	Mary Turner Tennyson's portrait painted by John Russell, RA
	George Clayton marries Elizabeth (Eliza) Fytche at Louth in August
1806	George Clayton and Eliza's son George born; dies in infancy
	George Clayton inducted to Somersby and Bag Enderby in December
1807	George Clayton and Eliza's son Frederick born
1808	Charles marries Frances Mary Hutton at Gainsborough on 1 January
	Matthew Russell MP for Saltash – 26 February until death
	George Clayton and Eliza's son Charles baptized on 23 August
1809	Elizabeth and Matthew's daughter Emma Maria born on 8 March; baptized on 1 April
	Frances and Charles move to Caenby Hall in June
	Frances and Charles's son George Hildyard born on 10 July
	Alfred Tennyson born at Somersby on 6 August

Timeline

1810	Frances and Charles's daughter Julia Frances born on 13 October
	Matthew's visit to London in December
	George Clayton and Eliza's daughter Mary born
1811	Arthur Henry Hallam born in London on 1 February
	Prince of Wales appointed Prince Regent on 5 February
	Young Mary marries John Bourne at All Saints Church, Tealby, on 13 August
	George Clayton and Eliza's daughter Emilia born
1812	Frances and Charles's daughter Clara Maria born on 27 June
	John Turner, junior, Mary's brother, dies on 12 November
1813	Frances and Charles's son Edwin Clayton born on 4 July
	George Clayton and Eliza's son Edward born
1814	Frances and Charles move to London
	Frances and Charles's son Louis Charles born on 23 July
	Frances's mother, Mary Hutton, dies on 22 October
	George Clayton and Eliza's son Arthur born
	George's sister, Ann Raines, dies
1815	George Clayton and Eliza's son Septimus born
	Mary and John Bourne foster 'little Hugh'
1816	Frances and Charles's son Eustace Alexander born on 24 March
	Mary and George's niece, Elizabeth Raines, marries George Inman on 1 May
	George Clayton and Eliza's daughter Matilda born
1817	William Russell, senior, Matthew's father, dies; buried at St Brandon's Church, Brancepeth, on 13 June
	Frances and Charles's daughter Ellen Elizabeth born on 17 July
	George Clayton and Eliza's daughter Cecilia born
1818	Charles elected MP for Great Grimsby
1819	Matthew's stepmother, Anne Russell, dies at Brancepeth on 19 May
	Frances and Charles move from Lincoln's Inn Fields to Park Street, Westminster
	Frances and Charles's son William Henry born on 29 August; dies in early September
	George Clayton and Eliza's son Horatio born
1820	George III dies on 29 January; at subsequent election, Charles re-elected as MP for Great Grimsby
1821	Coronation of George IV on 19 July

1822	Matthew dies on 8 May; buried at St Brandon's Church, Brancepeth, on 23 May
	In August, Elizabeth begins an equity suit at the Court of Chancery to challenge the executors of Matthew's will
1825	Mary Turner Tennyson dies on 20 August; buried in family vault at All Saints Church, Tealby, on 31 August
	Dr Gooch recommends continuing separation for Frances and Charles
1826	Charles becomes MP for Bletchingley
1827	*Poems, by Two Brothers* published anonymously in April; includes 'And ask ye why these sad tears stream', Alfred Tennyson's elegy for his grandmother
	Alfred joins Frederick and Charles at Cambridge in November
1828	Emma Maria marries Gustavus Frederick Hamilton on 9 September
1830	George IV dies on 26 June
	Charles appointed Clerk to the Ordnance on 13 December
1831	George Clayton dies on 16 March; buried at Somersby on 22 March
	Coronation of William IV on 8 September
1833	Arthur Henry Hallam dies in Vienna on 15 September
1834	Arthur Henry Hallam buried at St Andrew's Church, Clevedon, on 3 January
1835	George Tennyson dies at Usselby on 9 July; buried in family vault at All Saints Church, Tealby, on 13 July
	Charles (by Royal Licence) changes name to Tennyson d'Eyncourt on 31 July
1837	Tennysons leave Somersby for High Beech in Epping Forest
	William IV dies on 20 June
1838	Coronation of Queen Victoria on 28 June
1841	Mary and John Bourne's home, Dalby Hall, destroyed by fire in January
1850	*In Memoriam A.H.H.* published anonymously by Moxon on 1 June
	Alfred Tennyson and Emily Sellwood married at Shiplake on 13 June
	Alfred Tennyson invested as Poet Laureate on 19 November
	John Bourne dies in Cleethorpes on 15 December
1852	Charles retires after twenty years as MP for Lambeth
1861	Charles dies in London on 21 July; buried in family vault at All Saints Church, Tealby
1864	Mary dies in Dalby; buried at St Lawrence's Church, Dalby, on 2 May
1865	Elizabeth dies in Cheltenham on 30 September
1878	Frances dies in London on 26 January; buried in family vault at All Saints Church, Tealby

1884	Alfred Tennyson takes his seat in the House of Lords as Baron Tennyson of Aldworth and Freshwater on 11 March
1892	Alfred Tennyson dies at Aldworth on 6 October; buried at Westminster Abbey on 12 October
1896	Emily Tennyson dies at Aldworth on 10 August; buried at Freshwater Church
1897	Hallam Tennyson's *Memoir* published

Tennyson Family Tree

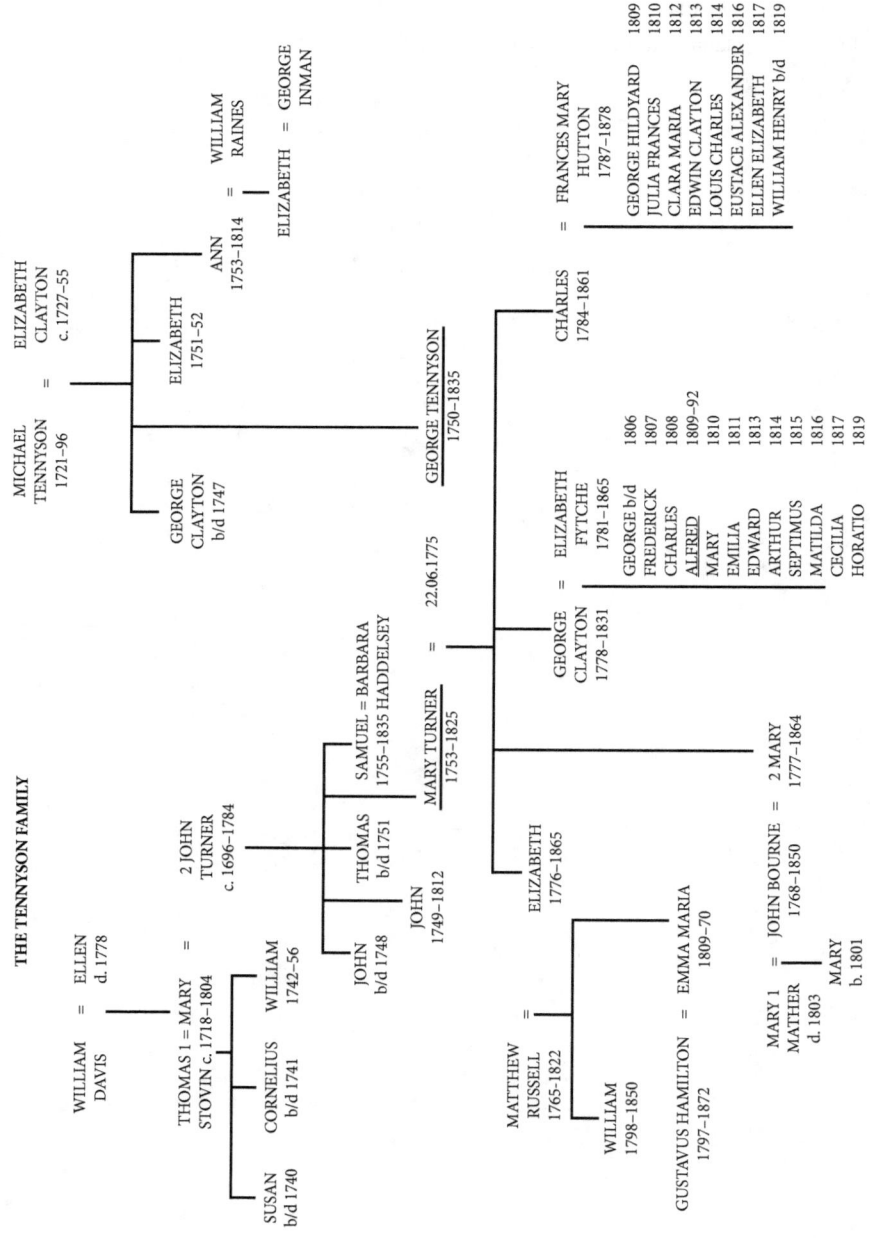

Acknowledgements

Grateful thanks to Mark Tennyson d'Eyncourt for permission to publish the Tennyson family letters and to Frances Tennyson d'Eyncourt for photographs of family portraits.

Despite Covid closures and restrictions, staff at the British Library, Durham County Record Office, Lincolnshire Archives and the National Archives did their best to provide copies, documents, information and photographs. Thank you.

Thanks to Garry Crossland and Vivienne Lowe, who provided background information on the Grimsby Haven Company and the Russells of Brancepeth.

Marion Shaw's reading of draft chapters was invaluable and is greatly appreciated.

Thanks to Susan Donovan Ibrahim and Claire Jones for help and encouragement.

Appreciative thanks to Ben Doyle and colleagues at Bloomsbury for bringing the letters and lives of the Tennyson women to a wider public.

Preface

Rosalind Boyce

When he retired in the early 1990s, my late husband, Douglas Boyce, an enthusiastic local historian, became aware that in Lincolnshire Archives was a collection of about a thousand letters relating to the forebears of Alfred Tennyson and their families.

Douglas spent the next ten years transcribing these letters. He became increasingly involved with the life and times of the Tennyson family and believed that their letters were of sufficient interest to merit publication. After his death in October 2002, I looked through this huge volume of research papers and realized they should not be abandoned. Publication would fulfil Douglas's wish and be a memorial to him.

The project was held in abeyance for several years. In 2015, I joined forces with Marion Sherwood who, with her knowledge and experience, was able to guide the project to completion. Thirty years since Douglas first discovered the collection, *Letters and Lives of the Tennyson Women* has come into being.

Introduction: Touching the past

Marion Sherwood

The four women whose letters and lives are the subject of this study are Alfred Tennyson's Lincolnshire forebears – Mary, his 'Grandmamma Tennyson',[1] her daughters Elizabeth and Mary and her daughter-in-law Frances. They were an inseparable part of the young poet's life until he left for Cambridge in November 1827 at the age of eighteen and, as his friend Benjamin Jowett later confirmed,[2] 'the persons and incidents of his childhood' remained 'very vivid to him'.[3] The woman who remained most 'vivid to him', evoking powerful feelings and clear images in the poet's mind throughout his life, was his mother, Elizabeth Tennyson, née Fytche (1781–1865), known as Eliza – 'one of the most angelick natures on God's earth'.[4] But Eliza's life and letters have been examined in detail by many Tennyson biographers, and she is not included in this study.

With the publication of his early volumes, particularly *Poems* (1842), which established him as 'the foremost poet of his generation',[5] Alfred Tennyson, like *Ulysses*, became 'a name'.[6] By birth or marriage the four women shared his surname, but they have been overshadowed by their famous relative. Until Ann Thwaite published her ground-breaking biography, *Emily Tennyson: The Poet's Wife* (1996), biographers focused on the Tennyson men: the women were disregarded, dismissed as 'more than usually submissive',[7] or caricatured. Fortunately, however, the women were prolific and engaging correspondents; many of their letters survive, although few have been published. Reading, in memory, Arthur Hallam's letter, the poet was 'touched' by the spirit of his friend and inspiration – in a typically Tennysonian image: 'So word by word, and line by line, | The dead man touched me from the past, | And all at once it seemed at last | The living soul was flashed on mine'.[8] Today we can be in touch with the dead women, albeit more slowly, by reading – and being emotionally touched by – their 'silent-speaking words'.[9]

Mary Turner Tennyson (1753–1825):[10] The poet's paternal grandmother is particularly important to this study, the first book-length study of the Tennyson women. Throughout her fifty-year marriage Mary wrote innumerable letters to several generations of her large family. She had an acutely observant eye and through the immediacy of her writing we are directly in touch with their daily lives and developing relationships and catch an occasional glimpse of the changing times through which they lived.

Mary was married to George Tennyson (1750–1835), known to Alfred and his siblings throughout their lives as 'The Old Man of the Wolds'. As a wife in the patriarchal Georgian era, Mary was subject to her husband's decisions and disposition. George's decisions affected more than his immediate family. Paternal preference for his younger son continued into the next generation, with the Caenby Hall children of Charles and Frances favoured over the Somersby Rectory children of George Clayton and Eliza. Decisions made by George on the premature death of George Clayton in 1831, and the legacy of his own death four years later, created 'The myth of the Tennyson disinheritance'.[11] Succeeding generations were also affected by the 'Tennyson black blood' (perhaps more correctly 'a Clayton characteristic')[12] – a predisposition to depression, irascibility and, in males, to epilepsy, fear of which delayed for years Alfred's marriage to Emily Sellwood. In Mary and George's daughters, these characteristics lessened to 'nervous excitability'[13] and a tendency to say things they later regretted.

Mary was twenty-two in June 1775 when she married George, an ambitious lawyer of twenty-five, and they set up home in Market Rasen. George's profession defined his social status, placing the Tennysons firmly in the 'growing ranks of the genteel and middling'.[14] Mary and George's eventually close relationship took some years to develop; in the unsettled early years Mary's confidante was her mother, Mary Turner. Mary began writing to her mother soon after the wedding and the vividly informative, often anxious letters form the surviving half of a correspondence that lasted for nearly thirty years. In 1778 she wrote movingly of the 'inward joy unspeakable' [10.03.1778 Tenn 2/1/15] she derived from her mother's letters.

Unlike many contemporaries Mary and George had only four children, all of whom survived into adulthood. Elizabeth, the poet's favourite 'Aunt Russell', was born in April 1776. Young Mary, the future 'Aunt Bourne', was baptized a year later. George Clayton, the poet's father, was born in December 1778. Young Mary and George Clayton spent much of their childhood with grandparents, young Mary in Caistor and George Clayton in Yorkshire. Elizabeth remained at home until she went to boarding school, and the resulting close relationship with her parents was strengthened by her childhood ill health, which was 'entirely nervous' in origin [24.03.1789 Tenn 2/5/47].

Three pregnancies and births, followed by a miscarriage, undermined Mary's health and in December 1783 she was initially distressed to become pregnant again. Mary and George's fourth and last child, Charles, the poet's uncle, was born in July 1784. Charles, like Elizabeth, remained at home until his schooldays and 'endear'd' himself to both parents 'by the strongest tyes' [09.04.[1801] TdE/H/60/1].[15]

In the 1790s Mary and George moved to Lincoln, later to Clayton House in Grimsby, which George inherited from a Clayton uncle and symbolized his increasing prosperity and contentious bequests. As the children grew up, moved away and married, Mary tried through her letters to connect and advise her increasing and sometimes fractious family. In January 1798 Elizabeth married the wealthy Matthew Russell (1765–1822) and ten months later gave birth to William, the first Tennyson grandchild.

Mary Turner was with the family at Elizabeth's wedding. But her health deteriorated, and she died in February 1804. Confined to Caistor by bad weather after the burial, Mary wrote of her 'severe disappointment' at being separated from George: 'my treasure on earth I consider very great – so long as the lives of my dear family are preserved & in health' [25.02.1804 TdE/H/62/3].

Maturity and faith allowed Mary to accept her mother's death and acknowledge 'my dear family' as her 'treasure on earth'. Mary's earthly treasure increased. George Clayton married in 1805, Charles three years later, and when Mary died in 1825 there were twenty surviving Tennyson grandchildren. Alfred, just turned sixteen, marked her passing with an elegy – 'And ask ye why these sad tears stream'.

Elizabeth Tennyson Russell (1776–1865): Elizabeth was Mary and George's first child and favourite daughter. In her early years she was called Bessy or Bess, and Mary's letters make clear the empathetic bond that developed between mother and child. As an adult, known as Eliza and married to Matthew Russell, she became her nephew Alfred's favourite aunt: 'My dearest Aunt (or if you will allow me to call you by a name that pleases me as well) My dearest Azile'.[16]

Biographers describe Elizabeth as 'the most charming' of the Tennyson children.[17] Charm is clearly apparent in her later letters, but her earliest surviving letter, written to Mary Turner in September 1797, is self-satisfied and occasionally waspish: 'we have no news stirring which will entertain you or be worth penning I am ashamed to send this scrawl but a bad Letter is better than none' [22.09.1797 Tenn 2/1/31].

After their marriage the Russells moved between Hardwick Hall and Brancepeth Castle in County Durham. Their social round was on a grand scale and Mary feared 'these everlasting parties' [01.06.1799 TRC 4682] would affect Elizabeth's health. Eleven years after William's birth, Elizabeth endured a difficult second pregnancy. Mary remained with her until Emma Maria was born in March 1809.

George Clayton marked Elizabeth's marriage with *Verses Addressed to a Lady on Her Departure*: 'Star of the North farewell – thy ray | Shall happier skies illumine'.[18] But with the 'overpowering excitability of [her] nervous system' [13.07.1821 TdE/H/86/4], Elizabeth shared an element of the Tennyson 'black blood'. Her relationship with George Clayton deteriorated, and she did not attend his funeral.

Elizabeth remained close to Charles. Her devotion and the developing gift for language she shared with her mother and sister are reflected in the moving letter sent to Charles and Frances on the death in 1819 of their eighth and last child:

> I did weep, my ever dear Charles ... There is something in the death and burial of an infant which touches the tenderest chord in our hearts, especially when it has belonged to those who are inexpressibly dear to us.[19]

In May 1822 Elizabeth was suddenly widowed. Her 'mental sufferings' and 'grief of Heart' [02.03.1823 TdE/H/90/6] suggest that she was happy in her marriage and may explain the legal action that biographers appear to have overlooked. Three months after Matthew's death she applied to the Chancery Court to challenge his executors, the most active of whom was her 'most beloved' Charles.[20]

Litigation did not affect her relationship with Charles. After their mother's death in 1825 she wrote in renewed distress:

> I need not tell you my most beloved of brothers what are my feelings. ... Thank you, my dearest Charles, for your beautiful descriptions of her last hours, they are, & will always be my first treasures. [August/September 1825 4TdE/H/33L]

Alfred's elegy for Mary was published anonymously in *Poems, by Two Brothers* in April 1827. A volume by unknown young poets was unlikely to cover its costs and Elizabeth may have paid for the publication. Seven months later Alfred followed his brothers to Cambridge, intending to stay 'until the 100£ you kindly promised him is exhausted' [23/11/1827 TdE/H/148/12]. Elizabeth's generous gift, worth more than £10,000 today, became an annual allowance that continued into Alfred's Laureateship.²¹ His affection is clearly apparent after Elizabeth's 'terrible fall' in May 1856:

> I now write to ask whether you *are* going on well … pray, dearest Aunt, let me know, for though I write seldom I have not the less affection for you, do not the less joy in your joy, and grieve with your grief … Ever yours affectionately A. Tennyson.²²

Throughout her widowhood Elizabeth continued the 'locomotion' she recommended 'for spirits like ours when depressed' [[28.07.1825] TdE/H/144/182]. She died in Cheltenham on 30 September 1865 in her ninetieth year.

Mary Tennyson Bourne (1777–1864): Mary was the Tennysons' younger, less favoured daughter. Unlike Elizabeth, who married young and immediately became pregnant, Mary married at thirty-four and had no children of her own. As her faith deepened with time, she moved from Anglicanism to Nonconformism. And from the late nineteenth century Mary has been harshly treated by Tennyson biographers, who continue to define her as 'a gloomy, pessimistic Calvinist'.²³

Before she turned three, Mary was living with her maternal grandmother, Mary Turner. Four years later, as her mother noted, 'her Attachment to you is certainly very great' [21.09.1784 Tenn 2/7/18]. She remained in Caistor until 1788, when George 'wishe[d] her to know and be Attach'd to home … before she goes to school' [08.01.1788 Tenn 2/1/29]. Mary was taken back to Market Rasen just before her eleventh birthday.

Mary did not become 'Attach'd to home'. On leaving school she began to travel and by 1794 her mother 'long[ed] to know where she has taken up her residence' [27.04.1794 4TdE/H/2/7]. She returned to Caistor in April 1803, when her grandmother's health deteriorated, and remained with Mary Turner until her death.

Mary's earliest surviving letters date from 1805. George Clayton and Eliza Fytche married in August, and Mary describes with vivid humour a wedding where 'trouble was nothing, expense was all'. She gives a touching early glimpse of Eliza, who in 1809 would give birth to Alfred: 'Eliza is really a sweet tempered creature and the very woman for George' [[August 1805] TRC 5052].

On 13 August 1811 Mary married John Bourne (1768–1850), a widower and 'dissenting squire'.²⁴ For the Somersby siblings until they left Lincolnshire, the Dalby home of 'Aunt Bourne' became 'the *second home* of their childhood'.²⁵

Biographers believe the marriage was 'held together by their shared faith',[26] but the Bournes' letters confirm their mutual love and understanding and the marriage lasted until John's death.

Although the Bournes had no children, their lives were not childless. They had frequent contact with many nephews and nieces, and Mary's unpublished letters reveal that she fostered an unwanted, possibly illegitimate, young boy called Hugh. Her wish for 'the Child [to] go to the <u>Chapel</u> instead of the Church I do not wish him ever to be a Church Bigot' [26.08.1815 4TdE/H/55/33] implies that 'Church Bigot[ry]' towards young Hugh impelled Mary to her husband's faith.

From 1818 Mary's health deteriorated. Biographers accuse her of hypochondria,[27] but family correspondence provides evidence of frequent illness. Her affectionate letter to Frances and Charles's young son, George Hildyard, confirms that despite ill health she enjoyed children's company: 'we have much pleasure at the thought of receiving you soon at the Sea & of giving you a good ducking ... Your truly affec^{te} Old Aunt Bourne' [20.06.[1819] TdE/H/146/5].

Mary's sensitivity to others' suffering and her firm and sustaining faith are reflected in her moving letter to Charles after their mother's death:

> My own sorrows do not abate my sympathies for those I love & my dear Father especially ... but I am sustained by the Joyful & <u>Scriptural</u> persuasion that our dear departed parent is now one among the thousands spoken of in Revelation. [23.09.1825 TdE/H/33e]

Mary was devoted to Charles, but she had a particular affinity with George Clayton, who spent much of his childhood with his paternal grandfather. During his final illness in March 1831, Mary was a constant visitor to Somersby, and she was 'visibly affected' by his funeral.[28]

After her mother's death, Mary became distanced from her father. With her independent spirit and the 'nervous excitability' she shared with Elizabeth, perhaps Mary, like her sister, regretted a remark 'she was carried away to say'.[29] After John's death she continued to travel and was buried in Dalby on 2 May 1864 aged eighty-seven. Alfred regretted that Mary had become 'hidden from me ... since we left Lincolnshire' and, after the event, believed he 'ought to have gone' to her funeral.[30]

Frances Mary Hutton Tennyson (1787–1878): Frances was known to the family by the diminutive, Fanny. Born at Morton Hall near Gainsborough on 22 September 1787, she was the only child of Mary and the Reverend John Hutton, who died when she was two.

Frances and Charles had a protracted courtship. At sixteen, Frances had formed an unsuitable attachment. Apparent female impropriety could jeopardize the negotiation of a marriage contract and George insisted that 'the Lady's temper, conduct and character' [25.05.1807 TRC 4658] were scrutinized. When the marriage was approved, Frances wrote to Mary expressing 'my grateful sense of that attention and goodness I experienced both from you and Mr Tennyson' [22.10.1807 TdE/H/144/65].

Frances and Charles were married on New Year's Day 1808. They moved into Caenby Hall in June 1809 and two months later, on 6 August, Frances became the aunt by marriage of the future Poet Laureate. In the first ten years of her marriage, which lasted fifty-three years, she gave birth to eight children, seven of whom survived. Today we can touch the lives of the Tennyson women through the indirect legacy of their son, Louis Charles, whose descendant placed the Tennyson family papers in county archives.

Charles inherited his father's ambition. He travelled often to London, initially to his law practice and from 1818 as MP for Great Grimsby. Frances wrote to him regularly. As an only child, without the inspiration of imaginative siblings, she did not develop the Tennyson sisters' gift for language, but her letters come alive when she writes of her children. In 1812 she mentioned George Hildyard, soon to turn three:

> On the night you left Caenby, he ingratiated himself in a wonderful manner into your father's and Mother's good opinion by his innocent but as your father termed it 'noble conversation'. [12.05.1812 TdE/H/154/5]

Frances was a Tennyson woman by marriage, not birth, and viewed family relationships in a new light. She saw George Clayton's sons (Frederick, Charles and Alfred) as '3 fine Lads – who behaved themselves all the time with decorum' [14.09.1812 4TdE/H/6/25]. Her mother-in-law feared their roughness towards Charles's children, whom she and George favoured. After George's death, Frances maintained that Alfred 'was quite incapable of the remarks attributed to him'.[31]

The poet's grandson dismissed young Frances as 'a pretty, lively girl' of limited intelligence.[32] Her letters confirm, however, that with her mother's support in the early years of marriage, Frances became the confident manager of a wealthy political household. After her mother's death, Frances, Charles and the five children moved to London, where three further children were born. Frances was a small woman, for whom childbirth was 'tedious and suffering'. An obstetrician advised Charles in 1825 that physical 'separation must continue', as future childbearing would be 'attended by danger' [01.10.1825 TdE/H/33/(25)].

Separation perhaps became more than physical: by December 1825 Frances needed money: 'I have calculated my bills and fear I cannot do with less than a hundred pounds' [09.12.[?1825] TRC 4646].[33]

In 1801 Mary and George had moved from Clayton House in Grimsby to Tealby Lodge, later renamed Bayons Manor. After George's death, Charles (by Royal Licence) added d'Eyncourt to his surname and transformed Bayons into a mock-medieval castle – in the Laureate's lines: 'Seeing his gewgaw castle shine, | New as his title, built last year'.[34] Frances retained her impartial perspective. When Alfred and Emily visited Bayons in 1857 she showed them the house and 'seemed very friendly'.[35] Charles died in July 1861 aged seventy-seven. Frances outlived him by seventeen years and died in London aged ninety on 26 January 1878. Six years later Alfred was elevated to the peerage and acquired a new title. On 11 March 1884 he was introduced to the House of Lords as Baron Tennyson of Aldworth and Freshwater.[36]

Frances was born into a wealthy family, but on marriage her 'considerable fortune'[37] went to Charles. The Tennyson women lived 'under the conditions of coverture', which made a husband and wife one under law and gave husbands financial and legal control over their wives.[38] The Tennyson men are therefore also important to this study, and their letters are included when they reveal relevant information. Biographers note that after George Clayton's death the Somersby children's future was planned by Charles and George.[39] Writing to Mary from Tealby, John Bourne makes clear his own involvement: 'The Somersby concerns are always uppermost in your Fathers mind they are a little complicated, & I have been arranging them all' [[1831–2] 4TdE/H/42[35]]. Few of the family letters refer so precisely to contemporary 'concerns' and narrative has been added throughout to clarify the context.

The poet's 'Grandmamma Tennyson' is central to this study. Mary's legacy of letters connects us with her life and family relationships and with the early years of her daughters, Elizabeth and Mary. Nothing is known of Frances's childhood, as no early Hutton family letters survive. Chapter 1 considers Mary's letters to her mother, Mary Turner. Mary began writing as a newly married, self-absorbed young woman. The letters continued for almost thirty years and movingly reflect their increasingly close relationship. Early letters touch on worries that recur, strengthen and are inherited, with family health a constant preoccupation. Parental preference is soon apparent and continues in the next generation. Although concerns are constant, the letters' language and tone are transformed as Mary experiences birth, miscarriage and grief, and as her feelings for George deepen.

Mary Turner and George Tennyson were married on 22 June 1775 and, despite family problems, loneliness and recurring ill health, the marriage lasted until Mary's death just over fifty years later. Chapter 2 examines Mary and George's long and eventually happy marriage. There are no surviving letters to Mary from George; the unsettled early years, her concerns, her growing confidence and contentment and her deepening feelings for George are all revealed through Mary's prolific correspondence.

Elizabeth is the subject of Chapter 3. There are gaps in her surviving correspondence, and we learn of many life events from other family members. Biographers rightly refer to her charm, but Elizabeth had other characteristics. Although she shared her mother's gift for language, her wit had a sharp edge; she was class-conscious, and her recurring depression was an element of the Tennyson 'black blood'. Despite litigation she remained close to Charles, but her relationship with George Clayton and her father deteriorated. Her affectionate support for Alfred continued until her death.

Chapter 4 studies Mary's relationship with her sons. Her preference for Charles intensified after the sons' marriages. Mary wrote often to Charles and Frances and was devoted to their children. No letters from Mary to Eliza survive; she mentions only the three eldest Somersby boys and references to George Clayton reflect compassion more often than love. Charles's early political success coincided with his brother's deteriorating health. After George Clayton's death in 1831, George's provision for Eliza and her children was seen by Somersby as financial disinheritance.

Chapter 5 is focused on Frances. She married Charles in January 1808 and the first of their eight children, seven of whom survived, was born in July 1809. Charles's ambition often took him from home, but there are no letters from Charles to Frances after the marriage. Frances was a prolific correspondent. Letters reveal her increasing confidence and lasting impartial viewpoint. She became the capable manager of a political household and throughout her long marriage regarded George Clayton's sons, particularly the poet, more kindly than Mary and George.

Chapter 6 is a study of Mary, the Tennysons' younger, less favoured daughter. Despite the evidence of her own letters and the correspondence of family and friends, biographers continue to misrepresent Mary. Her mother's letters refute the view that she was always a difficult child. Young Mary's own words reflect her sociability and wit. The Bournes' correspondence confirms their lasting mutual love. Her later letters reveal Mary to be a compassionate woman of deep faith, with a gift for language and a Biblical turn of phrase that biographers may have misunderstood.

Mary Turner Tennyson died on 20 August 1825 aged seventy-two, fifty years after her marriage to George. She is buried in the Tennyson family vault at All Saints Church in Tealby where, on a memorial plaque, an idealized account of Mary's life can be read. Today we may more closely touch and truly understand the lives of all the Tennyson women by reading their 'silent-speaking words' – the letters presented in this study.

Notes

1. *The Letters of Alfred Lord Tennyson*, ed. by Cecil Y. Lang and Edgar F. Shannon, Jr, 3 vols (Oxford: Clarendon Press, 1982–90), I, p. 2 ([October 1821]).
2. Benjamin Jowett (1817–93), English scholar, Master of Balliol from 1870, later vice-chancellor of Oxford University.
3. *Tennyson and His Friends*, ed. by Hallam Tennyson (London: Macmillan, 1911), p. 187.
4. The poet quoted in Charles Tennyson, *Alfred Tennyson* (London: Macmillan 1950), p. 14.
5. Christopher Ricks, *Tennyson*, 2nd edn (Basingstoke: Macmillan, 1989), p. 163.
6. *Ulysses* (1842), line 11.
7. Robert Bernard Martin, *Tennyson: The Unquiet Heart*, 2nd edn (London: Faber & Faber, 1983), p. 3. Honourable exceptions to this critical neglect are: 'Address given by Roger Evans at the Tennyson Memorial Service at Bag Enderby Church 7 August 1994', *Tennyson Research Bulletin*, 6:3 (1994), 183–90; Valerie Purton, 'Travels with an Aunt: Mary Bourne revisited', in *Lincolnshire People and Places: Essays in Memory of Terence R. Leach (1937–1994)*, ed. by Christopher Sturman (Lincoln: Society for Lincolnshire History and Archaeology, 1996), pp. 182–4.
8. *In Memoriam A.H.H.* (1850), XCV, 33–6, *Tennyson: A Selected Edition*, ed. by Christopher Ricks (London: Longman, 1989), p. 439.
9. XCV, 26.
10. In the Tennyson family circle there are three Georges, three Elizabeths, and six women and a baby named Mary. To avoid confusion, when a George has a middle name it is used throughout; Mary (the daughter) is 'young Mary' until she marries; US-style naming is used for married women, with the married surname following the full single name.
11. See, for example, Mark Girouard, *Enthusiasms* (London: Lincoln, 2011), pp. 19–29; Francis Hill, 'The disinheritance tradition reconsidered', *Tennyson Research Bulletin*, 3:2 (1978), 41–54.

12 Charles Tennyson and Hope Dyson, *The Tennysons: Background to Genius* (London: Macmillan, 1974), pp. 16–19.
13 Tennyson, 1950, p. 7.
14 Amanda Vickery, *Behind Closed Doors: At Home in Georgian England* (New Haven, CT: Yale University Press, 2009), p. 6.
15 The women's original spelling has been retained throughout.
16 Lang and Shannon, I, p. 88 (10 March [1833]).
17 Martin, 1983, p. 4.
18 Sturman and Purton, pp. 69–70.
19 Tennyson and Dyson, pp. 177–8.
20 Russell v Russell, NA C13/2791/9; C13/1739/31; the other executors were Elizabeth's son William and Sir Gordon Drummond, who was married to Matthew's sister Margaret.
21 https://www.bankofengland.co.uk/monetary-policy-inflation/inflation-calculator [accessed 19 October 2020].
22 Lang and Shannon, II, p. 149 (19 May 1856). Italics in the original.
23 John Batchelor, *Tennyson: To Strive, to Seek, to Find* (London: Chatto & Windus, 2012), p. 12.
24 Tennyson, 1950, p. 48.
25 J. Kolb, ed., *The Letters of Arthur Henry Hallam* (Columbus: Ohio State University Press, 1981), p. 700 (12 December [1832]). Italics in the original.
26 Martin, 1983, p. 5.
27 Peter Levi, *Tennyson* (New York: Scribners, 1993), p. 16.
28 Tennyson and Dyson, p. 78.
29 Lang and Shannon, I, pp. 59–61 (18 May 1831).
30 Lang and Shannon, II, p. 363 ([early May] 1864).
31 Tennyson, 1950, p. 158.
32 Tennyson, 1950, p. 17.
33 Equivalent to more than £9,550 today, https://www.bankofengland.co.uk/monetary-policy/inflation/inflation-calculator [accessed 13 September 2021].
34 *Maud: A Monodrama*, 1855, X, I, 346–7.
35 Martin, 1983, p. 414.
36 Martin, 1983, p. 546.
37 Tennyson, 1950, p. 17.
38 https://hist259.web.unc.edu/marriedwomenspropertyact [accessed 22 September 2021]. Women gained a degree of autonomy with the Married Women's Property Acts of 1870 and 1882.
39 Martin, 1983, p. 135.

1

'When I receive your letters I feel that inward Joy unspeakable': Mary Turner Tennyson's letters to her mother, 1775 to 1804

Marion Sherwood

Mary is of particular interest to Tennyson biography. She was the mother of Elizabeth and Mary, and mother-in-law of Frances, the three Tennyson women whose letters and lives are also the subject of this book. To Alfred and his Somersby siblings and Tealby cousins she was 'Grandmamma Tennyson',[1] an inseparable part of their Lincolnshire childhood until her death in 1825. Alfred, just turned sixteen, marked her passing with a poem – 'And ask ye why these sad tears stream?' – published anonymously in *Poems, by Two Brothers* two years later.[2] Throughout her fifty-year marriage to George Tennyson, Mary was a prolific correspondent. When first married, Mary's closest relationship was with her mother and letters linked her with the family home in Caistor. When her children were young, her mother was her confidante. As the children grew up, married and moved away, she sought through her letters to connect – and protect by her advice – her increasing and at times fractious family. Maturity and faith allowed Mary to accept her mother's eventual death and to acknowledge her love for George and their children, particularly for Elizabeth and Charles whose early years were spent at home.

Born in 1753, Mary was the only surviving daughter of John Turner (*c.* 1696–1784), an attorney in Caistor, a small town on the western edge of the Lincolnshire Wolds, and his wife Mary, née Davis (*c.* 1718–1804). Mary Davis Stovin was a widow when she married John Turner on 28 June 1747. The three children of her first marriage to Thomas Stovin, a Caistor apothecary, died in infancy or adolescence; of the five children born to Mary and John Turner, only

Mary and her brothers John and Samuel survived into old age. John (1749–1812) followed his father into the legal profession; Samuel (1755–1835) became a clergyman.

On 22 June 1775 Mary, aged twenty-two, married George Tennyson (1750–1835), later known to the Somersby Tennysons as 'The Old Man of the Wolds' but then an ambitious Market Rasen lawyer of twenty-five. Although there was no reason for haste, rather than waiting for banns to be called Mary and George were married by licence in Caistor by the Reverend Henry Thorold, who had officiated at the wedding of Mary's parents. George's profession defined his social status. In the social hierarchy of late-eighteenth-century England lawyers were included among the 'growing ranks of the genteel and middling', positioned 'below the nobility but above the vulgar'.[3] Accordingly the marriage meant 'the construction of a separate household' and Mary and George moved to Queen Street in Market Rasen, nine miles from Caistor. Soon after the marriage Mary began writing weekly to her mother and the vividly informative, often anxious and at times revelatory letters, which reflect the variable spelling and grammatical constructions of the age (and which have been retained in this study) form the surviving half of a unique correspondence that lasted for almost thirty years.

'It makes me very happy to find that my Dr Mother will soon be with me': August 1775 to February 1776

Mary's letter to her mother soon after the wedding foreshadows much of her later correspondence. She writes fluently, as if talking to the recipient, often at length and at times with humour. She has clearly been educated, probably at the 'boarding-school' run by 'Miss Wheeley, of Lincoln', with whom her family had been in touch.[4] In 1766 her brother John wrote to thirteen-year-old Mary 'at Mrs Wheeleys above Hill Lincoln' ('Mrs' was probably a courtesy title for professional purposes):

> My Father has been out Three or Four Times in Order (if he could) to find a large hare for Mrs Wheeley (but all to no purpose) he has met with Two Fine Leveretts which Mrs Wheeley is very welcome to if she thinks them worth her Acceptance. [19.11.1766 Tenn 2/9/1]

Writing in August 1775, distressed at being wrongly informed of her father's death, Mary's first thoughts are for her family. Newly married Mary refers to her husband formally as 'Mr Tennison':

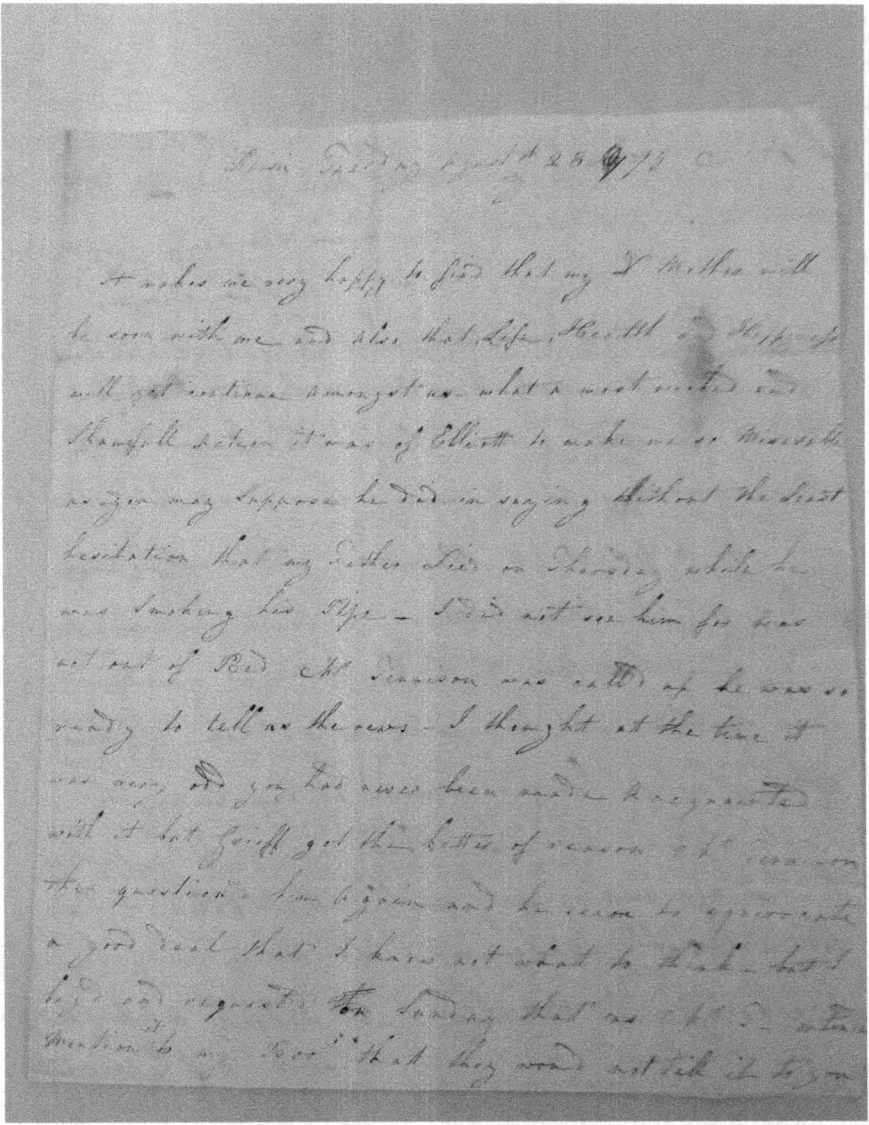

Figure 1 Mary Turner Tennyson to Mary Turner [28.08.1775 Tenn 2/5/18].

It makes me very happy to find that my Dr Mother will soon be with me and also that, Life, Health and Happyness will yet continue among us – what a most wicked and Shamefull action it was of Elliott to make me so Miserable as you may suppose he did in saying without the least hesitation that my Father Died on Thursday while he was Smoking his Pipe – I did not see him for was not out of Bed Mr Tennison was call'd up he was so ready to tell us the news – I thought at the time it was very odd you had never been made Acquainted with it but Grieff got the better of reason.

She mentions her own 'Health', which allowed her to fulfil the social obligations of a genteel wife for whom 'duty visits were hard to evade'.[5] Her letter confirms that in 1775 genteel households 'Dine'd' at midday. During the late eighteenth and early nineteenth centuries 'the upper classes ate later and later', the middle classes 'moved later to emulate them' and 'luncheons and afternoon teas' evolved to fill the gap:[6]

> I have been much better this week than I was ye Last – I paid 3 Visits Last Fryday as I always said I would – We Breakfasted at Mr Hinchmans Dine'd at Mr Croppers and drank tea at Mr Branstons and in our return call'd at Mr Boucherette as we heard he was not well.

Mary closes with her usual formal salutation:

> I am Dutifully & Affectionately Yours M Tennyson. [28.08.1775 Tenn 2/5/18]

But by September Mary is missing her family and friends. In the early letters she refers to Caistor as 'Castor' and Market Rasen as 'Raisin':

> I can take no Pleasure in anything Neither in working reading writing or company – but yet if it was a few Castor friends that live near me I believe I cou'd with some degree of Satisfaction enjoy 'em. Raisin I fear can never be Agreeable to me If I had but my Dr Mother and the rest of my friends in the Town with me I could then be happy … not but Mr T – is very tender and pitty me a good deal, yet a female companion is a great relief this most certainly is a dull stupid place.

Mary's pen portraits of family friends are vivid and endearing:

> Mr Grey is indeed an Agreeable sensible Man and dont seem to know that he is so – And I dare answer for him being a good Man in every respect he lives very strictly up to ye rules of Christianity and as everybody ought to live for which some wou'd call him a Methodist – a method most certainly he has which I'm afraid few follow – but he has not got a drawn out Sanctify^u face.[7]

As the reference to Methodism suggests, early in her marriage Mary is aware of but does not comment on the world outside her family and social circle. She closes by thanking her mother for items sent and returned 'by Goodman', a local carrier used by the Tennysons to transport their letters, belongings and occasionally themselves:

> I thank you in the first Place for the Table (also for the Napkins which I have sent by Goodman [)] – I imagine the Desk is forgot I should like to have it ye first opportunity. [[September] 1775 Tenn 2/8/6]

During their marriage the Tennysons travelled widely in England, George often on business, Mary to visit family and friends. In October 1775 they plan a 'great journey' to London. Mary wants her mother to travel with them, even though 'George' (Mary now refers to her husband by his forename) has engaged a suitable female friend to accompany her:

> I wish much for your company with us – George says tho he has engag'd Miss Coltman there is yet room for you as he will ride on horseback if you agree to go with us … I'm very throng in writing a Sermon to Mr Grey which I [k]now youll be glad to hear – and another Long letter to Miss Tennyson – meaning my Sister. [31.10.1775 Tenn 2/6/4]

An occasional dialect word or phrase appears in Mary's early letters; here 'throng' means 'busy'. 'Miss Tennyson' was George's sister Ann, born in 1753. She married William Raines in 1788 and they had one daughter, Elizabeth.

After their return Mary relates 'our Adventures':

> I made an attempt to write yesterday by the Post but all the whole day I found I must solely devote to my Neighbours that came in with a how do ye do, and now being quite alone I have leasure to give you some account of ourselves … the Journey was agreeable enough but could not have thought before I went, that ten Days wou'd have satisfied me and I can say with truth that I was thoroughly satisfied with London – after one has seen a Play or two there is nothing further to amuse – as to the rest of the Places we soon look'd over – such as Westminster Abbey, St Pauls & the Waxwork &c, &c, but the weather being so foggy and the streets so uncommonly dirty made it uncomfortable walking about – I did at last see Mr Garrick[8] – but if I say he did not Please me you'll say nothing could … it was the same Play we could not before get in to see – it was performed again that same week – much Ado About Nothing and in my private opinion a very stupid Play.

She was unimpressed by the city: 'I never wish to see London again at such a disagreable season'. For Mary 'the latter part of our Journey was the most agreeable', when they visited Samuel at Queen's College, Cambridge, and saw 'the Library and Senate House and Chappel &c, &c'. She adds a postscript:

> I forgot to tell you how very Genteel Mr Johnson was … he took Places for us in the Play house to see Mr Garrick knowing we were very desirous to see him, and invited us to dine that day. [24.11.1775 Tenn 2/1/7]

'Genteel' was Mary's highest term of praise. And for genteel households finding a reliable female 'Servant' was often difficult. Servants could be acquired through advertisements or hiring fairs, but as the following letter suggests, 'the most popular means was personal recommendation':[9]

> I sho'd be obliged to you (if you have not already[)] to enquire if Mrs Johnson has got a Servant or engag^d one – as this Young Woman you saw at our House – is very desirous of going again to service I think that Place might suite her as well as any. [08.12.[1775] Tenn 2/8/36]

Four days later Mary is worried by news of her maternal grandmother, Ellen Davis, and the plight of a neighbour:

> I'm truly sorry to read your Account of my Grandmother and also of Mrs Scott but am afraid it is not in my Power to soften their Hearts as you term it was I certain that I cou'd be of any service to her – I wou'd readyly do my utmost towards her relief – if I see Mr Scott or Miss Wickham this week I will make he[r] Case known to them and so try how far their Charity extends – Mr Scott has got a Name – but am afraid Miss Wickhams will prove a Heart of Adamant – I have sent Half a Crown by Miss Coltman. [12.12.1775 Tenn 2/5/19][10]

Mary continues to be concerned:

> I told you I might perhaps see Mr Scott or Miss Wickham and represent Mrs Scott's case to them – but unknown to me George this afternoon went to Mr Scotts and told him in what a distress'd situation poor Mrs Scott was in – and I do Suppose talk'd in so very Pathetic a strain, that it moved the old Gentleman to draw out Half a Guinea – Pleas'd enough he came home – but says he will yet fight hard to get somthing from Miss Wickham ... But this I will say of George that I never yet have discover'd a more compassionate disposition in any-body than in him ... Mrs Walker was brought to bed of a fine Boy Yesterday in the Afternoon about 5 o C^k ... Her Husband [a doctor] deliver'd her – I never saw any-body so well as she is – and in such spirit George says he wou'd give a Hundred pound to be certain I shall be as well. [15.12.1775 Tenn 2/3/3][11]

George Tennyson is described as 'driven by his hunger for wealth and status',[12] but as a recently married young lawyer he shows compassion for 'poor Mrs Scott' and concern for Mary, who is now pregnant with their first child. His concern would be less apparent in subsequent pregnancies. Mary, however, retained her sympathy for the suffering. Eleven years later she writes:

I am going to see poor Mrs Haslehurst she had Lost the use of a Hand last Saturday and on Sunday a whole side … Mrs Watson you may be sure in great distress I go in two or 3 times a day. [05.12.1786 Tenn 2/1/26]

By mid-February 1776 Mary is preparing for the birth:

Ive only just time to beg my Dr Mother will be kind enough to Procure me Half a dozen Yards of Flannel from Brigg ye first opportunity as I can get nothing here of ye kind but what is so very thin … I heard yesterday from Miss Rewcastle she tells me she will come next week which I dont thank her for as I dont wish to have anybody with me at the time I Lay in but yourself and my Sister … I have not time to add more than that it vexes me

I am my Dr Mother Your dutyfull Daughter M Tennyson. [17.02.1776 Tenn 2/5/20]

Mary's closing salutation changes with her mood. Here she is 'vexe[d]' and no longer 'Affectionate'.

'It gave me great Pleasure to hear of my Sisters happy delivery': April 1776 to April 1777

Mary and George differed from many of their contemporaries. They had only four children (although Mary suffered at least one miscarriage), all of whom survived into adulthood.[13] Their first child, Elizabeth – the future 'Aunt Russell', called by her nephew Alfred 'My dearest Azile'[14] – was baptized at Market Rasen on 18 April 1776, ten months after the wedding. We learn of the birth from Samuel's letter to his father:

It gives me great Pleasure to hear of my Sisters happy delivery, and do not doubt of its being mutual throughout the Family, pray give my sincere love and kiss, and thank her for the honourable Title of Uncle which she has confered upon me. [27.04.[1776] Tenn 2/4/7]

Mary's letters to her mother initially contain few references to Elizabeth, known as 'Bessy' or 'Bess'. She writes at greater length during Bessy's later childhood illnesses, which Mary feared 'will bring her to the grave' [24.03.1789 Tenn 2/5/47] but which strengthened the mother–daughter relationship. In May 1776 she notes:

As Bessy is much better she changes Collour a good deal but seems quite easy and well – I'm very happy to hear you do realy intend coming but not a word of my Father & Bro^r – do Prevail with 'em both if you can to come – I think it is in your Power – it will have a very odd Appearance if they dont – therefore I wou'd not fill other peoples Mouths with disagreements that happen amongst us. [02.05.1776 Tenn 2/1/8]

Disapproval of gossiping neighbours recurs in Mary's early letters to her mother.

Although maternal breast-feeding was increasing at this time, many genteel women continued to employ a wet nurse.[15] By the end of May six-week-old Bessy is with a wet nurse and the Tennysons' social visits resume:

we are all well and Bessy in her new situation finds no ill Effects – Mrs Somerscales came from Lincoln on Saturday evening and on Sunday afternoon they departed ... Mrs Cropper din'd with us – I am not certain whether she stays all Night or not. [28.05.1776 Tenn 2/6/5]

In late July Mary's letter contains a brief reference to Bessy and a startling sentence:

We got safe and well home on Sunday Night ye rain came before we got to Nettleton – and (therefore stop't thinking it would only be a Shower) as I thought at Mr Suttons it being the House where he did live – it Prov'd to be one of the Saundersons – the Rain Continued and we stay'd to Drink Tea – had an Ash heap Cake and his Sister came to make tea[16] – we were about turning back to Castor but George recollected that he wanted to go out the next Morning or we should. However as it was not very violent we ventur'd – the Servant that lives with Saunderson is Betty Jordan's Daughter she lent me an old Hat as the Rain would certainly have spoil'd my Bonnett which I left there & received today by Goodman. The umbrella we found of infinite service as it kept us entirely dry & the Horse went very safe but my Husband and I were very Quarrelsome & he hath Horsewhipt me two or Three times a day ever since. [28.07.1776 Tenn 2/6/6]

Although it is not listed in contemporary dialect dictionaries, horsewhipping may have been a local term for a verbal tirade.[17]

A month later Mary experienced the first of many problems with servants:

I am just now left in very great distress for a Servant. (Nanny and I parted last Night – we had agreed only a day or two before to continue together the year out – but upon Neds Appearance it threw everything into confusion again – he abus'd us and said he cou'd come whenever he pleas'd and go the same she went out before tea and did not return till bed time) that as I found there wou'd be no end of it – the best way wou'd be to part immediately ... I shou'd be glad if you can recommend one to me – but am great[l]y afraid there is none about you at this time of the year that wou'd suit I may as well be alone as have the Girl I have, she is so very ignorant. [17.08.1776 Tenn 2/4/9]

Mary defines her servants by role or gender, which cannot have improved their relationship:

> I have sent our Boy with ye Grey Horse and hope you are not Particularly engag'd so as to prevent your coming ... And that you may be in no hurry in Packing your Clothe's – I have sent him over Night that you may set off compos'dly in the morning ... If you can bring a Silk Gown do – as Mr Scotts are full of company and we may happen to be Amongst 'em. [21.08.1776 Tenn 2/7/2]

The 'Boy' is sent with the horse so that Mary Turner may leave 'in the morning', more 'compos'dly' than the young servant who must travel 'over Night'.

After her mother's return, Mary is again in need of 'Flannel':

> I am Making Bessy 2 or 3 Frocks, She yet wears her Jam^s, and first blankets, which now starves her legs as they dont meet before that I shall be quite rejoic'd to make her some comfortable Petticoats.[18]

> Mrs Booth has been near a Month at Mr Scotts if you remember her Daughter, you wou'd know her at first sight as she is exactly like her in Person face and conversation, only making some Allowance for Age in my opinion a very trifling Woman. [27.08.1776 Tenn 2/6/7]

She continues to have strong views on the character of friends, neighbours and servants.

Mary's close relationship with her mother is already apparent; the closeness perhaps enhanced because she is Mary Turner's only surviving daughter. Mary wants her mother to travel with them and share the social life she clearly enjoys. She finds her children companionable only when they are older and her close relationship with George takes some years to develop.

When five-month-old Bessy develops 'Hooping cough' in September Mary is not unduly concerned: 'I dont find it very violent that I hope she'll get over it very well' [10.09.1776 Tenn 2/6/9]. Mary worries more that 'company' keeps her from Caistor, wishing 'I cou'd prevail with you to return to Raisin' [08.10.1776 Tenn 2/2/3].

Mary's mother did not 'return to Raisin' and in early November Mary feels 'Bannish'd' from the family:

> Your letter on Wednesday last gave me much uneasyness as you wou'd give me no Promise of ever coming this Winter ... I look upon my-self as Bannish'd from you ... I cannot come so often to see you as I cou'd wish as somtimes I'm not

well, at others engage'd by Busyness in my House such as making and mending of Cloth's – being now free from company I find my-self much more at Liberty to work – and – read – and even – think – but it is unhappy for me my thoughts are not of ye most Pleasing kind – one of which reigns more predominant in my breast than the rest is that selfish wish I always have of conversing with my Dr Mother as I us'd to do. [05.11.1776 Tenn 2/5/22]

On New Year's Eve she again 'lament[s]' their separation:

The weather it is true my Dr Mother is at presant bad for traveling but will hope e'er this week be out that the Snow will Abate and the road a good passable track against your coming the next ... You tell me you eat your Cake and Pudding with peace and thankfullness – I can say the same but yet cou'd not help lamenting the being from you at the time and once or twice occasion'd a few tears to drop but took care to dry 'em up least my Husband shou'd [see] them – he is indeed very good and I believe studies to make my life as comfortable as possible. [31.12.1776 Tenn 2/4/10]

She is still waiting in mid-January:

I wish my Dr Mother that you cou'd have com'd to day for my Bro^r tells me the roads are exceeding good, and I'm Afraid the longer you stay and the worse as most likly the Ground will be lighter so Consequently worse travelling. [14.01.1777 Tenn 2/6/10]

From Mary Johnson's letter to her 'Dear Sister' Mary Turner in early February, we learn the probable reason for Mary's low spirits – she is six months pregnant with her second child:

you Intimate you thought my Amiable Nece was again in a way, to present you with another grand Child. I pray God she may have good Health and a Happy time which I shall be very glad to here, you [k]now, She must not be in feare. Tho she may be quick in breeding so soon, as I hope. She will have the Happyness to Live to see her Children Settled in the world, and Receve great Comfort in the prospect of thare doing well. [06.02.1777 Tenn 2.6.11]

Despite her aunt's prayers, by March Mary is feeling the weight of her second pregnancy:

I thank my Dr Mother for her kind advice – but ... to use exercise out of doors much, dont by any means Agree with me – As I find my own weight, too Burthensome to get on – or even support myself – It is very extraordinary that I shou'd feel more a Load to myself with this Child than ye Last as I am not yet near the Size – as I was before – I can but one way Account for it – which may very possibly be yᵉ case – being perhaps somthing weaker than I was. [04.03.1777 Tenn 2/6/12]

During her final weeks of pregnancy Mary has many visitors:

Having have had [*sic*] an unusual number of people call'd in to Day I scarce have ten Minutes to send a Line and as it is a Pleasure to my Dʳ Mother I wont deprive her of it … poor Mʳˢ Weston I pity her much, It is realy hard upon her to be depriv'd of her daughter entirly and it is nearly the same as Death for they can scarce ever meet Again – how happy are we my Dʳ Mother – to be situated so as to be within a Cupple of Hours ride – Miss Rewcastle came Yesterday – and also the party from Willingham came to Dine. [25.03.1777 Tenn 2/6/14]

Learning of Mrs Weston's separation from her daughter, presumably through marriage, Mary is grateful that her mother is only 'a Cupple of Hours ride' away. By early April she feels very unwell:

Tho Almost unable to write thro'ugh a faintness and Sickness which I have had these two or 3 days – I yet was unwilling to let my Father return without a letter to my Dʳ Mother … I believe I was mistaken in saying I shou'd not keep up longer than this week – at that time I suppos'd the 18th wou'd fall in this week – which was the longest reck'ing I can make – If you cant with convenience come this week I wont desire you till the next As I dont think Im likly to fall down yet – The Young Gentleman or Lady which ever it is being rather too Alert and not compos'd enough for coming into the World so soon. [08.04.1777 Tenn 2/4/11]

'The Children are become great Friends': May 1777 to April 1778

Mary and George's second daughter came 'into the World' a year after her sister Elizabeth and was baptized at Market Rasen on 4 May 1777. Named after her mother and maternal grandmother, young Mary is the future 'Aunt Bourne', whose Dalby residence became 'the *second home*' of the Somersby siblings' childhood.[19] When Mary writes in early May she is missing 'My Ever Dʳ Mother', who again helped with the birth:

I lament yᵉ loss of you very much as I have no more my Husbands company than I had – he is always employed out of Town or in the Office … I hope I keep in the mending way – Yesterday I din'd below which was the first day being a Most delightful Warm Day I put on a Pair of Clogs and a Cloke Extraordinary & took a walk of 2-or-3 turns in the Garden which I think must do me good – tho' I felt myself weaker After it than I cou'd suppos'd I shou'd have been – the Children are become great Friends … I like to hear of [Bessy's] generous temper as she gives her sister her Breast without repining – she strokes her face too and treats her very tenderly.

By giving 'her sister her Breast', Bessy is imitating the wet nurse.

Mary's closing reference to 'Magnesia' foreshadows a preoccupation with her bowels that was inherited by her grandson Alfred. As Edward FitzGerald wrote despairingly to E. B. Cowell in 1848, 'this really great man thinks more about his bowels and nerves than about the Laureate wreath he was born to inherit':[20]

> I have gone on tolerably well as to being open in my body since you left me The Night following after you left I took ye quantity of Magnesia you did and the same the next Morning without Effect. The next night I took a full teaspoon and the next morning a full teaspoon and on Saturday Morning it gave me a Stooll – [02.05.1777 Tenn 2/1/11]

Bessy returned from the wet nurse when she was fourteen months old: 'Bessy came home Yesterday and has never yet seem'd to want her Nurse – but has been quite good temper'd ever since she came' [10.06.1777 Tenn 2/7/3]. Two weeks later young Mary is placed with a wet nurse and the Tennysons again resume their social visits:

> We are happy at present in having nearly every comfort we can wish for, which is a great deal for any one to say … cou'd I have the society oftener of my Dr Mother with ye rest of my near and Dear Friends I think I shou'd come as near to a Completion of my happyness as I cou'd wish – if it be possible I intend to enjoy as much of your company this summer as I can … Yesterday I an[d] George went to drink tea with Mr Ward … in our Return we call'd to see Mary at Middle Raisin And I think without Partiallity I never saw a finer Child. [24.06.1777 2/1/12]

Mary could not enjoy her mother's company during the summer:

> I'm constantly disappointed of coming to see my Dr Mother at the times I fix – I therefore will now leave it to Chance to come ye first opportunity fine Weather or Foul – I wish'd much this week to have been with you – and had no Busyness of my own to prevent me But George went to Lincoln last Wednesday upon a Commission and thought he shou'd be at home on Saturday but Yesterday wrote to inform me he cou'd not be at Home till Wednesday.

Mary believes her mother makes herself ill by worrying about her father. John Turner was twenty-two years older than his wife:

> My Dr Mother – I'm Afraid brings on Complaints by uneasyness on my Fathers Account I shou'd hope she has no Occasion everybody say how well he looks and to Appearance I realy think I never saw him look better – you are better I hope of your Complaint at your Stomach – I Pray and Beg of God Almighty to spare you Both in Health many Years (for what is Life without Health) for ye Comfort of your Children. [25.08.1777 Tenn 2/1/14]

She writes again the following day:

> Considering every thing that has happen'd and might have happen'd had I been from home for this week was our washing week and at all times ye Girls are very careless with Bessy that upon ye whole perhaps it was better I was at home George too wrote for things which nobody cou'd have got him but myself and had he receiv'd no answer he wou'd not have been Pleas'd. [26.08.1777 Tenn 2/4/12]

Mary had reason to be wary of George's displeasure.

From the age of eighteen months Bessy was no longer 'quite easy and well'. (Her childhood ill health is discussed in Chapter 3.) In November 1777 she suffered a series of nightmares caused by teething:

> I sent immediately for Mr Walker [a doctor] for I thought every moment the Child would lose her Sences and be in fitts – She continu'd so whilst he came and somtime after ... I never in my life was so distress'd ... she has since that been very fretfull with her teeth – but I hope we shall have no return of such scenes. Georges father is here so he'll be doctring her. [07.10.1777 Tenn 2/8/7]

George's father, Michael Tennyson (1721–1796), was an apothecary, later surgeon. Two weeks later, after an accident in 'the Wisky',[21] Mary was 'doctored' by her father-in-law. He sent a brief and rather pointed note to John Turner, an 'Attorney at Law':

> Prognostes in Physic are almost as uncertain as in Law I don't wonder you are anxious a^{bt} y^r Daughter's wellfare, and I can now with Truth assure you the Report I last night sent you is confirm'^{d} This Morning she being chearful without any <u>considerable</u> Complaint now below Stairs.

Mary added a reassuring note:

> I thank God my Dr Mother for his great Goodness in preserving my Sences and Limbs and that you was not with me this I do to show you that I am Able to write

and to Assure you I feel nothing at present but a Headach and a Stifness in my joints. [20.10.1777 Tenn 2/6/15]

The following day she mentions her father-in-law's treatment:

I'm rather lame of my Arms – As Mr Tennyson cou'd not get Blood at the first he prick'd me 3 times in my Right Arm but one drop came – he then try'd ye left Arm and I then began to be warm and bled pretty Plentyfully ... from what I think at present I'll never get into it again – the Wisky I mean. [21.10.1777 Tenn 2/7/4]

Contemporary medical thought, inherited from ancient Greece, attributed disease to an imbalance among the four humours (black bile, yellow or red bile, blood and phlegm).[22] Releasing the excess could help restore the patient to health.

By early December Mary feels the lack of social gatherings:

As my Father has been so kind as to dine with us have but little time to say anything but to tell you the Truth I have as little subject to treat upon for we go on at the same bat you have seen us here we have no Assemb[l]ys to talk of or Visiting of any kind. [09.12.1777 Tenn 2/4/13]

Three months later, as her sense of isolation continues, Mary movingly expresses the joy and comfort she derives from her mother's letters:

I did not at one time think that writing wou'd have ever been to me of ye service and Satisfaction, I have found it, since the beginning of my weekly correspondence with my Dr Mother – tho, we have neither of us any-thing to communicate of material Consequence yet when I receive your letters I feel that inward Joy unspeakable which if you was to deny me off thro' any Misfortune or Illness – which God be Praised has never yet been the Case, I shou'd then be Lost indeed as I shou'd lose one of the greatest comforts <u>I now enjoy & I hope will still continue to do.</u> [10.03.1778 Tenn 2/1/15]

'3 Children all together must be a Great Trouble': December 1778 to summer 1780

Not all family events 'of material Consequence' are recorded in the letters. Mary's maternal grandmother, Ellen Davis, was buried at Caistor on 23 June 1778. Mary was again pregnant. The Tennysons' third child, George Clayton – future father of Alfred and his siblings – was baptized at Market Rasen on 10 December.

We learn of the birth from Samuel's letter to his brother John:

> I imagine my Mother is yet at Raisin, nursing ye good Woman in ye straw, who I hope long ere this has produced us a Nephew, & does as good Matrons say very well. [26.12.1778 Tenn 2/2/8]

'The woman in the straw' was a contemporary euphemism for birth, deriving from the medieval practice of placing rushes under a birthing chair.[23] But Samuel, recently ordained and writing at Christmas, may be making a religious allusion.

Mary makes no reference to George Clayton in a series of letters dated 'c. 1778–79'. She writes of difficulties with servants:

> the Girls realy they are become a Towns talk so infamous the Boy has told it in several places in the Town that he has laid with both of 'em for many times together … the Boy is Afraid they may both prove with Child & is gone to London. [[c. 1778–79] Tenn 2/8/18]

She refers to medical treatment:

> my Chief reason for writing is to tell you that I was Blooded on Sunday – for had very uneasy nights – cou'd get no rest – but since the opperation – (which I went through with great Courage) – I have found relief. [[c. 1778–79] Tenn 2/8/31]

And she mentions Bessy's health: 'she has been so poorly of late her eyes have been so weak and her Appetite so bad' [[c. 1778–79] Tenn 2/8/27].

The letters also make clear that young Mary, who would turn two in May 1779, is living with her grandmother. (Her move to Caistor and eventual return are explored in Chapter 6.) With her letters Mary sends clothes and shoes for the child: 'I have just sent Mary a Cupple of Frocks 4 shifts 1 Pr of Old Shoes & shall have more things to send her on Tuesday' [[c. 1778–79] Tenn 2/8/22].

Mary's plans to visit Caistor are often changed by bad weather:

> The weather is yet only Dr Mother so Precarious that I scarce can tell you what to determine upon I did think the next week of being with you if convenient to you surely the wind will not Always be in this cold quarter. [[c. 1788–79] Tenn 2/8/10]

The lack of available horses and Mary's reluctance to travel on the Sabbath are also delaying factors:

> I am put off coming to day the Horses are all wanted … If they want the Horses tomorrow I dont intend to be disappointed as I will have a Chaise I dislike it much travelling on Sundays. [[c. 1778–79] Tenn 2/8/33]

Mary and George lived in Queen Street, Market Rasen, for almost four years. In May 1779 they moved to a new house in King Street, next to the Vicarage. Her elderly father, about to arrive at the house, has recovered from a recent 'indisposition':

> I can easyly Guess the terror you was in About my Father It was indeed very Alarming as every little indisposition must at his Years ... But was you to Lose my Father I hope you might still find comfort in your Children Comfort such as to keep Life from being a Burthen ... But I hope both you and we all may enjoy his company many years – hear he comes. [10.08.1779 Tenn 2/1/16]

Young Mary has also been unwell:

> I hope as you make no Mention of her she is mending fast ... But if she is to suffer and at Last to be taken Away we must Submit Patient as we are Able to the will of Heaven I must own I shou'd be unhappy to part with Any of 'em but more Particularly either of the Girls. [17.08.1779 Tenn 2/4/15]

George Clayton, aged eight months, is already less favoured than 'the Girls'. But as the letters reveal, Mary was soon to 'part with' her younger daughter.

Apparently 'mispair[ed]' shoes reveal occasional tensions in Mary's close relationship with her mother. In late August Mary writes: 'I quite Admire the shoes but cant get any on but the Lealock & only one of them I will try a thiner p^r of Stockings and if I cant get the other on I can wear none of 'em' [20.08.1779 Tenn 2/5/24]. She reports again at greater length:

> if I am to keep any of the Lealock ones I must have these as I have now Paid 'em and whoever wants the other I shou'd suppose they wou'd rather Chuse to have 'em as I have put 'em together than to Pair 'em; as every Pair is a little one and a great one – I did not make a Mistake as you imagin'd & told George that you cou'd never make me understand anything I saw a small inconvenience in mispairing 'em which was turning the Tab of the shoes one inside and one outside but if they are worn with Knots it Matters not a Pin how they are. [August [1779] Tenn 2/8/13]

Mary's later mishap with 'the Ruffle' may also have frustrated her mother:

> enclos'd you have the Ruffle I brought home to finish, but I'm sorry to tell you it has not Prov'd so handsom as I intended ... what was the first thing that Spoil'd it was owing to the unevenness of the Thread I brought none home of ye same it was began withall but netted some of my own which prov'd worse than the other At the finishing of it ... I have been quite unlucky in this poor Ruffle throughout the Piece (for I put it upon the fire this Morning to Boil expecting it wou'd come

out very White – But to my great Mortification it was quite yellow – Oweing to the Saucepan not being well tinned it was a small Copper one and the tin Almost all worn off – it was Vexatious because it was Netted quite Clean and did not want Boiling but I thought I wou'd have it look better than well … it is unnesessary [sic] to say will you come I imagine; I have receiv'd so many refusals. [25.01.1780 Tenn 2/1/17].

Mary is saddened by her mother's reluctance to visit: 'I think it very unkind of you never to come all this Long Summer' [16.09.1779]. By early December she fears the family is 'Weaning your selves from me … I am not accusing you of any such thing – I only say it had very much the Appearance of a decline of Motherly Love' [07.12.1779 Tenn 2/7/7].

Three months later her disappointment intensifies:

You have no desire to see how we live in our House or what we are doing with the Garden all is now finish'd and I think it is a compleat a Place for the Size of it; as it cou'd Possibly be made But if neither <u>Affection</u> or <u>Curiosity</u> will bring you I have nothing to do but sometimes to come myself and if I have lost ground in Your Affection by taking my self out of the Family I must strive to regain it as well as I can –

But it frets and teazes me very much – You cant imagine how it greives me … Was I situated at a Hundred miles distance from you I shou'd have been with you upon every opportunity that offer'd. [21.03.1780 Tenn 2/4/17]

Mary, now aged twenty-seven, is clearly unhappy. George is often away; she is disappointed in her mother and feels unwell:

Being not in my Power to get to Castor to Day as I told my Father on Tuesday if nothing particular happen'd I wou'd be with you this evening … but I'm afraid I must not Venture to ride yet as I have had a great discharge lately of my Monthly complaint and since that have be[en] brought very low by a weakness that follow'd. [c. early 1780 Tenn 2/8/14]

She writes again in February of 'my Complaint' that causes 'great weakness' [22.02.1780 Tenn 2/3/6]. Mary's health, perhaps undermined by three pregnancies in just over three years and by excessive menstrual bleeding, may be the cause of the decision taken in the summer of 1780 – young Mary will remain in Caistor with her grandmother:

You are very kind in offering to keep Mary it will I redily Accept your Offer it will Most certainly save me a great deal of Trouble and expence As I am sure if we had all three at home we cou'd not do without another servant 3 Children all together must be a Great Trouble and one Persons work to take care of 'em – I am sensible that Mary is better Care taken of her than we can do than she cou'd Possibly be here and I think both her and we are greatly Oblig'd to you. [*c.* summer 1780 Tenn 2/8/12]

The decision regarding young Mary's future is mentioned only in the final paragraph, implying a lack of concern. Mary argues that three 'Children all together' will cause her 'a great deal of Trouble'. However, 'all three' are rarely 'at home' together. Each child spends many months with a wet nurse, 'little George' did not return until April 1780 [25.04.1780 Tenn 2/2/9] and by September 1783 he is with his grandfather in Holderness. Young Mary has already spent much of her life with her grandmother. Mary claims she will need 'another servant', but the 'genteel' Tennysons already employ several servants.

Mary usually writes fluently and neatly, but in the final paragraph – trying to explain her belief that young Mary would be better looked after in Caistor than at home – her syntax and handwriting deteriorate: 'I am sensible that Mary is better Care taken of her than we can do than she cou'd Possibly be here'. The writing becomes a scrawl and punctuation dashes increase in length. Perhaps she accepts her mother's 'Offer' only at the end of the letter because it is a painful decision.

'What for my self and your sake I wish'd never wou'd have happen'd again': April 1780 to September 1784

Early in her marriage Mary tells her mother that when 'at Liberty' she likes to 'read' [05.11.1776 Tenn 2/5/22]. From May 1780 they begin to discuss, exchange and 'wager' on books. According to Peter Levi, Mary 'read young Alfred' Byron's *The Prisoner of Chillon* (1816) 'very tenderly',[24] but her letters mention only prose fiction:

I dont know how my Dr Mother will settle this Affair concerning our wager I have found Maria's death in the same book but not in the Part wrote by Yorrick You'll find it Mention'd Again in a very few leaves after <u>the other where she is</u>

<u>Sitting under a Poplar</u> it is call'd a Continuation of the Sentimental Journey by Eugenious[25] – You'll find some Part of the continuation very Pleasing and some I dare say You'll observe fall short of his Style as it cannot be suppos'd imitations of any kind can Equal nature however it may Amuse you as being somthing new. [02.05.1780 Tenn 2/8/29]

Mary seems to recommend Laurence Sterne's *A Sentimental Journey*, published in two volumes three weeks before his death in 1768. (He defines himself as a 'Sentimental Traveller' who travels 'out of *Necessity*' and wanderlust.[26]) The underlined words allude to the narrator Yorick's encounter with Maria, parodied as an 'icon of sentimental distress'.[27] But as Mary explains, albeit confusingly, she is referring to *Yorick's Sentimental Journey Continued*, published in London in 1769, probably by Sterne's Cambridge friend, John Hall-Stevenson.[28] In time Sterne would also 'Amuse' Mary's grandson Alfred, who owned copies of *Tristram Shandy*, including the author's own copy of volume one of the 1760 London edition.[29]

During the autumn Mary worries about her parents' health:

Your letter Confirming my Father's good state of Health I need not add gave me Pleasure & not only on my account but more Particularly yours – Tho' I believe all his Children feel as great an Affection for him as is Possible from Children to Father – Yet I'm well asur'd his death wou'd be more sensibly felt by my Mother than others of the Family & It is natural to suppose it wou'd be so as your loss indeed wou'd be great. [13.09.1780 Tenn 2/1/8]

Mary's father, now aged eighty-four, is less well in November:

I'm indeed truly sorry to find by your letter my Dr Mother that my Father is no better I hope in God he will get relief by taking a Vomit his complaint is certainly of a very extraordinary kind that it dont show itself what it is. [07.11.1780 Tenn 2/5/26]

Mary has also been unwell:

I thank you my Dr Mother for the Affectionate concern you express for me But I have had no return of my Fainting so hope in God I shall not … I am of the opinion that the only reason that can be Assign'd for it, is the not being regular. [21.11.1780 Tenn 2/5/27]

Eventually she found a remedy for 'not being regular':

it is compos'd of oil of Almonds, Tincture of Senna and the infusion of Senna, made as Tea – The Yolk of an Egg – and made palatable by the syrup of Violets – I take 2 spoonsfull over Night and the same in the Morning which just operates so as to give me a stool every day. [24.06.1783 Tenn 2/2/12]

In November 1781 George Clayton, soon to turn three, is 'Inoculated' against 'the Small Pox':

I said the Last time I wrote to you that there was no prospect of my being with you so soon as I wish'd to be but it is now farther off than I expected at that time – for we have since Inoculated George & poor thing I cant leave him till he is turn'd the Heighth the Small Pox came so near us that we cou'd not rest satisfy'd and I hope God will give a Blessing to us, as he has done to Thousands under the same operation. [30.11.1781 Tenn 2/5/31]

The first successful inoculation in England was during a smallpox outbreak in 1721. Lady Mary Wortley Montagu (1689–1762), following 'folk practice' observed in Turkey where her husband had been ambassador, deliberately infected her three-year-old daughter with a tiny amount of smallpox matter; she developed a mild case of the disease and survived.[30] One of the male physicians invited to watch the child's recovery successfully inoculated his son; others administered too large a dose and patients died. From 1775 Edward Jenner (1749–1823) began to examine the similar protective use of 'cowpox matter', which led to the development of a safer vaccine in 1796.[31] Twelve months of opposition followed, until more than seventy London physicians and surgeons signed a declaration of total confidence in the practice. It is not surprising that in November 1781 Mary invokes God's 'Blessing'.

At the end of January 1782 she feels very unwell:

for this fortnight past I have been sick Always at one time of the day or other & I have now had a stop of more than 7 weeks and at other times I have been sick all day which has oblig'd me to lay in bed 3 days this last week ... the sickness I have is not like a breeding sickness I used to reach and never had it Accompany'd with a Pain at my stomach before – I shall certainly know soon ... If I am breeding I shall strive to make myself as happy as I can – hopeing it may Possibly be much for the best was it otherwise I might have some dreadful Illness. [29.01.1782 Tenn 2/7/10]

Mary's next letter is dated almost three months later, but in the meantime we have 'heard by' Mrs Somerscales, who writes to 'Dear Mrs Turnor':

We have just heard by our Neighbour Mr Johnson, that our Worthy friend Mrs Tennyson is very Dangerously ill ... beleive me my Dear friend, we were all greatly shock'd when the Melancholy news came into the Parlor as you told me when I was at Caistor, that she was got as well as cou'd be Expected, in her Situation. [18.03.1782 Tenn 2/1/22]

To be in an interesting condition or 'Situation' was a euphemism for pregnancy. Mary had been 'breeding', but as the Tennysons' fourth child was not born until July 1784 the dangerous illness was a miscarriage.

Mary recovered by April, when visits to Caistor resume:

I am now got perfectly well in Health & I Heartily thank God for it, Nevertheless I shall have the same Pleasure in coming to see my Dear Mother nay more satisfaction to me As I do not come for my Health sake. [23.04.1782 Tenn 2/7/12]

Mary and her mother continue to exchange the books they clearly value: 'I'm oblig'd to you for the last books I will take great care of 'em, & if either my Father or Bro[r] comes to day I will read Roxana but I dont mean to trust 'em in any other hand' [19.11.1782 Tenn 2/4/21].

The books travelled with family members between Caistor and Market Rasen, but Mary does not mention where they were obtained. Late-eighteenth-century readers could subscribe to circulating libraries or purchase books from 'booksellers' who stocked books only as one of several lines.[32] A notable exception was James Lackington, whose London bookshop was founded in 1774. The catalogues of Lincoln's two booksellers, Drewry and Brookes, are dated 1794 and 1801,[33] too late to supply the books Mary mentions, and Jackson's of Louth was not established until 1797.[34] Mary's books and love of reading passed to her descendants – her grandson Alfred wished for 'a novel to read in a million volumes, to last me my life'.[35] Hence the books were bought rather than borrowed, perhaps during George's visits to London when his letters were sent to Will's Coffee House in Russell Street, close to the Inns of Court.

Roxana has a complex textual history. Mary 'will read' a novel with a title not chosen by Daniel Defoe,[36] and before the term 'novel' became established at the end of the eighteenth century.[37] Published anonymously in 1724 as *The Fortunate Mistress*, *Roxana* was first recorded as the title in 1742, eleven years after Defoe's death: he was named as author only in the 1770s. *Roxana*'s many editions reflect its commercial success. In January 1783 Mary 'at last' obtains a copy of a more recent success – Fanny Burney's *Cecilia: or Memoirs of an Heiress*, published in five volumes in June 1782. As with *Roxana*, Mary writes before reading *Cecilia* and her unpunctuated sentences result in an unexpected juxtaposition of thoughts: 'I've at last got Cecilia but have only just dipt into it that I can give you no Account of it your Nose I hope is better' [14.01.1783 Tenn 2/5/35].

On 10 December 1783, the fifth anniversary of George Clayton's baptism, Mary writes in anguish to her mother, confirming the 'unwelcome' news that at the age of thirty she is again pregnant:

I have been very not well this last Month or 6 weeks past – last week I brought over a Heavy time indeed – with sickness and inward pain which brought on fainting fits ... I thank God it's now over but I was determin'd you shou'd not be made unhappy with the knowledge of it till I was able to tell you all myself as I am well convinc'd the <u>Cause</u> will be sufficient and what for my self and your sake I wish'd never wou'd have happen'd again.

Mary is also concerned for her mother, who helped at the births of all her children:

I ought not to repine [she continues] but Oh my Dear Mother I have had a hard struggle to feel happy and compos'd under what has fall'n to my lot – After the keen edge of my grief was a little subsided – I call'd reason to my Aid and said to myself am not I in the situation of Thousands in this respect (and perhaps one half of 'em dont enjoy a tenth part of ye comforts of this World as I now do ... I have now got over that Miserable time & that <u>Great</u> and <u>Good</u> God has thought fit to hear my Prayers and compose my mind ... I shall put my whole trust and confidence in <u>that Being</u> that can extricate me out of all difficultys. [10.12.1783 Tenn 2/3/10]

Mary remained 'very not well' throughout the pregnancy:

you may recollect perhaps how I used to be when with Child of Bessy in a Morning seiz'd with a faintness and weakness all over – I am now every day in that way but I think effects my breath more now – & leaves me so low I with difficulty hold my pen. [16.03.1784 Tenn 2/7/14]

Less than a month later, on 13 April 1784, Mary's father was buried at Caistor. She writes at the beginning of June:

I am as well as I can expect to be – the weather has been cool two or 3 days which agrees much better with me – but am often very much oppress'd with pain & last Night I was Alarm'd and thought I had got the end of my journey as the pains I felt were not common however thank God It went of[f] but I began to wish for you and <u>shall</u> more and <u>more</u> that I hope you wont be so long as I first fixd for I shou'd be very unhappy if you was not with me at the last. [01.06.1784 Tenn 2/6/22]

The Tennysons' fourth and last child, Charles, was baptized at Market Rasen on 20 July 1784. Mary writes with love and gratitude to her mother on her return to Caistor:

It made me very happy my Dear Mother to know you got well home I hope you continue so and rest well of Nights I thank God am as well as you left me – but am at a great loss for your company – & as there is no making things more comfortable we must strive be happy as much as in us lay's and be thankful for the other blessings we enjoy – I'm sorry my Dear Mother shou'd think it necessary to thank me for any little civility that was in my power to shew you – was my duty as well as inclination – so Tender and kind a Mother deserves at least an equal return which can never be in my power to shew the grateful sense I have of it. [17.08.1794 Tenn 2/7/15]

'Charles ... as fine a boy as one can see': September 1784 to April 1787

Mary had been deeply distressed by her 'unwelcome' late pregnancy. In time, however, her younger son 'endear'd' himself to Mary 'by the strongest tyes' [09.04.[1801] TdE/H/60/1] and maternal favouritism is foreshadowed by Mary's anxious references to Charles in the weeks after his birth. She writes in September:

> This Town rages so with the small pox that people are dying dayly I'm greatly Afraid of poor little Charles he grows surprisingly and is as fine a boy as one can see I propose innoculating him if the weather continues cool. [14.09.1784 Tenn 2/7/17]

Contemporary burial registers indicate that Mary exaggerated the death toll.[38] A week later Charles is placed with a wet nurse:

> Poor little Charles is I think at a stand still, ye Nurses Children go on as they began and seem a little ill which I wish he did, I have not see him Awake to day but the flushing in his face is Apparently gone and looks pale and delicate, as he lays. [21.09.1784 Tenn 2/7/18]

When she writes again four days later, two-month-old Charles has been inoculated. Late-eighteenth-century England was a patriarchal society, and only the Tennyson boys were given the smallpox vaccine:

> Little Charles has been not well the 2 days last past got no sleep the night before last but yet no Spots Arise Excepting about his Arm where he was inoculated ... he is perfectly Safe from having 'em Again but I shou'd like more erruption or it certainly leaves a humour. [25.09.1784 Tenn 2/7/19)

By early October he was 'perfectly well again'. But six months after her father's death, Mary is worried by her mother's continuing grief:

> Your Melancholy letter last Night made me very unhappy indeed I'm afraid you will shorten your days ... the very thought to me is dreadfull this in[c]essant

grieving will bring on complaints of various kinds depend upon it how dubbly Miserable wou'd you be if that is to follow I hope when we come we shall be able to give you comfort. [03.10.1784 Tenn 2/6/2]

In a sign of her growing maturity, Mary seeks to comfort and reassure her grieving mother, particularly in the deeply felt letter written just after the first anniversary of her father's death:

> I began to think long of your not writing and was surpriz'd at not having a letter sooner believe me I always look for 'em with great anxiety ... I admit of late they have been wrote in a Strain of a too Melancholy cast which for your sake as well as my own I cou'd wish might be otherwise – but if a settled thorough composure of mind has not yet taken place, write to me often if it is any relief it will be a Means of making the Burthen sit lighter ... I am always ready to join you in talking of my Dear Father & your loss we must all Alow is Truly great – and no lasting happyness in this world is to be had for you but what is to be produced from y^r own more profitable reflections ... depend upon it my Father knew perfectly well the love and esteem you had for him I'm well convinced you shew'd it in many instances to him – that I beg of you not to let that distress you ... Therefore my Dear Mother strive and pray that you may enjoy the comforts dispenced so bountifully to us and that you may have some pursuit some amusements or a somthing in View to fill up this space Alotted us here I can easily picture to myself how miserable you are at somtimes in having lost a Steady friend and constant companion you I dare say feel yourself divested of every earthly comfort as he is not a partaker – I hope he is a partaker of more solid blessings – so you at present are the loser he the advantage of it.

The apparent disillusion suggested by the sentence that follows shows that Mary too is still mourning her father:

> I find myself so little dispos'd for the fashionable and polite modes of conversation and dress – that I rather brood than court the company of such. [26.04.1785 Tenn 2/7/22]

They continue to find 'amusements' in books. Early in 1785 five volumes of George Anne Bellamy's *An Apology for the Life of G.A.B., Late of Covent-Garden Theatre, Written by Herself* were published. A sixth volume followed in May, and a benefit was held on her behalf at Covent Garden. Bellamy was an English actress, born in Ireland in 1727 and named George Anne through a mishearing at her christening of the name Georgiana. She achieved success in Shakespeare's tragic roles, although her 1788 obituary states that 'her reputation as an actress rested largely on her good looks'.[39]

Mary received Bellamy's *Apology* soon after publication. Initially she was disappointed: 'We have Almost read Mrs Bellamy You will like it – tho it is nothing equal to Phillips if we had not read them this wou'd Answer better' [[1785] Tenn 2/8/25]. Mary's faith becomes increasingly apparent in her letters, and she refers to the religious writings of Catherine Payton Phillips, born in Dudley in 1727 and recognized as a Quaker Minister in 1748.[40] But Mary changes her mind about *Apology*, an unreliable memoir resembling the life story of one of Defoe's itinerant, self-fashioning narrators. By May she is quoting Bellamy, setting aside dressmaking silk with the comment: 'if I live and (as Mrs Bellamy often observes, no untoward Melancholy Event happens) it may lay till next Year'. Leaving to visit friends, she writes:

> I take Mrs Bellamy with me for all the family at Sixhills want to see 'em I see in the News-paper she has publish'd a 6th Volume and also that she Appeard upon the Stage to deliver an Address to the Public but cou[l]d not proceed so got a friend to do it for her – if you dont see it in the paper I will save it for you and bring it when I come I think it very pretty and moving that I dont wonder at her feelings being affected. [31.05.1785 Tenn 2/7/24]

Bellamy's inability to read her 'Address to the Public' calls to mind Alfred's reluctance to recite his prize poem, *Timbuctoo*, at Cambridge in July 1829.[41] In a more material connection between generations, volumes one, three and five of the third edition of *Apology* – the half-title page of volume three inscribed 'Mary Turner 1786' – formed part of the Turner bequest and passed to Alfred's brother Charles, later Tennyson Turner. The volumes are now in the Tennyson Research Centre.[42]

With *Apology* Mary's discussion of books comes full circle. Bellamy recounts the events of a turbulent life until, impoverished and repentant, she asks the 'recording Angel' of 'my favourite Sterne' to 'drop the tear of pity and obliterate my faults'.[43]

In March 1786 Mary's thoughts are still with her grieving mother. She is concerned by Samuel's neglect and hopes that young Mary is 'some consolation', although there is a certain irony in Mary's use of the term 'banish':

> I sincerely feel for you but all you can do, is to make the best of it. I must own I cannot help being surpriz'd at my Bro^r Sam that he dont tire of his way of life, and consider you more, he never shou'd spend more than an evening at a time from you … was I in his place I shou'd take great pleasure in amuseing you with the anecdotes of the preceeding day; otherwise where are parents to look for any satisfaction from their children if they banish themselves their Company – I'm

happy to find my Dear little Mary is some consolation to you. [08.03.1786 Tenn 2/5/41]

A year later Mary amuses her mother by describing a visit to London:

> You will be much surpriz'd I have not a doubt when you see this is dated from London, as I neither intimated to you or had an Idea of proceeding so far when I told you of my intended Visit to Kimbolton … George wish'd me to go on with him, but what cou'd I do without a female friend it was propos'd that one of the Miss Hutchinsons should go … we got into London before 5 in the afternoon and at our Lodgings drank Tea and sett of[f] immediately for drury lane Theatre tho' half the Play was over, so got in at half price Mrs Siddons was upon the Stage at our entrance in the Character of the Grecian Daughter[44] I need not tell you I was pleas'd as she certainly is beyond any-thing one can conceive … yesterday Morning we spent the greater part in Westminster Abby – & in the evening at Covent Garden Theatre at Love in a Village[45] but we went rather late to a Crowded house so consequently had a bad place in the 2 shillings Gall^y where we cou'd neither hear or see anything of the Play. [29/04/1787 Tenn 2/1/27]

Mary's last evening in London was spent at Covent Garden where, at her benefit two years earlier, their admired Mrs Bellamy could not deliver her 'Address'.

'The loss I shall ever deplore': June 1787 to February 1804

After Mary and George's return from London the lives of the Tennyson family began to change. The older children went away to school. George visited the Grays in York in June 1787 and took George Clayton to St Peter's School.[46] The following January Mary confirmed that eleven-year-old 'Bess' was also at school, although she does not say where:

> [Bess] mentions what a pleasure it will be to her the having Mary with her and is sure she will like school … Talking of Marys going to school will serve as a preface to mentioning her coming home … he [George] wishes her to <u>know</u> and be <u>Attach'd</u> to home he being too, totally ignorant of her disposition – & which he observes shou'd be all accomplish'd before she goes to school. [08.01.1788 Tenn 2/1/29]

As explored further in Chapter 6, George's wish was 'a preface' to the painful process of bringing young Mary 'home' to Market Rasen just before her eleventh birthday. She had lived with her grandmother since she was two.

Illness prevented Mary from visiting Caistor in January 1789:

> I am and have been for this week last past much better of my complaints ... I sho^d not wish to come to you to want nursing or to bring poor Bess as an invalid but at present she is very unwell. [05.01.1789 Tenn 2/5/44]

Bess's condition deteriorated in March. She remained 'very unwell', suffering from ill health whose origin 'appears to have been entirely nervous' [24.03.1789 Tenn 2/5/47] but which brought mother and daughter closer together. In January 1790 Mary was able to report that 'Bessy is rather better these 2 or 3 days last past' [30.01.1790 Tenn 2/7/30].

There is a gap of almost six years between Mary's report to her mother and a note sent in October 1795. Thereafter Mary writes less often, perhaps because – aware of future loss – she is drawing closer to the rest of her family, or possibly fewer letters have survived. Both during and after this period, however, we glean family news from her letters to George and from his correspondence.

George's letter to John Robinson in June 1793 confirms that nine-year-old Charles joined his brother at St Peter's School. The Tennysons moved to Lincoln between April 1790 and June 1793, and George writes from Deloraine Court. He thanks the Robinsons but doubts the boys' progress: 'George I am sorry to say speaks as bad or worse than ever'. 'My Wife & Girls', he adds, 'are returned from Bath' [30.06.1793 TRC 4657].

Mary's letter to George the following April has news of the 'Girls'. It also reveals the depth of Mary's feelings for her husband after almost nineteen years of marriage:

> Your letters of Wednesday and Friday I rec'd in due time & judge what were my feelings at reading ye purport of your first – this proof of your affectionate respect for me is more than I cou'd, or had a right to look for but believe me your great goodness to me shall never be forgotten ... I make no doubt but you have seen dear Mary I long to know where she has taken up her residence ... Bessy never was so well as at this time she is quite fat. [27.04.1794 4TdE/H/2/7]

Young Mary is with her mother when they visit Caistor in October 1795: 'At the time Mary wrote I did not think we sho^d be able to reach you by tomorrow dinner but I hope to see you by half Past one O C' [14.10.1795 Tenn 2/6/29].

George's father, Michael Tennyson, died on 6 October 1796.[47] Two days later George Clayton went up to St John's College, Cambridge. In 1796 Elizabeth – now Eliza, no longer Bess or Bessy – was twenty years old. She had already received an indirect proposal of marriage, but George thought her 'too young to marry at present' [29.08.1796 TRC 4606]. Two months later he approved a 'Connection'. Elizabeth was to marry Matthew Russell, a captain, later a major in the Durham Militia,[48] who inherited a mining fortune and several houses when his father died in 1817. Mary believes her daughter will be happy:

> I flatter myself my dear Mother that the dear girl may contemplate the prospect before her in being happy with the choice she has made ... I have only to add that I hope you will not delay coming in time to settle yourself that is at Least 10 days or a fortnight before and so to give me the comfort of your company after they are <u>gone</u> as well as <u>before</u>
>
> I am very busy preparing, as she will have everything new from Head to foot. [15.12.1797 Tenn 2/6/31]

Elizabeth and Matthew were married at St Mary Magdalene Church, Lincoln, on 23 January 1798. Their first child, William, was born on 9 November.

Living at Deloraine Court the Tennysons found that 'the Generality of Lincoln people are not pleasant' [22.09.1787 Tenn 2/1/31]. In May 1798 they moved to Clayton House in Grimsby, which George inherited from his uncle, Christopher Clayton. Three years later they moved to Tealby Lodge, eventually renamed Bayons Manor and transformed by Charles.

After Elizabeth's marriage to Matthew, Mary becomes more aware of the world beyond the family circle:

> their Visit to us I fear will not so soon take place as we had once reason to hope for – The Regiment is now removed to Chelmsford in great haste to make room at the Barracks for the poor sick & wounded from Holland. [21.09.1799 Tenn 2/6/32]

Mary refers to casualties of the Battle of Bergen on 19 September 1799, which resulted in a French-Dutch victory against the British and Russians.[49] 'The Major likes this life', she adds, 'but I think poor Eliza would be more comfortable with her child & Husband at home'. Matthew resigned his commission in December.

In April 1801 Mary tells George that his 'anxiety respecting my health' is shared by seventeen-year-old Charles: 'the affectionate tenderness he evinced will never be forgotten having endear'd him to me by the strongest tyes' [09.04. [1801] TdE/H/60/1]. Charles's unwanted conception caused his mother much anguish. However, as with Elizabeth, his pre-school years were spent at home and Mary grew to know his 'disposition'. Now his 'affectionate tenderness' has gained her enduring love.

Charles followed his brother to St John's College, Cambridge, on 6 July 1801. Five weeks earlier George Clayton had been ordained deacon; he was ordained into the priesthood on 19 December 1802.

Mary had been at Caistor in March 1802. Her mother was ill but, as Mary noted to George, 'is at present a little better' [22.03.1802 TdE/H/61/22]. The improvement did not last:

> my poor Mother has yet bad nights – bad appetite & bad digestion attended with a slow Fever – & which I fear in the end will wear her down – you are being very good in having given me the priviledge of staying to any period I may wish so long as I can be of use it is a great satisfaction to me to be with her – but I much dread the failure of every measure that may be adopted – It is a great comfort to her to have me with her – but she more than once in a day mentions the inconvenience that acrues to you – but yesterday your letter which I read to her gave her a great quiet, and her gratitude was extreme for your kindness to her – I could leave her really with great satisfaction – & come only occasionally to see her, if she could only get a night or twos rest … another day or two will soon deside whether she is ever to be better – However my dear husband rather than you shall be low or dispirited for want of society I will (except my poor Mother should be very considerably worse) fix Saturday for returning – Mary of course I leave. [03.04.[1803] TRC 4685]

Only at the end of Mary's letter do we learn that young Mary is with her in Caistor.

Young Mary remained with her grandmother until Mary Turner died the following February aged eighty-six. She was buried at Caistor on 24 February 1804. Mary wrote to George three times in the days following her mother's burial:

> Now that my dear departed Mothers remains are consigned to the earth and the tumult of my mind is abated to a calm resignation to the will of the Almighty – it is a severe disappointment to me not to have it in my power to return to you for though it is a great satisfaction to my Brother to have our longer continuance yet however my Affection may silence my complaints here – I must inwardly regret the longer imprisonment to this melancholy place where every thing reminds me of the loss I shall ever deplore.

Bad weather confines them at Caistor. Mary is separated from Elizabeth, who is at Tealby, and worried by George's 'Gouty symtoms':

> I pray Heaven to avert the violence of an attack & preserve a life so valuable to me – without which, what good would my life do me? I cannot bear to think of it and how unfortunate I am to be so situated with my dear Eliza – to have her

under my roof and within 7 miles, and neither be able to get to her or she to me ... tell me how she & you both do as soon as you can by the Post – I must have a letter as I cannot be happy without one, my treasure on earth I consider very great – so long as the lives of my dear family are preserved & in health – & may the God of the spirits of all flesh bless you all in this world & that which is to come is the most fervent Prayer of my Dear Husband your Affectionate Wife. [25.02.1804 TdE/H/62/3]

Replying to George and Elizabeth the following day, Mary eulogizes her mother:

Your letter found us in Tears – the family having gone to Church and we alone – we were as you may suppose led to talk of the many past & happy days spent here in the society of one so justly lamented and find consolation in the retrospect of a life spent so conformable to the will and Lesson of our blessed Savior – her trust & confidence in God for aceptance at the resurection was strong in faith through his merits – & I have no doubt of her final state of being happy –

Therfore rely upon our endeavors to throw off the weight of sorrow we have ... never was a dear creature so generally lamented – the poor have the most cause for she was ever doing good – all discription of people lament her – but she has rested from her labor & her work will follow her to those Mansions to which we are all hastening.

Mary turns to practical matters – fabric for mourning clothes, and the weather:

As to the Cotton or Cambrick Muslin my dear Eliza we have but one piece left in the Town and the colour is not near so good as the piece we have got It is true I could send it you to day – but am not tempted to do it as you may probably get better at Raisin ... Cooper seems to think the frost is breaking up – yet I cannot help fearing he may be mistaken – as it appears likely to freeze again to night ... so we wait our removal from hence with more patience – all here unite in best affection with dear Mary & myself to you my dear Husband Eliza Geo & Charles with your truly Affectionate Wife & Mother. [26.02.1804 TdE/H/62/1]

George Clayton and Charles have joined the family at Tealby. Mary sends a concerned final note to George:

My mind is so agitated to hear that you are worse rather than better, that I can only say that not anything should prevent me setting out this afternoon but that I cannot bring Mary with me neither dare I venture to leave her she has had a bad night pass'd without sleep ... I trust better news will await my arrival tomorrow when I mean to be with you as soon as possible.

She concludes with a blessing to her family: 'May God bless You my dearest life and preserve you to my comfort as well as all my dear children to whom my Love' [later at Caistor Feb 1804 TdE/H/62/2].

Afterword: 'And ask ye why these sad tears stream?': 1805 to 1835

Mary's letters to George after her mother's burial reflect how much she has changed in almost thirty years of marriage and family life. Writing in August 1775 as a young woman of twenty-two her tone was one of anxious self-pity: she disliked 'Raisin', missed her family and friends and complained that she was alone and unwell [28.08.1775 Tenn 2/5/18]. She is now a mature woman of fifty-one and her tone, as her mind, is one of 'calm resignation'. Although mourning the loss she will 'ever deplore', faith and maturity allow her to accept 'the will of the Almighty' and acknowledge that the lives and health of her husband and family are her 'treasure on earth'.

A year after her mother's death Mary's portrait was painted by John Russell, 'painter to George III'.[50] Mary is fashionably dressed and has a wistful expression; she is seated, her face turned to the artist. To her right, the painting of a substantial country house signifies her status. Her left hand holds an open book – an appropriate attribute: as genteel, town-dwelling women, Mary and her mother epitomized the late-eighteenth-century novel-reading public.[51]

At her mother's death, Mary acknowledged 'her dear family' as her 'treasure on earth' [25.02.1804 TdE/H/62/3]. During Mary's final decades her 'treasure' multiplied; when she died in 1825 she had twenty grandchildren, two more having died in infancy. And George was 'preserve[d]' – he died in 1835 aged eighty-five, outliving Mary by ten years.

Poems, by Two Brothers was published in 1827, two years after Mary's death. The volume includes sixteen-year-old Alfred's elegy for his 'Grandmamma Tennyson', 'And ask ye why these sad tears stream?' But as the following verse suggests, the young poet's dream vision of Mary foreshadows rather than represents his greatest work, written when – like *Ulysses* – he has 'become a name':[52] 'I saw her mid the realms of light, | In everlasting radiance gleaming; | Co-equal with the seraphs bright, | Mid thousand thousand angels beaming' (13–16).[53]

Notes

1. *The Letters of Alfred Lord Tennyson*, ed. by Cecil Y. Lang and Edgar F. Shannon, Jr, 3 vols (Oxford: Clarendon Press, 1982–90), I, p. 2 ([October 1821]).
2. *The Poems of Tennyson*, ed. by Christopher Ricks, 2nd edn, 3 vols (London: Longman, 1987), I, p. 127.
3. Amanda Vickery, *Behind Closed Doors: At Home in Georgian England* (New Haven, CT: Yale University Press, 2009), p. 6.
4. 'Miss Wheeley, of Lincoln, some years ago keeper of a boarding-school', 'Obituary of Considerable Persons; with Biographical Anecdotes', *Gentleman's Magazine*, April 1791, p. 382.
5. Amanda Vickery, *The Gentleman's Daughter: Women's Lives in Georgian England* (New Haven, CT: Yale Nota Bene, 2003), p. 205.
6. Pen Vogler, *Scoff: A History of Food and Class in Britain* (London: Atlantic, 2020), p. 7.
7. William Gray met George at Betsey Dales's Dame School in Hedon; they remained lifelong friends. Between 1767 and 1796 the number of Methodists in England increased from 24,000 to 77,000. Roy Porter, *English Society in the Eighteenth Century* (Harmondsworth: Penguin, 1982), p. 193.
8. David Garrick (1717–1779), celebrated English actor, manager and dramatist.
9. Vickery, 2003, p. 135.
10. 'Half a Crown' in 1775 (2s 6d in pre-decimal currency) is worth approximately £20 today. https://www.bankofengland.co.uk/monetary-policy/inflation/inflation-cal culator [accessed 9 January 2021]. For case studies of the impoverished elderly see Susannah R. Ottaway, *The Decline of Life: Old Age in Eighteenth-Century England* (Cambridge: Cambridge University Press, 2004).
11. 'Half a Guinea' in 1775 (10s 6d in pre-decimal currency) is approximately equivalent to £82 today. http://www.bankofengland.co.uk/monetary-policy/inflat ion/inflation-calculator [accessed 9 January 2021].
12. John Batchelor, *Tennyson: To Strive, to Seek, to Find* (London: Chatto & Windus, 2012), p. 11.
13. 'The "average" mother in this period bore six to seven live children'. Vickery, 2003, p. 97.
14. 'My dearest Aunt (or if you will allow me to call you by a name that pleases me as well) My dearest Azile', *AT Letters*, I, p. 88 (10 March [1833]).
15. Vickery, 2003, p. 107.
16. An 'Ash heap Cake' is baked on the hearth under hot wood embers. *The English Dialect Dictionary*, ed. by Joseph Wright, 2nd edn, 6 vols (Oxford: Oxford University Press, 1981), I, p. 79.
17. The term is not listed in dialect dictionaries edited by Edward Peacock, Joseph Wright or John Brogden.

18 'Starves her legs' means that the child's legs are cold because the blankets are too short.
19 *The Letters of Arthur Henry Hallam*, ed. by J. Kolb (Columbus: Ohio State University Press, 1981), p. 700 (12 December [1832]). Italics in the original.
20 *The Letters of Edward FitzGerald*, ed. by Alfred McKinley Terhune and Annabelle Burdick Terhune, 4 vols (Princeton, NJ: Princeton University Press, 1980), I, p. 623 ([late November] 1848).
21 A 'Wisky' was an open, two-wheeled vehicle drawn by one horse, so called because its light weight enabled it to whisk about. https://www.britannica.com/technology [accessed 4 November 2018].
22 https://www.sciencehistory.org/distillations/let-it-bleed [accessed 2 March 2020].
23 Kyra Cornelius Kramer, 'The woman in the straw', http://www.kyrackramer.com/2019/11/08 [accessed 20 January 2021].
24 Peter Levi, *Tennyson* (New York: Scribner's, 1993), p. 16.
25 In the eighteenth century the name was traditionally applied as a compliment; Yorick converses with *Eugenius* in *Tristram Shandy* and *A Sentimental Journey*.
26 *Laurence Sterne: A Sentimental Journey and Continuation of the Bramine's Journal with Related Texts*, ed. by Melvyn New and W. G. Day (Indianapolis, IN: Hackett, 2006), p. 15.
27 New and Day, p. 157.
28 Hall-Stevenson's authorship has been challenged by Arthur H. Cash, *Laurence Sterne: The Later Years* (London: Routledge, 1993), p. 331.
29 *Tennyson in Lincoln: A Catalogue of the Collections in the Research Centre*, ed. by Nancie Campbell, 2 vols (Lincoln: Tennyson Society, 1971), I, pp. 97 and 122.
30 https://www.theguardian.com/society/2021/mar/28/how-mary-wortley-montagus-bold-experiment-led-to-smallpox-vaccine-75-years-before-jenner [accessed 25 May 2021]. See also Jo Willett, *The Pioneering Life of Mary Wortley Montagu* (Barnsley: Pen & Sword, 2021).
31 *Chambers Biographical Dictionary*, ed. by Magnus Magnusson, 5th edn (Edinburgh: Chambers, 1990), p. 779.
32 Richard D. Altick, *The English Common Reader: A Social History of the Mass Reading Public, 1800–1900*, 2nd edn (Columbus: Ohio State University Press, 1998), pp. 58–9.
33 Drewry, LA UP 1082; Brookes, LA UP 858.
34 Richard Goulding, *Notes on Louth Printers and Booksellers of the Eighteenth Century* (Louth: Goulding, 1917).
35 *William Allingham: A Diary*, ed. by H. Allingham and D. Radford (Harmondsworth: Penguin, 1985), p. 293 (entry for Sunday 29 August 1880).
36 Daniel Defoe, *Roxana: The Fortunate Mistress*, ed. by John Mullan (Oxford: Oxford University Press, 1996), pp. 331–9.

37 Ian Watt, *The Rise of the Novel: Studies in Defoe, Richardson and Fielding*, 5th edn (Harmondsworth: Penguin, 1970), p. 10.
38 Burials in Market Rasen in late 1784 – none in August and December, four in September, two in October, three in November.
39 The obituary adds: 'riotous living, including a legal and a bigamous marriage, took its toll on Bellamy's beauty' and reputation. https://www.britannica.com/print/article/59740 [accessed 24 January 2017].
40 'Obituary of remarkable Persons; with Biographical Anecdotes', *Gentleman's Magazine*, I (1795), p. 259. Phillips' active engagement 'in the Gospel Ministry' led her to visit Quaker congregations throughout England, Ireland and North America.
41 Because of the poet's 'horror of publicity', *Timbuctoo* was read by Charles Merivale. Hallam Tennyson, *Alfred Lord Tennyson, a Memoir, by His Son*, 2 vols (London: Macmillan, 1897), I, p. 47.
42 Campbell, ed., I, p. 109.
43 Bellamy, II, p. 208; V, p. 85.
44 Sarah Siddons, née Kemble (1755–1831), late-eighteenth-century theatrical celebrity. Euphrasia in *The Grecian Daughter* by Arthur Murray (1727–1805) was her most famous role, https://www.tregeaglefineart.com/en-GB/historical-items/sarah-siddons-as-euphrasia-in-the-grecian-daughter [accessed 7 April 2020].
45 *Love in a Village*, ballad opera composed and arranged by Thomas Arne (1710–1778) First performance London 1762. *The New Oxford Companion to Music*, ed. by Denis Arnold, 2 vols (Oxford: Oxford University Press, 1983; repr. 1984), II, p. 1085.
46 William Gray's brother-in-law, Reverend John Robinson, was headmaster of St Peter's School.
47 He was buried in the nave of Hedon parish church in Yorkshire with his wife Elizabeth, who died in 1755.
48 Since the Civil Wars the British had been wary of a standing army under a monarch's control; county militias were designed 'to balance this centralised force and to be a professional reserve'. Jenny Uglow, *In These Times: Living in Britain through Napoleon's Wars, 1793–1815* (London: Faber & Faber, 2014), pp. 34–5.
49 French and Dutch forces defeated the Russians and British under the Duke of York who had landed in North Holland. https://dbpedia.org/page/Battle_of_Bergen_(1799) [accessed 16 April 2020].
50 John Russell, RA (1745–1806) English portrait artist and painter to George III, Magnusson, ed., p. 1278. Mary's portrait is stored in the Usher Gallery, Lincoln (LCNTE 2016/59).
51 Watt, p. 157.
52 *Tennyson: A Selected Edition*, ed. by Christopher Ricks (London: Longman, 1989), p. 141.
53 Ricks, ed., 1987, I, p. 127.

2

'The tenderest and best of Husbands': Mary Turner Tennyson and George Tennyson, 1775 to 1825

Rosalind Boyce

'A dull stupid place': 1775 to 1794

Mary Turner and George Tennyson were married on 22 June 1775 at Caistor parish church by the Reverend Henry Thorold, rector of the Lincolnshire villages of Cuxwold, Ludborough and Swallow, who had officiated at the wedding of Mary's parents. The witnesses were Mary's brothers, John and Samuel Turner. Mary was twenty-two and George twenty-five. They became a devoted couple, and the marriage was long and eventually happy but beset by family problems, loneliness and ill health.

Caistor is a small market town on the edge of the Lincolnshire Wolds. Caistor House, the home of the Turner family, a fine five-bay, three-storey house still stands today. The date above the porch with its Ionic pillars is 1682, but the façade is Georgian.

Mary was the daughter of John Turner, an attorney, and his wife, also called Mary. There were two sons who feature from time to time in these letters: John, born in 1749, and Samuel, at times a source of anxiety to the family, born in 1755. Two other sons died in infancy.

It is not known how Mary and George met, but George would certainly have encountered Mary's father on business. They were both single and of marriageable age, and in a small town it would not have been long before George was introduced to the family. There is no information about the period of their engagement except, according to family tradition, Mary told her grandson Alfred many years later that when she and George were courting on the steps of Caistor House a large piece of stone fell from the parapet to the steps where they had been sitting, adding, 'It was a special Providence, my dear, but for that where would you have been?' Evidence for this story cannot be found.

The marriage was to last for fifty years until Mary's death in 1825. Before her marriage she seems to have been a lively, spirited girl: 'I believe Miss Neve will stay rather more than a week I am her bedfellow we are very merry', she wrote to her mother during a visit to friends in 1774 [21.01.1774 Tenn 2/6/3]. At the time it was usual to share beds, particularly when space was limited. But in the early years of her marriage she was lonely and missed her Caistor friends and regarded Market Rasen as 'a dull stupid place' [[September] 1775 Tenn 2/8/6].

Despite this uncertain start, Mary was to develop into a strong, capable woman, very much involved in family matters as shown in her letters. But, typically for the times, she was subservient to her husband, an ambitious man who was often away furthering his business interests leaving her with only the servants and later, the children, for company. She was a deeply religious woman. Illness struck frequently, and in an age when doctors could do little, she turned to her faith: 'commit yourself to the healing hand of the Almighty – he is the great Physician of both soul and body' [14.01.1809 TdE/H/149/4].

On one occasion when George was away, Mary wrote to him: 'God bless you I went to bed with a heavy Heart last night not having you near me and shall continue to mourn your Absence' [14.02.1809 TdE/H/67/3]. Many years later Mary explained to Charles that they were 'fashionable sleepers':

> I am writing these few lines before I have seen your dear Father <u>and before breakfast</u> – we remain yet fashionable sleepers, <u>separate</u> beds and <u>chambers</u> – to speak of no other inconveniences than the great fires he has had night and day – would alone drive me away from the perpetual roasting. [16.03.1822 TdE/H/87/27]

The Tennysons' first home was in Market Rasen, a small market town nine miles from Caistor, where George had his law practice. It seems that until 1779 Mary and George lived in a house in Queen Street on the corner of Waterloo Street, after which they moved to a new house in King Street next to the vicarage. Later buildings now exist on the sites of the two houses, and the garden of the King Street house forms part of a car park.[1]

Mary and George had four children: Elizabeth, Mary, George Clayton, who was to become father of the poet, and Charles, who was born several years after the others. As Mary's letters reveal, all four were to be the cause of much anxiety as time went by.

After four pregnancies and a miscarriage in eight years, Mary's health became poor, but she made light of it and often apologized to George for it, as in this letter of 1799:

> I have to my sorrow given you so much anxiety respecting my health as will never I fear be in my power to recompence even if a series of health and long life should be granted me.

George suffered severely from gout, 'a crippling inflammation of the joints of the extremities, especially the big toe' and in the same letter, Mary has some advice for him:

> I much fear (talking of your lameness) that you walk a great deal too much – consider a little and keep of[f] the Gout if possible – fatigue you may remember has sometimes brought it on. [01.06.1799 TRC 4682][2]

The Tennysons were a genteel family and kept several servants, probably three or four, but exactly how many is not clear. They often caused difficulties: 'We have never yet been comfortable amongst the servants', Mary wrote to her mother [02.03.1789 Tenn/2/5/45]. Magdalen King-Hall says that 'Complaints about servants, which occur frequently in 18th-century letters and diaries, are a sign of the new age, and of a new, less stable relationship between employers and their domestic servants … The feudal spirit was wearing thin'.[3]

According to Robert Bernard Martin, George appears as a strong, forceful, perhaps intimidating character, 'overbearing with friends, bully to his family, susceptible equally to choleric rages and to maudlin self-pity about his treatment by his own children'.[4] However, the letters reveal that there was a kind, caring, perhaps indulgent father underneath, particularly towards Charles and Elizabeth. During the courtship of Charles and Frances Hutton there was intense correspondence amongst all the parties involved regarding the marriage settlement. A letter from George to Charles at this time shows not only his affection but also his severe attitude towards his son:

> My happiness depends on yours, you know how much your Mother and myself love you and on so material a transaction of your life, we can but think, and think deeply … I would not for the worlds wealth have you made unhappy, but be prepared for any circumstance that can possibly arise. [20.06.1807 TRC 4665]

Letters from George to Mary are sometimes referred to but none have survived. However, his affectionate feelings for her are expressed in a letter to Mary's brother, John Turner, when he was preparing John's will: 'You will know your Sister is the best & most amiable of women, her relative duties of a Child, of a Mother of a Sister & a Wife she has fill'd as she ought' [1808 or 1809 TdE/H/63/75].

George had great faith in a gout remedy called colchicum or colchicine, which is derived from the autumn crocus and is a key ingredient of the medicine known as *l'eau médicinale d'Husson'*, patronized by George IV when he was Prince Regent. It was used as a treatment for gout until the 1960s and 1970s but is highly toxic and has largely been replaced by safer drugs.[5] George often asked Charles to purchase his medicine and other items in London, which were not available locally:

> I wish you cou'd procure me by means of Mr Boucherett half a Doz^n Bottles of the Gout Medicine Dr Harrison is in Town at a Mr Bickerstaffs Bookseller a corner shop in Essex St Strand, perhaps he co^d help you better by means of Sir Joseph Banks. If you do not find yourself <u>quite</u> well take the earliest opportunity of consulting him on your own acc^t. [06.06.1810 TdE/H/68/8]

The Boucherett family of North Willingham were friends of the Tennysons, and Ayscoghe Boucherett was MP for Great Grimsby. Sir Joseph Banks, son of a wealthy Lincolnshire landowner, was a distinguished explorer and naturalist. In 1778 he was elected President of the Royal Society.[6] Robert Bickerstaff (1758–1835) was a bookseller, stationer and bookbinder in the Strand, London, from 1787 to 1818.[7] The Tennysons would have enjoyed having such distinguished friends.

'A country solicitor turned country gentleman': 1774 to 1835

George Tennyson was born in 1750 at Hedon in the East Riding of Yorkshire to Michael Tennyson (1721–1796), an apothecary and surgeon, and his wife Elizabeth, née Clayton. They were married in 1745. A son, George Clayton, was born to them in December 1747, but died soon after his birth. Their second son, who was to become Mary's husband, was also called George following common practice at the time to call a later child by the name of a child who had died, but his mother's maiden name was not included this time.[8] There were also two daughters: Elizabeth, who was baptized on 21 February 1751 and died the following year, and Ann who was baptized on 13 January 1753.

Young George met his lifelong friend William Gray when they were pupils at Dame Betsy Dale's school in Beverley. In about 1770 both boys were apprenticed to William Iveson, a Hedon attorney, and in 1774 George set up in practice at

Market Rasen. His uncle William Tennyson, who had worked as a solicitor at Barton on Humber, moved to Market Rasen in 1779 and joined George in the business, but he is not thought to have been a partner.[9] George worked hard to build up the business and a good relationship was established with the local landowners. Because a bank had not yet been established at Market Rasen, banking was added to his activities.

George had ambitions to climb the social ladder and was active in building up his landed estates. Joseph O. Baylen and J. Norman Gossman describe him as 'A country solicitor turned country gentleman'.[10] According to them, he was a Justice of the Peace and Deputy Lord Lieutenant of Lincolnshire, but this has not been confirmed despite an extensive search. Later he was briefly Member of Parliament for Bletchingly (1818–19).

At this time many parishes were being enclosed. Enclosure was the replacement of two or three large open fields around a village by small individual fields cultivated by new owners. From the 1750s enclosure by parliamentary act became the norm, requiring costly surveys and parliamentary approval, thus involving large fees for lawyers. George prospered during this time and was able to buy a considerable amount of land in the area. In 1783 at the age of thirty-three, he purchased half of the Beacons Manor estate at Tealby from Sir Wharton Amcotts[11] for £1,000, and in 1787 bought the rest from the Reverend Brownlow Potter for £1,100.[12] It was then a small seventeenth-century manor house situated just below the high ground where the foundations of an earlier manorial stronghold had stood.[13]

In 1781 George was balloted and drawn to serve in the militia for three years, but a William Hardy was paid £7 by the parish to serve in his stead.[14] The militia was the oldest reserve force. Organized in county regiments, it was recruited by ballot from able-bodied men on lists drawn up by parish constables, and its officers were local gentlemen. It trained part-time, but might be embodied for full-time service when there was a risk of invasion, and in the Napoleonic wars it provided many recruits for the Regular army.[15]

George was one of six parishioners in 1786 each lending seven guineas to build a workhouse so that the poor could be employed in industry.[16]

In the 1790s George took a lease on Deloraine Court, a large house near the cathedral in Lincoln which still stands today. The receipt for the purchase is signed 'J. Field', presumably a lawyer: 'I acknowledge to have heretofore received of Mr George Tennyson the sum of six hundred pounds in full for the purchase of the House at Lincoln now in his Occupation – which I undertake to Convey'[17] [26.09.1794 2TdE/H/94/2].

By moving to Lincoln George had hoped to establish closer links with social leaders of the county. But the venture was not successful, and in 1797 the family left Lincoln for Grimsby to a house which he had inherited from his uncle, Christopher Clayton. From Grimsby the family moved in 1801 to the Beacons estate at Tealby. 'My Father thinks of building a House from the old foundations at Tealby, we none of us regret quitting Lincoln every body agreeable seems tired of the place & talk of leaving', wrote Elizabeth Tennyson to her grandmother, Mary Turner [22.07.1797 Tenn 2/1/31].

'Beacons Manor' or 'Tealby Lodge' eventually became 'Bayons Manor'. The name 'Bayons' is said to be a corruption of 'Bayeux'. Bishop Odo of Bayeux, brother of William the Conqueror, was granted land at Tealby. He was the cousin of Walther of Aincourt (hence d'Eyncourt) who fought at the Battle of Hastings.[18] George kept the Market Rasen house and his interest in the firm until 1811.

George was closely involved with a major project to improve Grimsby Haven, which over many years had fallen into decay, and then to construct a new dock. The aims of the scheme were partly to divert traffic from the rival port of Hull, across the Humber, and partly political. It was hoped that the resulting prosperity would encourage Grimsby voters to 'show gratitude to those whose plans brought them new prosperity and the docks would provide jobs with which to reward political supporters'.[19] George owned a great deal of property in the area of the scheme which he had inherited from the Clayton side of his family, and hoped to gain considerable advantage from it. After many vicissitudes the dock opened in 1800, but the company was in financial difficulties from the start and was never successful until the railway company took it over in the 1840s.

'Without you I should indeed be a forlorn creature': 1799 to 1804

George was frequently away on business in London and Mary often took the opportunity to ask him to obtain items not available locally:

Mary [her daughter] & I have only to repeat our thanks for all your kindness in offering to make what purchases we may want but cannot give you such commissions as we in short know not what we want present [*sic*] us but your dear self and we shall be happy as you can make us – your Sister and little Bess arrived on Saturday to dinner poor woman I feel for her she is low in spirits as you may expect … You ask'd me in a former letter what you could buy that would be acceptable to Bessy – as she cannot wear at her age any ornaments – &

suppose you make your Sister a present of a small silver Snuff-box – she takes a little and has a Horn one in her pocket – she thinks mine pretty so If you have time do look for one suitable for her. [17.06.1799 TRC 4683]

'Your sister and little Bess' are George's sister Ann Raines and her daughter Elizabeth, aged about nine. Ann may be in 'low spirits' after the death of her husband William Raines, which may have occurred in 1798, although no record of his death has been found. Snuff was a pulverized form of tobacco, which became popular from the mid-1600s to the mid-1800s and was more popular than smoking.[20]

In the summer of 1800 Mary was staying with her daughter Elizabeth Tennyson Russell at Hardwick, County Durham, and wrote to George from there. She is very subservient to him:

Till yesterday coming out of Church I had thought your silence very long indeed – & feared your late great enemy had seiz^d you by the right hand and quite disabled you from taking up the pen – but when I seriously reflected (which I could calmly do after reading your letter) how many matters of busyness you had and always have upon your hands I blam'd myself extremely – knowing that all the time you are absent from me you are despatching as fast as possible every weighty matter that occupys your thoughts almost night and day – to be in readyness to meet all your dear family again … I have not expressed all my joy at your perfect recovery from the Gout – but I feel thankful to God. [Summer 1800 TRC4684]

George's 'late great enemy' is gout.

In April 1801 Mary was staying with her elderly mother at Caistor. George was in London, and she wrote to him at Will's Coffee House:

Yours dated Friday I have this moment rec'd and hasten my reply to satisfie you that with the greatest readiness I accede to your wish of fixing to be at home two or three days before your arrival so that when you send for Horses there may be no impediment – My poor Mother is very desirous of seeing you by this road I have not a wish of the sort except I could be certain that the subject so often treated on could be discuss'd to your satisfaction and the comfort of all parties – … I shall be at home on Thursday. [04.04.1801 TdE/H/61/2]

The 'subject so often treated' is the behaviour of Mary's brother, the Reverend Samuel Turner, born in 1755 who, according to Martin, was 'notorious for his profligate life'.[21] He had always been something of an embarrassment to the family and the cause of much anxiety to Mary. As she wrote to her mother in 1780: 'His (my Bror's) behaviour of late to me has been very unbrotherly I dont believe there is in him the Least spark of Affection for anything anybody but himself or his Cards & they are the ruin of him' [22.02.1780 Tenn 2/3/6].

There was an ongoing disagreement between Samuel and George. George was teetotal and disapproved of Samuel's drinking: 'My Bror Sam was so good as to call upon me on Sunday & the Sunday before also – I wish'd to have ask'd him to return'd at night to have taken a Bed but as George gave him so cool a reception at the door the first Sunday I co'd not mention it to him' [10.03.1789 Tenn 2/5/46].

Mary was with her mother at Caistor again the following year and was missing George. Samuel's behaviour was still causing trouble:

> As you would receive my answer (to a former letter you speak of) on Wednesday Morn^g last I did not hasten yesterday a reply to that received yesterday – but am truly sorry the delay of one day should have given you so much uneasyness – for it is all my desire and happiness to <u>have</u> and <u>see you so</u>, and shall be my <u>study</u> for I hope I am not insensible to the gifts of providence in so ordering that the principle part of my days should be pass'd with the tenderest and best of Husbands O' may he grant me this blessing the residue of my years – for without you I should indeed be a forlorn creature – but to find that heart burnings and strong resentment is still kept alive against my Bro^r Sam … I speak my real sentiments & upon the strongest foundation that he bears you not the least enmity on the contrary quite the reverse … I shall drop the unwelcome subject and pray that the topic may be coolly touch^d upon – so that peace may be restor'd …
>
> I am sorry to read that your Sister the day was sitting in her chair apparently well – when on a sudden a fit seiz'd her and for a quarter of an hour she seem'd as dyeing – when she was recover'd in some degree she complain'd of a numbness in her Head and one Arm – I think a bad symptom – she adds that she wishes her to take advice but which she (your Sister) is averse to believing it nothing worse than a fainting. I think we should go to see her soon poor woman this is a warning for somthing worse to follow we are all well and happy to find you the same. [2.04.1802 TdE/H/61/21]

Despite suffering what may have been a stroke, Ann was to live for another twelve years.

Mary liked clothes and fashion. Although the family had become increasingly prosperous through George's business interests, she was careful rather than extravagant and not tempted by the prospect of the expensive straw hats, which George had offered to buy for her and their daughter: 'Many thanks to you for your intended presents but we really are sorry you should think of buying such expensive things as the straw ha[t]s – if they are not purchas'd pray dont – we have enough for this year' [12.06.1802 TdE/H/61/17].

Mary was often at Caistor during her mother's illness and was anxious about George being on his own:

> However my dear husband rather than you shall be low or dispirited for want of society I will (except my poor Mother should be very considerably worse) fix Saturday for returning … Perhaps you will be so good as take a ride over in the interim – <u>all partys</u> Im sure will receive you gladly. [03.04.1803 TRC 4685]

'My mind is so agitated': 1804 to 1808

Mary was in Caistor again in early 1804 and wrote to George:

> My mind is so agitated to hear that you are worse rather than better, that I can only say that not anything should prevent me setting out this afternoon but that I cannot bring Mary with me neither dare I venture to leave her she has had a bad night pass'd without sleep – but having taken rest from nine this morning (when I left her) till within the last half hour now half past two – refresh'd but not equal to the travelling to night – though I remain here on thorns
>
> I trust better news will await my arrival tomorrow when I mean to be with you as soon as possible. [February 1804 TdE/H/62/2]

When her mother died in February 1804, Mary could not return home straightaway:

> My dear dear Husband
>
> I must inwardly regret the longer imprisonment to this melancholy place where every thing reminds me of the loss I shall ever deplore, nor do I see from the present appearance of the weather a probability of an early removal. [25.02.1804 TdE/H/62/3]

In November 1808 Mary was at Hardwick with Elizabeth, who was expecting her second child. Although she was conscious that George must be lonely without her, she was becoming impatient with him. After thirty-three years of marriage, she was more confident and becoming more assertive:

> Charles having said almost everything I would wish for your information concerning us – I have only to add my sorrow that our dear Elizas weakly state of health contracts me to make this melancholy separation from you, but God be prais'd you are I trust well for which I cannot be too thankful – but why are

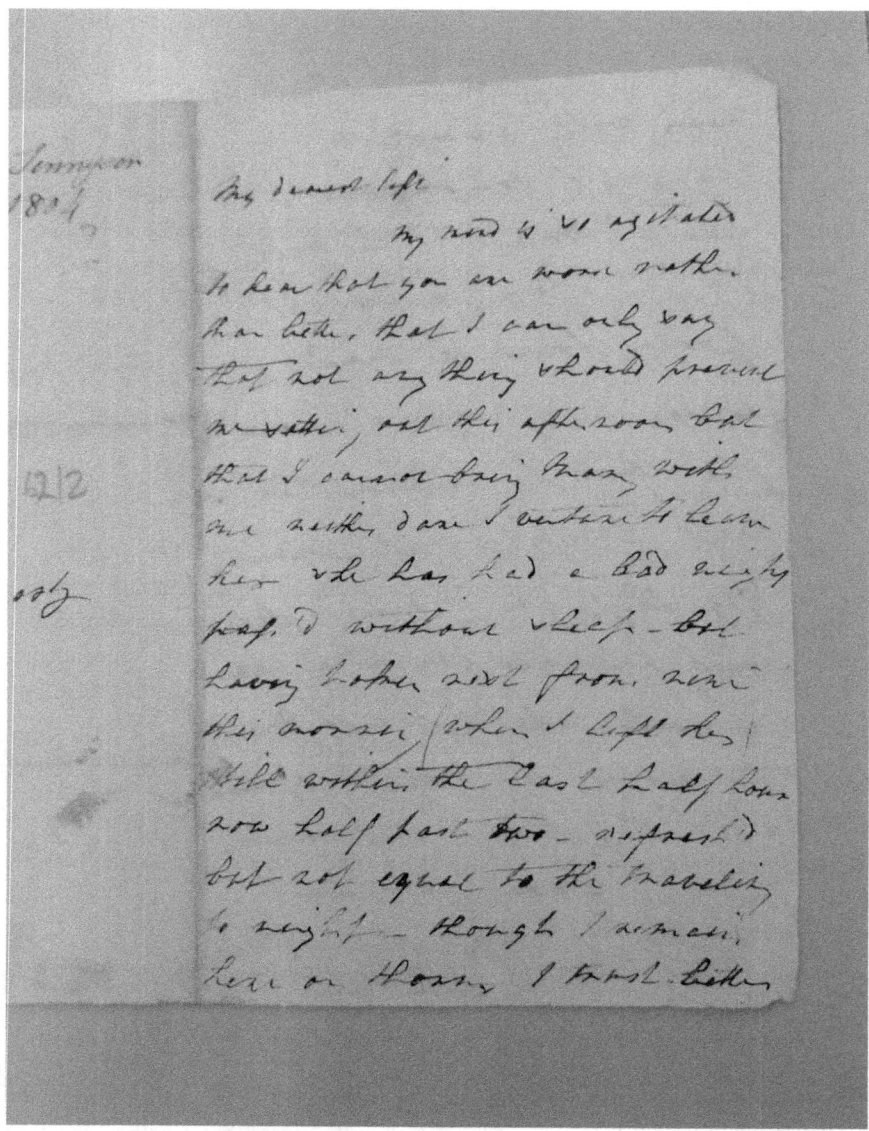

Figure 2 Mary Turner Tennyson to George Tennyson [February 1804 TdE/H/62/2].

you alone? Pray have somebody or get out – have you found your wig [? ...] Adieu my dearest life and believe me your truly Affectionate Wife M Tennyson. [27.10.1808 TdE/H/65/31]

According to Amanda Vickery 'dearest life' was a routine address between husbands and wives.[22] In the eighteenth century wigs would have been worn by men with some social standing, but by the time of this letter, their popularity was fading.[23] George is bare-headed in the portrait by Sir Thomas Lawrence, *c.* 1800, now stored in the Usher Gallery, Lincoln, so it is not known what type of wig he would have worn.[24]

A few days later Mary regretted her impatience:

> Indeed my dear Husband I most truly feel your lonely situation and grieve at the distance & time that is still to come before we meet again – but most of all I lament your lost appetite & remember this to have occurr'd before at this particular Season – you are a little Billious – Eliza with me agrees that to sometimes take a Pill of <u>Calomel</u> or sometimes a cup of <u>Chamomile</u> Tea would be of infinite service to you – pray do try one or both of these, and I have no doubt of you regaining your Appetite – for it is most disgusting to sit down to dinner to eat anything – and neither can it be properly digested – pray tell me what you have done and how you feel yourself from time to time – I shall be happy when Charles and Fanny get back to you – to relieve the tedious hours – and you must have many. [02.11.1808 TdE/H/65/28]

Calomel is mercurous oxide, a white powder formerly used as a purgative.[25] Chamomile has anti-inflammatory and antiseptic properties and was used to treat a wide range of health issues.

By December 1808 George had become aware that he had responsibilities to his tenants. In a letter to Charles he writes: 'If this [? weather] lasts something must be done for the poor of Tealby & I wish Hill wo^d make out a List with the Number of each in a family & the Ages of the Children & let us have it, but to do this privately & not give any hint of our intention' [24.12.1808 TdE/H/66/2]. However, there are no further references in the letters to 'the poor'.

George Hildyard Tennyson, the eldest child of her son Charles and his wife, Frances, was born on 10 July 1809. Mary was more fond of her grandchildren than she had been of her own children, but favoured Charles's children, particularly George Hildyard, over the Somersby grandchildren, referring to them affectionately as 'twigs' and 'the chickens', although they were often rowdy – 'I hear my Chickens very merry below' [29.01.1823 4TdE/H/31/25]. Mary and George were to have twenty surviving grandchildren.

The following letter to George was written when Mary was recovering from an illness, the nature of which is not known:

> Your letter of to day has given a fillip to my Spirits which were beginning to droop for the want of it – and therefore unnecessary to add that I rejoice at your safe arrival and good health ... as to your spirits my dearly beloved Husband let

them not suffer the slightest depression on my account, comparatively I am well & suffer no longer either in my stomach or side and indeed have not a complaint but a diminution of my strength – which time and care (with the blessing of God) will over come – I have been down stairs two days – and yesterday attempted to walk down the Gravel Valley towards the Garden but did not accomplish the intended stretch – from failure of strength but it was intensely hot – to day I am going an airing in the Carriage – and which I propose pursuing constantly till I can use my Legs to better purpose. [26.05.1810 TdE/H/68/2]

In the early years of their marriage the Tennysons would have travelled on horseback 'riding double', with Mary behind George. Over thirty years later they had become prosperous and were now the proud owners of a carriage. As Roy and Lesley Adkins observe: 'Wealthy gentry and the aristocracy would own at least one carriage that was solely for passengers'.[26]

A year passed before the next letter, suggesting that George had been at home. However, by May 1811 he was in London and Mary was worried about him:

My dear Husband it will indeed be a period most happy to me to receive you here again – but much fear you hurry yourself beyond the strength of your Nerves … Tomorrow Charles joins us and tomorrow, or Perhaps Saturday – I shall know the day when you my dear Husband have fix'd to head our party when we shall look as we should do – God bless you & preserve you from accident says your / Truly Affectionate Wife / M Tennyson … I am quite well. [02.05.1811 TdE/H/69/12]

'We go very slowly on in the drawing room': 1801 to 1810

The family moved from Grimsby to Tealby Lodge in 1801. Although the following letter is sent from Grimsby, it is likely that the improvements Mary mentions are for the house at Tealby. No doubt George, now a prosperous landowner, felt that Tealby was a suitable location for him to present himself as a country gentleman, and the work described was all part of the plan. In the 1830s, after his death, Charles continued the process when he rebuilt the house as a mock medieval castle. In a letter to both George and Charles, Mary wrote:

We go very slowly on in the drawing room – the Painter has gone 3 times over the pillars – & the other parts twice and he now must stop – till the paper is put up – but which I have really given over expecting – having enquir'd every where for it – Miss Swan who came to me the other day – I desired to search the warehouse at Lincoln as well as ask at [? Otters] the Druggists but without success – the same at Louth – do when you have time ask the people who sent it – & by what conveyance for I am also prevented making the Carpets.

According to Adkins: 'Apothecaries (druggists) were allowed to prescribe, prepare and sell substances for medicinal purposes, but many of these were little better than the strange concoctions sold by itinerant quacks'.[27] The connection with wallpaper is not clear.

The letter continues:

'Adieu my dear Husband but not without thanking you for your intention of presenting me with your picture – and may God preserve the original'. [21.04.1801 TdE/H/60/36]

The 'picture' refers to the portrait of George by Thomas Lawrence.

In the early nineteenth century, although many people never ventured far from home, others travelled a great deal. Despite anxieties about their health, Mary and George appear to have been perpetually on the move – Hardwick in County Durham visiting the Russell family, Harrogate for the waters, Scarborough, York, Bristol, Cheltenham and many other locations closer to home.

The following letter is from Mary to George when she and the rest of the family were staying at Clifton near Bristol in May 1808. George was in London on business:

We have had a very pleasant drive to Kings Weston this morning our party being joined by Eliza and the Russells propose to go with us to morrow to Stapleton in order to see the French Prisoners barracked there & perhaps to see the Duke of Beaufort's place at Stoke on our way. [03.08.1808 TdE/H/65/15]

The Napoleonic Wars were in progress at the time, and the French prisoners would have been regarded as curiosities. Stoke Park at Stoke Gifford near Bristol was the seat of the Duke of Beaufort.[28]

Mary expressed a wish to call at Windsor on the way home to see the king (George III). In those days it was possible to visit the king informally. According to Lucy Worsley: 'In the eighteenth century the curious custom of watching the royal family eat was still occasionally performed'.[29] The only information about Mary is through her own writing, but in a letter to his father Charles's reaction to this idea gives a brief but revealing insight into her character and confirms her deep religious faith:

My mother desires me to say she feels very much obliged by your liberality & disinterestedness in wishing her to gratify herself at Windsor and I agree that she is the last person on whom self denial has any claim. She has not how[r] determined whe^r we shall stay at Windsor to see the king etc; at any rate we shall I believe go that way but sho^d ye great object of viewing Majesty be [? ...] we must stay at Windsor Sunday Night & proceed to Town on Monday as my mother objects to travelling on Sunday. [03.05.1808 TdE/H/65/15]

But later Mary had second thoughts 'for to gratify my curiosity in seeing our Earthly King I should surely bring upon myself and all of us the displeasure of my Heavenly one to travel the remaining part of Sunday and stay at the Castle Inn all night would be very expensive so shall wave for the present my ardent desire to see him' [May 1808 TdE/65/14a].

This letter also shows her prudence in money matters.

Mary enjoyed fashion, but preferred to choose something herself, rather than trust George to do it for her. In the matter of clothes, she was not quite so subservient to him, and her language is more decisive:

Mary [Mary and George's younger daughter] continues very attentive and kind she joins me in love and thanks for your offer of purchases – as to myself I could not tell how to direct you to buy anything for me – but this Summer I want every thing yet how is it possible you can judge of the Fashions or what would be proper for me in Gowns, Hats, Bonnets – or Caps so I will spare you the trouble & fatigue of excercising either yourself or your faculties yet again accept my thanks – I shall have reason enough to be supremely thankful when you bring your dear self to me safe. [26.05.1810 TdE/H/68/2]

The subject of money continues. Mary was soon deciding on costly new 'Table China', which she hoped George would obtain for her, probably in London. It is likely that the items were intended for the new home in Tealby:

You would receive my 2nd letter to day I have got yours concerning the Table China – Rich green and Gold must be handsom – but I can form no idea of the appearance the difference is great in the price between each – 23 guineas and 30 – the Supper Plates small in the 23 G^s Sett is not necessary nor can I do anything with them at dinner ... but act my dear Husband as you best like to buy one of the setts or either as you feel disposed or neither – one thing I would observe to you don't buy them with any roughness of enamel on them for it wears the spoons and the knives wear the Plates shabby for it comes off.[30]

I must now say something of myself or you will not be satisfied I am thank God quite well have anticipated your wish of getting out dayly in the Carriage and gain strength – so that I trust by the time you get home I shall not have even weakness or [? means to] complain of – to know that you are in health & spirits is a great consolation & I pray to God for a continuance and a happy Meeting – the weather is here intensely cold with a cutting east wind. [28.05.1810 TdE/H/68/3]

The 'enamel' refers to the glaze on the dishes. Although money was plentiful, Mary seemed to prefer the less expensive set but left the final decision to George.

The Tennysons did a great deal of entertaining and would have enjoyed showing off their new purchases to their friends. In those days when travel was difficult visitors often stayed the night, but Mary was not daunted by the inconvenience of extra guests. Perhaps they played cards in the evening, or if Frances was present she might play the piano.

Dr Zephaniah Barton was a well-known and respected doctor in Market Rasen and a founder of a 'dynasty' of doctors Barton in the area. He was a close friend of the Tennysons and a frequent visitor. Born in 1780, he was of a similar age to Charles and missed the family when they moved to London. He lived in a house called Sheffield Manor, which still stands in George Street opposite the church. His grave can be seen in the town churchyard.

Other friends were the Robinson and Alington families from Louth, the Boucherett family of North Willingham and the Vanes and Mains, partners in George's business. Family members were often present at gatherings as well.

By 1810 Mary was feeling settled in Tealby and taking pleasure in the home and garden:

> How much your letter has delighted me to know that you continue in good health & spirits and that I am soon to behold you again [she wrote to George] – I did not disappoint you about the reply to your letter concerning the China but answer'd it on the return of post – this is a most delightful day I have been [? airing] to see your Ludford Farm and find it in such a state of improvement I scarce knew it again Tomorrow I intend going to see the <u>Castle on the point</u> – it seems to beckon me to the spot it's walls advancing higher every day – in short I think out of doors we look very neat about home, the lawn before the house you will find improved and if it was not for <u>frost</u> – <u>east winds</u> and a <u>lack</u> of <u>Rain</u> we should look beautiful – God bless you my dear Husband – and <u>send you</u> and me a happy meeting – I had for got to say I am quite well and in good spirits as you may perceive. [31.05.1810 TdE/H/68/5]

The 'Castle on the point' refers to the building of Castle Farm, a castellated house, still standing today, situated in a spectacular location on the Lincolnshire Wolds about a mile from Tealby. The 'Ludford farm' was on part of George's estate.

Among Mary's papers is a 'House Inventory' [TdE/D/20/5]. It is not known to which Tennyson house it refers. It is not dated, but as it is a comprehensive list of items in a large household with 'A front parlour east', a 'front parlour west', a kitchen', a dairy, 'stables', a 'brew house', at least three bedrooms, two rooms in the 'garret', probably to accommodate servants, it is most likely to be the house which later became Bayons Manor. The many items in the 'front parlour east' include 'A Wilton carpet', '6 Mahogany chairs', 'a large dining table', 'an oval looking glass'; in the kitchen are a 'fixed range', 'an ironing board' and 'fender and fire irons'. Outside are 'A yard, stable and field' with horses, 'a brown and white heifer', 'an ass and a fool', pigs, poultry and an assortment of carts and agricultural implements. The 'fool' is a misspelling of 'foal'.

Mary's teeth often caused problems. Rachel Bairsto says, 'Prior to the introduction of sugar in the eighteenth century, tooth problems were most often the result of excessive wear of the teeth from grinding hard, coarse food … However it was the introduction of sugar that was to have a major impact on our oral health'.[31] 'Sniftering' is another of Mary's descriptive words:

> I have had a cold most oppressive [she wrote to Charles] and conclude you and I were both [? …] sniftering at one moment; but what remains of my cold is still worse to support a perpetual pain in my face nothing less the cause, than that old villainous tooth – that Mr Barton good Man contrived to keep great by filling its great cavity and which lasted till a day or two of our setting out for Hardwick – when to my dismay, on eating a piece of an old buck Rabbit and coming in contact they had such a battle pulling and tugging till alas I lost all hold of comfort no time or opportunity to repair the ruins being in pain – I went my journey but had had no peace for a whole day Together since that encounter … The Candles are arrived and very nice ones they appear; previously we were under the necessity of borrowing at Willingham they are all wax, something thicker than these threes but very yellow I like what you have sent much better – and thank you for all the trouble we have given you … how you surprize me at the cheapness of your poultry &c. …
>
> I saw Fannys Piano at Gainsboro' and have settled to send for it soon – I also have got 4 tablespoons for you that Gibson gave me from Morton – we have just had Mr Chambers the Rector of Scartho – Oliver came with him the former the merriest Man I ever saw – we play'd a Rubber in the even^g and they left us this morning – your uncle from Castor [Samuel Turner] has also been with us from Tuesday till friday – rubbers every night – ringing changes between our Curate & the Vanes. [03.01.1816 4TdE/H/11d]

'Rubber' is a unit of play in card games. The game may have been whist as it was too early for bridge which dates from later in the nineteenth century. King-Hall confirms that 'Card playing was the great recreation of 18th-century society'.[32]

The Tennysons' diet appears to have been relatively healthy. Vegetables and fruit were grown at home. In a letter to her mother in September 1776, Mary says, 'I have sent a few Peaches as they are just upon the turn and very eatable' [10.09.1776 Tenn 2/6/9]. Meat was obtained from the butcher, with additional produce being caught in the wild, such as the 'old buck rabbit'. *The Art of Cookery Made Plain and Easy* contains a section on 'How to Market' including 'Butcher's Meat'.[33]

Amongst a bundle of letters in Lincolnshire Archives are a few recipes, one of which, for 'almond cheesecakes', is in Mary's hand:

> A quarter of a pound of Almonds/ditto, of sifted loaf Sugar/four Yolks of Eggs, and three ounces of fresh butter. Bruise your Almonds in a Mortar with a little Orange Flower Water, or, Rose Water, or, Brandy, or simple water merely to keep them from oiling – Put the Sugar to the Eggs and beat them till the mixture is light – add the Almonds, and then the Butter, which must previously have been dissolved over the Fire and put in very small Tins. [4TdE/H/42-49]

Others include 'Indian pickle', 'gingerbread cakes' and 'honeycomb gingerbread'. Ginger, sometimes combined with rhubarb, was often used for digestive problems. On one occasion Mary asked Charles to obtain 'some Chilly vinegar – also a little Cyane Pepper & some good [? Apricots]' [15.08.1819 TdE/H/81/20]. A few days later she requested cocoa:

> which we usually buy here perhaps there may be a sort more like Chocolate for I cannot take Cocoa such as we have – the Milk Chocolate I know is excellent but perhaps not very high prized – however send us of two sorts – viz. ... Sloanes – & of the other Humphrey being at Grimsby I do not know whether we want Candles or not – he having the key of the place you may venture to send a couple of papers of Spermacite. [22.08.1819 TdE/H/81/26]

Chilli vinegar is a variety of malt vinegar infused with chopped or whole chilli peppers. Hannah Glasse includes a recipe for chocolate, which was introduced to Europe by the Spaniards and became a popular beverage by the mid-seventeenth century.[34] Spermaceti is a pearly white wax-like material found in the head cavity of the sperm whale, and during the whaling era it was used for making candles and various other items.[35]

George's state of health was a perpetual source of worry as Mary related to Charles:

> Your poor Fathers immensely swell'd Foot – the last 3 days he has been obliged to use both his crutches threatening to take another portion of 'Eau Medicinale'

aware my acquiescence was wanting he waved it last night – pass'd it tolerably well and this morning came down to breakfast a little after Ten O'C, feeling weakened and enervated as might be expected this relaxing weather, but which on the whole I trust will prove salutary, for after a drive down to Rasen on which I accompanied he evidently was revived – and enabled too to put his foot to the ground. [13.12.1814 TdE/H/72/14]

A few weeks later Mary was becoming increasingly anxious about George:

Your father I am sorry to say has been laid up of the Gout ever since he wrote his last letter to you, his Hand swell'd enormously but am happy to satisfy your fear for him so far that we are in no danger from a too free use of Eau Medicinale having persuaded him to give it up for the present and in its place to try Mr Bartons Indorifics – and which last night seems to have answer'd all our wishes he is poor thing very weak & highly Nervous – having had a great deal of fear – of course taken little Nourishment – we had too much company last week which I think accelerated the Acme of the disease & I trust (for this bout) the worst is past. [11.01.1815 TdE/H/149/12]

Mary feared that George was taking too much of his gout medicine, which raises the question that he may have been slowly poisoning himself:

We have dreadful cold weather here and which I conclude is general throughout the kingdom experiencing one day the most heavy Rains – another Snow and cold Sleet, with sharp frost agreeing very ill with Mr Tennyson – his hand yet remains stiff and swelled though much mitigated – by a fresh affliction of Gout in his Feet – for which on Saturday night he took another half Bottle of Eau Medicinale. I always give it him with fear, apprehensive that some [? …] poison may lurk under so flattering immediate and powerful effect, and can only pray that the Almighty may be pleased to avert such an evil.

Mary closes with the happy news that George's niece, Elizabeth Raines, daughter of his sister Ann, is to be married to the Reverend George Inman of Skeffling in Yorkshire:

I now turn to a different scene to take place on Wednesday the first of May – when Miss Raines is to enter the Holy State of Matrimony she drove over to take leave on Saturday and invite us to the Wedding – they are to Breakfast at Mrs Yorkes after the ceremony, and then depart for their habitation at Skifflington in Holderness – she e[n]quired after yourself Ch^s & family – I sincerely wish her happy and by Mrs Yorkes account he seems a steady gentlemanly and suitable Man – tho no very advantageous match for her. [15.04.1816 4TdE/H/11c]

The last comment suggests that Skeffling was not a wealthy living.[36]

Although Mary was still concerned about George's health 'he is certainly better than when I last wrote – ate a Pidgeon with a small bit of Ham to his dinner yesterday with some Pleasure … I write this by stealth as yesterday when writing to Eliza he said "My dear who are you writing to? adding don't say to either Charles or Eliza that I am ill it will make them uneasy"' [17 July 1816 TdE/H/96/1].

We cannot know what was making George 'highly nervous'. Perhaps, contrary to Mary's letter, it was overuse of the *eau médicinale*. Indorifics are defined in '*A rare antique 1800s handwritten doctor recipes*', which seems to indicate that they were cure-all medicines prepared by individual doctors.[37] However, the *eau médicinale* may have had a good effect on George after all as some time later, Mary, writing to Charles, says:

> I seize the opportunity of inserting the best news in <u>this</u> cover (which covers by the by should be put a stop to in future) the weather having been changed to soft from severe, the Gout (with the use of the Medicine received from you this day week) has almost altogether disappeared – from the feet entirely, and only a little blackish spot remains on the knee – he has taken a little walk for a few minutes round the house on the gravel – and to day we are going an airing in the Carriage. [17.02.1818 TdE/H/ 78/6]

Later that year when George was away on business, Mary, still very dependent on him and feeling uncomfortable without him, stayed with their friends the Gray family in York and described the visit to Charles and Frances: 'I have been an inmate of our friends the Grays in you fathers absence – and in such society I did not feel so much the loss of your dear father as I otherwise should, had I remained in this my house & alone. They studied to make everything pleasing to me' [28.12.1818 TdE/H/80/15].

'A great sufferer': 1819–1825

The first real concern about Mary's health dates from 1819 when Charles expressed his anxiety in a letter to George. Dr Belcombe was from York:

> I feel under considerable alarm about my ever dear Mother. Dr Belcombe indeed has not been accustomed to witness her dreadful spasms but still to justify ye alarm he expresses to you he must think them quite beyond what he is accustomed to in practice. [29.01.1819 TdE/H/82/1]

In June of the same year Mary described herself as 'a great sufferer' [29.06.1819 TdE/H/84/2]. A few months later, in a letter to Charles, she mentions the problem from which she eventually died:

> I am in perpetual fear of taking cold lest all the misery of the last year should be repeated – having felt acute [? stingings] in my front Teeth – but I camphorate them well … but <u>no more</u> for this complaint, which <u>I trust</u> will subside without the rage I experienced is not to be cured by <u>Tooth-drawing</u> – … I have had no furious return of my Heart complaint yet a harry every day assails me as on the verge when I walk into the cool air of the Passage and it is gone so that it requires this management. [23.03.1820 4TdE/H/23/35]

A few weeks later she wrote:

> At present I am pretty well but about this time last week having had one of my severest attacks of impeded pulsation on my Heart – Barton recommends Calomel being persuaded he says that the liver is at fault viz: too inactive having felt some little pain in it the calomel has relieved me, but I am fearful of repeating it because of the nerves, about the Teeth.[38] [29.04.1820 TdE/H/85/23]

Despite the 'impeded pulsation on my Heart' the Tennysons travelled to Wetherby shortly afterwards en route for Harrogate where George was to take the waters:

> Having overcome all difficulties you will be glad to know that your Father and myself are pretty well considering, that in the beginning of this week we have been almost dying of heat – and now at the close of it shivering with cold – but the travelling has been particularly pleasant both to us and our Horses which brought us hither … We intend making but a fortnights stay at H-gate as long as will be proper for your Father to use the Waters – since we came here we are inform'd that Russell, Eliza &c &c – only pass'd on <u>this morning</u> to H:- I conclude that the place will be almost empty of company – as London at this moment swallows up every one of note or name, what the issue of this affair of the Queen's is difficult to guess – to me, it means a formidable appearance as it would seem there is not any prospect of a Coronation in August. [01.07.1820 TdE/H/85/44]

George IV and Queen Caroline had lived separately since 1796. A few months after the king's accession in 1820, Caroline, who had been living in Italy since 1814, returned to claim her rights as queen consort. A bill to deprive her of those rights and to dissolve the marriage on the grounds of her adultery was introduced into the House of Lords but was never put to a vote in the Commons. The problem was solved by Caroline's death on 7 August 1821.[39]

George's health was a constant worry, and this time he was suffering from boils as well as gout. Mary's problems do not seem to have been considered:

> And is very often saying to me – 'My dear I feel myself breaking – you may depend upon it I am giving way and shall not live over next year' to hear this sunk my spirits. [Dr. Barton] has stopt the night on account of your poor father's fever running very high, [and as George] is being so charged with Gout as he has been Mr Barton has concurred in his wish of taking Colchicum, or rather the Eau Medicinale. [26.01.1822 TdE/H/87/19]

Despite his fears George was to live for another thirteen years. Dr Barton often stayed the night with Mary and George when George's ailments were giving trouble. He would not have done this with all his patients, only with friends such as Mary and George and those with the social standing and means to pay his bills.

A few days later George was a little better, but Mary was again uneasy about the overuse of colchicum, as she wrote to Charles:

> 'Alas' I greatly fear this is accomplished by that dreadful 'Medicine' that 'care [? ...] & Antidote' your suspicions are but too true and I am sensibly alive to unfavorable impressions – however I may rejoice in present good, the Eau Medicinale has been taken twice, but I never see it swallowed ... this is an endurance not to be described however, as I have no remedy but trust in the Almightys mercy to give a blessing to the medicine, I endevor as heretofore to be happy as I can under the tryal. [31.01.1822 4TdE/H/26/-]

In June 1823 Mary's letters again refer to her health problems:

> Your dear Father in expressing to his fearful and tender interest respecting my present state of health- may in you have undesignedly excited undue alarm, mentioning my asthmatic disorder, which from having taken cold has certainly increased upon my proper care and attention – through the blessing of God to mitigate – Mr Barton attends me in administering the Medicines prescribed by Dr Gibney at Brighton – together with any alterations he may judge necessary. [21.06.1823 4TdE/H/33s]

On 10 February 1825 George was involved in an accident with a gig when returning to Tealby from Market Rasen and was fortunate to escape serious injury. Mary described the incident to Charles: 'he arrived something later than the usual dinner hour on open^g the door he said in a feeble voice My dear you have nearly had a dead Husband brought home to you' [10.02.1825 2TdE/H/103/5]. A gig Is a light two-wheeled carriage pulled by one horse.[40]

By May 1825, Mary's health was seriously deteriorating. On 6 July George wrote to Charles: 'Your beloved Mo^r is certainly no worse of her Asthma, tho' it does not leave her, I hope & trust that her complaint is not worse than asthma'. In the same letter he expresses his devotion to Mary: 'Your beloved Mo^r & myself have been married half a Century on 2^{3rd} Inst, if we attain to that time. How happy we sho^d be to see you, & all or any of yours that day' [06.07.1825 4TdE/H/36/1]. They did, just, 'attain to that time'.

The following day Mary wrote her last letter to Charles:

> I must in a measure speak of the happiness it conveyed, as well as the gratitude that remains to God for giving me so affectionate a Child what to tell you of my disorder, I know not how scarcely to convey, my asthma or <u>short breathing</u> – you will be sorry to hear – I am perpetually combating i.e. I cannot move even from Chair to Chair without heaving or rather palpitation of Heart – yet by slow movement & care get out not only from room to room, but an airing every day – & Barton gives me hopes of being better, but <u>how much better</u> not any of us can guess – he is most earnest and even affectionate in his attention to me, & I feel very happy in having a Medical Man for my friend … At present do not show this letter to poor Eliza as I would not have her for a moment roused to think worse of my case that she has done in short all is yet <u>dark</u> but I am so happy as to be. [07.07.1825 4TdE/H/33/-]

Her 'asthma or <u>short breathing</u>' is likely to relate to heart problems. Apart from the breathlessness, 'the face and extremities may be blue and ankles swollen, and exercise makes the condition markedly worse, often in paroxysms. Breathing is easier if the patient is propped up'.[41]

A few days later Doctor Barton wrote the following letter to Charles. The tone is reasonably positive:

> From the time (10 o'Clock) I wrote last night until ab^t one o Clock this morning Mrs Tennyson was much distress'd from difficulty of breathing after wch she became more compos'd and got some small portion of sleep during the night, more than she has had for ye last 2 or 3 nights, when I saw y^r Mother this evening Ab^t 7 o Clock, I thought her looking rather better, and felt somewhat refresh'd from the little sleep she had obtain'd in the night … upon the whole the day has been rather better, but I dare not say <u>at present</u> there is any real amendment. [July 1825 4TdE/H/33e]

On 5 August the situation again seemed more hopeful. George wrote to Charles:

Your beloved Mo^r is, I hope, in a recovering State & feels all your attentions & hopes to be well enough when you arrive to make you happy & cheerful as Mr Barton will write to you about what you are so anxious to know (your Dr Mothers state of health) I will say no more on this kind and I beg of you to be as happy as you can, for shall any things happen to require your sooner being here you shall hear from me. [05.08.1825 4TdE/H/33/1]

Despite the 'recovering state' Mary died on 20 August 1825 at the age of seventy-two.

The following day Charles passed on the news to Samuel Turner. Relations with his uncle had always been difficult, and the following letters suggest a rift in the family:

My Affectionate Mother and your Affectionate Sister is no more ... I do not know whether you would desire to attend the Funeral – tell in reply & in that case I will send you the earliest notice of the day fixed – It is a thing we do not at all request & therefore must follow your own inclination ... My Father has been much afflicted but this evening is totally composed. Excuse my poor scrawl ... my head ackes very much. [21.08.1825 T2/10/23]

Samuel replied:

I feel greatly obliged by your kind attention to my feeling on this melancholy occasion, my affection leads me to attend her dear remains to the Grave, but perhaps all things considered, it is better avoided, – it might derange your general Plan and, as you observe, can answer no real purpose. I give up the thought. [22 08.1825 TdE/H/33j]

A few days later Elizabeth sent the following tribute:

Thank you my dearest Charles, for your beautiful descriptions of her last hours, they <u>are</u>, & will <u>always</u> be my first treasures which life is continued in me – If ever an <u>innocent</u> Life (so protracted) attained a happier, she has done so, her <u>pure</u> – <u>intentioned</u>, upright, humble ... & <u>Charitable</u> Heart, have seldom been equalled. [Aug/Sept 1825 4TdE/H/33l]

Mary Tennyson Bourne wrote to Charles a few weeks later: 'my sympathies for those I love & my dear Father especially weigh heavy on my heart but I am sustained by the Joyful & <u>Scriptural</u> persuasion that our dear departed parent is now one among the thousands spoken of in Revelation' [23.09.1825 TdE/H/33e].

The funeral took place at Tealby on 31 August. It was a grand affair as befitted the social status that the family had attained. A sheet of instructions found in Lincolnshire Archives informs mourners that 'The procession to move just before 2 O clock. The church bell to commence tolling at ½ minute to time at ¼ past [? ...] & to continue until the body shall arrive at M^r [? Broadgate's] House, when it will toll in the usual [? manner], until the Body arrives at the north gate of the church y^d. the parties will proceed 2 & 2' [31.08.1825 TdE/H/13/24].

The procession was led by the Reverend J. C. Young and Dr Zephaniah Barton, followed by bearers, Mr A. Clarke the undertaker and his assistants, then the hearse. The mourning coach bearing Mary's children preceded 'Mr Tennyson's carriage' with 'Horse & carriage craped'. The rest of the family and friends, including Mr and Mrs Vane, Mr Simkiss, Mr Boucherett, and Mr Heneage, followed, with tenants and servants in order of seniority bringing up the rear. The 'crape' (crêpe) refers to the black silk pall covering the carriage, bier and hearse.

Mary is buried in the family vault under the chancel in All Saints church at Tealby. On her memorial plaque are the words: 'after a union of 50 years she was survived by her husband who deeply lamented her loss'. A handsome tribute follows, describing her 'devoted tenderness as a wife and mother; her constancy, sincerity and active benevolence; by her pure mind, amiable manners and affectionate disposition, she was so endeared to her family, friends and the poor, that by them and all who knew her, she was justly respected, beloved and mourned'.

Afterword: George, 1825 to 1835

George was grief-stricken, perhaps belatedly realizing what a comfort and support Mary had been throughout their fifty years together. It is ironic that after so many years of devoted care for him, Mary was to die first. George survived her by ten years and lived a lonely life, first at Bayons Manor, then at nearby Usselby: 'My health is better, but the better I feel in health, the more I feel my great & irreparable loss & recollections crowd upon me more frequently & more strongly, every things a trouble & over much for me but no more of this' [April 1826 4TdE/H/37/3].

Four years after Mary's death, George wrote this melancholy letter to Charles. His grandsons Charles and Alfred, sons of George Clayton, aged twenty-one and twenty, respectively, had been staying. It seems the visit had not been a great success:

> Char^s & Alfred left me on Friday they did not act disrespectably to me but they are so untoward & disorderly & so unlike other people I dont know what will become of them, or what can be done with, or about them. I tried to impress them with the feeling that they and Fred^k was spending or wasting half their

Father's Income, & he had only half to maintain himself his wife & to Educate 4 other Boys & 4 Girls … these 3 boys so far from having improved in manner or Manners are worse since they went to Cambridge … The snow is here so deep and drifts I cannot get to Rasen … I keep well and live in the Housekeepers room for warmth. [26.01.1829 2TdE/H/86/3]

Frederick, aged twenty-two, was George Clayton's eldest surviving son.

In 1833 George sent a strange and incomprehensible letter to Lady Ingilby. It suggests he may be suffering from the early stages of dementia:

I hereby give your Ladyship, your Lord Sir W^m, my Son the Rt Honble C Tennyson & also Julia & Clara Tennyson spinsters, that I mean to indite you all for a conspiracy against me a poor old man who on the 7th Inst / if he lives so long will arrive at the great age of 83, by your threatening Letter of the other day … I will send you a pat of butter from the Cow Lady pasture, I mean to make you a charge for her keep, therefore the sooner you can be here to partake of warm milk honey etc the better for you

I am Dear Lady Ingilby your oblig'd and Affect. Friend Geo Tennyson Not D'eancourt. [2 February 1833 TdE/H/64/34][42]

George died on 9 July 1835 'in his 86th year'. The *Stamford Mercury* of 16 July contained a long report of his funeral, part of which is quoted here:

His remains preceded by the Rev. Atkinson, Vicar of Usselby, attended by his tenantry, and followed by his son, the Right Hon. Charles Tennyson, M.P., were removed in the night between Sunday and Monday last from Usselby to Bayons Manor, and on Monday at two o' clock were interred in the family vault in the Chancel of Tealby church … Sixty individuals from the town and vicinity followed his remains on horseback. … The number of persons who assembled to obtain a sight of the last receptacle of their kind departed landlord and friend, showed the affection with which his memory was regarded after a continued residence among them during the greater part of a century.

Mary is not forgotten:

Nor was the remembrance of his amiable and most benevolent lady less vivid during this impressive scene.[43]

In 1836 George's lifelong friend, William Gray, wrote in his notebook:

The only social privation I have to notice lately is the death of my very old friend George Tennyson Esq which took place during last summer. He was a year and a quarter older than myself and our acquaintance and intercourse was kept up for about 80 years, having commenced at a Dame's School in our infancy.[44]

Notes

1 Douglas Boyce, *The Tennyson Family in Market Rasen: Notes for the Exhibition in Market Rasen Parish Church 2nd and 3rd October 1992* (Market Rasen: Market Rasen Society, 1992), p. 2.
2 Roy and Lesley Adkins, *Eavesdropping on Jane Austen's England* (London: Little, Brown, 2013), p. 300.
3 Magdalen King-Hall, *The Story of the Nursery* (London: Routledge & Kegan Paul, 1958), p. 117.
4 Robert Bernard Martin, *Tennyson: The Unquiet Heart* (Oxford: Clarendon Press, 1980), p. 2.
5 '*T*' newspaper 1 May 2018.
6 https://www.britannica.com/biography/Joseph-Banks [accessed 2 December 2019].
7 https://www.royalacademy.org.uk/art-artists/name/robert-bickerstaff [accessed 11 October 2021].
8 Confirmed by George Tennyson's will [LCC Wills 1835/326].
9 Boyce, 1992, p. 2.
10 Joseph O. Baylen and J. Norman Gossman, *Biographical Dictionary of Modern British Radicals*, 3 vols (Hassocks: Harvester, 1979–88), p. 120.
11 Sir Wharton Amcotts (1740–1807) MP for East Retford, Nottinghamshire, 1780–90 and 1796–1802. https://www.historyofparliamentonline.org/ [accessed 15 August 2020]. No information about the Reverend Brownlow Potter has been found.
12 £1,000 in 1783 = £151,906.67 in today's money. £1,100 in 1787 = £174,059.72 in today's money. https://www.bankofengland.co.uk/monetary-policy/inflation [accessed 11 November 2020].
13 Information from the Drakes family website. The estate was purchased by Reginald William Drakes (1894–1969) in 1944: http://www.drakesfamily.org/id42.htm [accessed 10 November 2020].
14 Douglas Boyce, 'The Tennyson family in Market Rasen 1774–1835', *Tennyson Research Bulletin*, 6:2 (1993), 122–9 (124).
15 http://www.bbc.co.uk/history [accessed 28 February 2019].
16 £7 in 1780 = £1,265.89 in today's money. https://bankofengland.co.uk/monetary-policy/inflation [accessed 11 November 2020].
17 £600 in 1794 = £80,421.18 in today's money. https://www.bankofengland.co.uk/monetary-policy/inflation [accessed 11 November 2020].
18 Jim Murray, 'The Tennyson connection', in *Facets of Tealby*, ed. by John Howard (Tealby: Tealby Society, 2002), p. 49.
19 See Gordon Jackson, *Grimsby and the Haven Company, 1796–1846* (Grimsby: Grimsby Public Libraries & Museum, 1971).

20 Geri Walton, 'Snuff and snuff-boxes in the 1700s and 1800s', *Unique Histories from the 18th and 19th Centuries*, https://www.geriwalton.com/?s=snuff [accessed 23 June 2020].
21 Martin, 1980, p. 3.
22 Amanda Vickery, *Behind Closed Doors: At Home in Georgian England* (New Haven, CT: Yale University Press, 2010), p. 9.
23 Adkins, pp. 131–2.
24 LCNTE: 2016/53.
25 *Concise Oxford English Dictionary*, 2006.
26 Adkins, p. 243.
27 Adkins, pp. 295–6.
28 *Bartholomew's Gazetteer of the British Isles* (London: George Newnes, 1904), p. 757.
29 Lucy Worsley, *If Walls Could Talk* (London: Faber and Faber, 2011), p. 300.
30 23 guineas in 1810 = £1,898.83 in today's money. 30 guineas in 1810 = £2,452.66 in today's money. https://bankofengland.co.uk/monetary-policy/inflation [accessed 11 November 2020].
31 Rachel Bairsto, *The British Dentist* (Oxford: Shire, 2015), pp. 5–6.
32 King-Hall, p. 150.
33 Hannah Glasse, *The Art of Cookery Made Plain and Easy* (New York: Dover, 2015 (1805)), p. 7.
34 Glasse, p. 248.
35 https://www.whalefacts.org/spermaceti/ [accessed 15 March 2020].
36 The village is Skeffling in East Yorkshire. *AA Concise Road Atlas, Britain*, 38th edn (Basingstoke: AA Publishing, 2015), p. 61.
37 https://www.worthpoint.com/worthopedia/antique-1800s-handwritten-doctor [accessed 5 April 2021].
38 *Concise Oxford English Dictionary*, 2006.
39 https://www.britannica.com/biography/George-IV [accessed 9 March 2022].
40 *Concise Oxford English Dictionary*, 2006.
41 Joan Gomez, *A Dictionary of Symptoms* (St Albans: Paladin, 1973), p. 132.
42 Sir William Amcotts-Ingilby, 2nd Baronet 1783–1854 of Ripley Castle, N. Yorkshire & Kettlethorpe Hall, Lincs. He was MP for East Retford. Presumably he is the husband of Lady Ingilby, and perhaps the son of Sir Wharton Amcotts from whom George purchased lands at Tealby. https://www.historyofparliamentonline.org/ [accessed 15 August 2020].
43 *The Lincoln, Rutland and Stamford Mercury*, 9 July 1835. Typewritten copy from the newspaper by Douglas Boyce.
44 Almyra Gray, *Papers and Diaries of a York Family, 1764–1838* (London: Sheldon, 1927).

3

'Star of the North': Elizabeth Tennyson Russell, 1776 to 1865

Marion Sherwood

Elizabeth was Mary and George's first child and favourite daughter, 'our dearly loved Eliza' [03.07.1821 TdE/H/86/22]. A particularly close bond developed between Elizabeth and her mother during recurring childhood illness. As an adult, married to the wealthy Matthew Russell and living in County Durham, Elizabeth became the beloved 'Muse'[1] of her brother George Clayton and her nephew Alfred's favourite aunt. She continued an affectionate correspondence with the poet, enclosing a substantial annual cheque, until the end of her life. Tennyson biographers refer to Elizabeth's charm,[2] which is clearly apparent in her letters – like her mother and siblings she had a gift for language. But with the 'overpowering excitability of [her] nervous system' [13.07.1821 TdE/H/86/4] she shared the family's perceived and inherent 'spell against concord'.[3] Her relationship with George Clayton deteriorated, she did not attend his funeral or that of her father and she challenged the executors of Matthew's will, two of whom were her son William and her brother Charles. During Elizabeth's long widowhood the nervous excitability that accompanied or, as her mother believed, caused her childhood ill health deepened into depression, for which the only cure was constant 'locomotion' [[28.07.1825] TdE/H/144/182]. The earliest surviving letter written by Elizabeth herself dates from September 1797 when she was twenty-one. For insight into her early years we must therefore rely on the letters of other family members, predominantly those of her mother, Mary Turner Tennyson.

'Bessy ... seems quite easy and well': February 1776 to *c.* summer 1780

Elizabeth, known in childhood as Bessy or Bess, was baptized at Market Rasen on 18 April 1776, ten months after Mary and George's wedding. She was perhaps named in memory of George's mother, Elizabeth Tennyson, née Clayton, who died in 1755 aged twenty-eight when George was almost five and his sister Ann just two.[4] We learn of her birth from Mary's younger brother Samuel, who writes to their father John Turner in late April:

> It gave me great Pleasure to hear of my Sisters happy delivery ... pray give my sincere love and kiss, and thank her for the honourable Title of Uncle which she has confered upon me. [27.04.[1776] T2/4/7]

Mary's early letters to her mother, Mary Turner, contain few references to Elizabeth. She is mentioned only after all other news has been included. Mary writes in greater detail when the child is ill and as she grows older, becoming a companion for Mary when George is away. In early May 1776 she comments briefly: 'As Bessy is much better she changes Collour a good deal but seems quite easy and well' [02.05.1776 Tenn 2/1/8]. Like her siblings she was placed with a wet nurse at the age of six weeks and 'Bessy in her new situation finds no ill Effects' [28.05.1776 Tenn 2/6/5]. By the time she came home in June 1777 Mary and George's second child, young Mary, was five weeks old.

'Bessy' became less 'easy and well'. In October 1777 she suffered a series of nightmares and apparent hallucinations caused by teething:[5]

> we have had two or 3 such bad nights with Bessy that if she continues so I cant Possibly leave her She awak'd on Saturday night in a most shocking fright ...
> Molly got a light and went up to her (it was betwixt 12 and one O Clock) Betty had her in her Arms and was walking about with her – when she saw Molly and the Candle she took no more notice than as tho' she had not seen 'em but look'd at the farther end of the room, and still kept screaming they brought her down into my room and very Glad she was to come to me ... I sent immediately for Mr Walker [a doctor] for I thought every moment the Child wou'd lose her Sences and be in fitts – She continu'd so whilst he came and somtime after; he felt in her mouth but said it was too soon to Lanach her Gums ... she has since that been very fretfull with her teeth. [07.10.1777 Tenn 2/8/7]

Molly and Betty are two of the Tennysons' servants. Mary adds, 'Georges father is here so he'll be doctring her' as the Walkers 'leave Raisin next week'. George's father, Michael Tennyson (1721–1796), was an apothecary and had the right to practise medicine.⁶

Mary and George's third child, George Clayton, was baptized at Market Rasen on 10 December 1778. He came home from the wet nurse in April 1780. By then young Mary, soon to turn three, had already spent much of her life in Caistor; during the summer of 1780 this arrangement became permanent when Mary 'redily Accept[ed]' her mother's offer 'to keep Mary' [*c.* summer 1780 Tenn 2/8/12]. By September 1783 George Clayton was living with Michael Tennyson in Holderness, where 'he has had the Hooping Cough' [16.09.1783 Tenn 2/4/23]. Elizabeth was the only one of Mary and George's three older children to remain at home until she went to boarding school. The resulting close relationship with her parents was strengthened by her childhood illnesses, which Mary feared 'will bring her to the grave' [24.03.1789 Tenn 2/5/47].

'Bessy ... has been so poorly of late':
c. 1778–79 to January 1788

Between 1778–79 and 1789 Elizabeth suffered periods of ill health, which added to Mary's concern for her own and her parents' well-being:

> I imagine my Father acquainted you with my intention of going to [? Saltfleet] – I once thought of taking Bessy with me she has been so poorly of late her eyes have been so weak and her Appetite so bad that she never eats one hearty Meal ... Bathing wou'd do you good & I'm thoroughly perswaded it will do me good with the Blessing of God I have almost always a Pain in my Head and at all times exceeding weak. [*c.* 1778–79 Tenn 2/8/27]

Spa towns and seaside resorts became popular during the eighteenth century. 'Bathing' increased as sea water was thought to share the health benefits of mineral springs. Saltfleet is on the Lincolnshire coast about eight miles north of 'Mablethorpe', the 'infant Ilion' of the poet's mind 'when a child'.⁷

Elizabeth was again unwell in February 1780. Mary 'imagine[s] her Complaint is worms for she cant sometimes keep her Breakfast or dinner upon her Stomach' [22.02.1780 Tenn 2/3/6]. Attributing 'her Complaint' to worms reflects continuing belief in the four humours. Based on 'Hippocratic and Galenic medical traditions', this held that living creatures consisted of four fluids or humours – blood, choler, melancholy and phlegm.⁸ Their balance altered during the life cycle and illness resulted when humours became corrupted or unbalanced. Children, being 'more warm and moist than other ages', were 'very apt to produce Worms'.

Her digestive problems returned a year later. Writing of 'Neighbourly visit[s]', Mary concludes with a graphic account of her illness:

> she has had a purging upon her these 3 weeks but is now getting better – she Purg'd the very slime of her Bowels away and her stools were Nothing but Jelly and Blood and was 3 days before that could be put a stop to. [02.01.1781 Tenn 2/1/20]

Three months later she was suffering from a skin condition. Mary's relationship with her father-in-law was not always harmonious, but on this occasion he intervened to help her:

> Bessy's face has been better latly but I forgot to tell you that her Grandfather when he saw her said nothing cou'd be of so much service to her as an Issue – Physick she was to have none upon any Account – George said as you know he Always has done that a few doses wou'd do her good – I foresaw what wou'd be the case when his father left us – that she was to take Physick – so I took his father Aside and told him that he must frighten him from pursuing his inclination – by all Means so he went directly to George to tell him (After some little Altercation) – <u>that every dose of Physick that Child takes is one more Nail in her Coffin</u> – as he did not look upon her constitution to be good – It had the desir'd Effect – as to frighten him from it … she looks better – and had an Issue set the day After we got home he says we may dry it up in the Course of half a Year if we Chuse if her humors Abate. [23.07.1782 Tenn 2/1/23]

An Issue is the discharge of blood or other fluids from the body.[9] It can also mean a surgical cut to allow an abscess to drain and the comment 'we may dry it up' suggests she has a running sore. Michael Tennyson's concluding advice gives an insight into the 'diet' thought suitable for a convalescent child: 'her Grandfather has order'd her to have what Plain diet she wishes All sorts of Butchers Meat Plain drest and broths New Milk as often as she will'.

In December 1783 Mary was distressed to find herself pregnant again and had 'a hard struggle to feel happy and compos'd under what has fall'n to my lot' [10.12.1783 Tenn 2/3/10]. Mary and George's fourth and last child, Charles, was baptized at Market Rasen on 20 July 1784. Charles, like Elizabeth, remained at home until he went away to school and formed a close relationship with his parents.

By January 1785 Elizabeth, who would turn nine in April, has become a companion to Mary. Young Mary, almost eight, is still in Caistor and six-year-old

George Clayton is in Holderness. 'I am many hours alone in an Evening', Mary tells her mother, 'so make the same company of Bessy you do of Mary she reads exceedingly well' [25.01.1785 Tenn 2/3/11].

George Clayton was taken to St Peter's School in York by his father in June 1787. Elizabeth had turned eleven two months earlier, and the following January Mary confirms that she too is away at school:

> Bess wrote another to me a Post or two since wherein she says she is almost well & mentions what a pleasure it will be to her the having Mary with her and is sure she will like school …
>
> Talking of Marys going to school will serve as a preface to mentioning her coming home. [08.01.1788 Tenn 2/1/29]

As related in greater detail in Chapter 6, Mary's 'preface' set in train the painful process of bringing young Mary 'home' to Market Rasen.

Family letters give no details of the school. Unlike St Peter's School, founded in AD 627,[10] the girls' school was probably one of the new commercial schools whose numbers expanded during the late eighteenth and early nineteenth centuries. These were 'private ventures dependent on fees and run for the profit of their teachers': existing grammar or public schools were charitable or endowed foundations.[11] Most commercial schools took boarding and day pupils. Girls' schools were the greater educational innovation, offering an alternative to private education in the home, and by teaching useful subjects (reading, writing and arithmetic) and polite accomplishments (French, dancing, drawing and music) they became extremely popular.

'The origin appears to have been entirely nervous': March 1789 to April 1794

Elizabeth was back at Market Rasen in March 1789, seriously ill and presumably sent home from school to recover. Amanda Vickery states that in Georgian England 'after childbirth itself, life-threatening illness was the supreme trial that parents faced'.[12] Watching their children's acute suffering 'was a virtually universal ordeal' yet, she adds, one 'which merits barely a sentence in many accounts of genteel life'. This is not the case with Mary. Her letters relate in painful detail not only Elizabeth's suffering and her own 'ordeal' but also the agony of other 'genteel' families enduring contemporary medical treatment. In early March she mentions the Hinde family, now living in the Tennysons' former home in Queen Street:

> young Mrs Hinde Lay-In About 3 weeks since of a very fine Boy to the great Joy of the Family – but in a few days their joy chang'd to sorrow for the Child began to be very uneasy from having no Stool poor little creature it was often you may suppose in great pain and began to swell till its body was ready to burst it continu'd in this State more than a fortnight they try'd Blisters and Syringes and Medicine to no Effect – and found it inevitably must die if they did not try what cutting a passage might procure Accordingly it underwent a very painful operation of probing and cutting the first gain'd the first black Stool and after that one of a common collour but poor thing it continues in great pain often screaming out … They dont know where they cut it must be in the dark for it was 2 inches in it's body at first they thought it was a thin <u>Skin grown</u> over but dont now appear so – it's stools keep always coming so they in all probability have cut at the side of the Gutt. [02.03.1789 Tenn 2/5/45]

A 'Blister' is 'a plaster smeared with a harsh caustic substance placed on the body' to provoke blistering and force out 'any toxins'.[13] Parish registers do not record a Hinde baptism in 1789; unsurprisingly therefore the child died.

Eighteen days later a distressed Mary describes her own suffering child:

> The poor child is only able to take Lemons and Oranges which seems to correct an uncomfortable Nausea she has had at her stomach & thank God to day she dont complain of such deadly weakness as yesterday two or 3 hour in the Morning of yesterday she was so irritated by continual reaching that she told us if we walk'd in the room or even wisper'd to each other she felt so harried it wo^u kill her when she settl'd I did not venture to raise her head from the Pillow lest Sickness sho'd follow … my Spirits are rather cheer'd from a seeming change for the better & I have from the beginning my dear Mother put my trust in that great Physician of all or I co^u not have been hitherto supported … what I most dread are the horrors which night brings on me & the consequences that may ensue but a harry of spirits at present keeps me up for the childs sake at times her poor heart feels afraid for me which the more distresses me. [20.03.1789 Tenn 2/6/26]

Mary's empathetic identification with her daughter intensifies as she grows weaker:

> I scarce know whether to say this poor dear Girl be better or worse her strength gradually is worse for though the sickness is remov'd & appetite increas'd yet it is whimsical … her sleep is such as to give her no refreshment she seems to have many complaints for half an hour together and the next they are fled the

origin appears to have been entirely nervous but I fear will bring her to the grave ... poor dear Creature she is now on the outside of the Bed with only half her cloaths having twice fail'd in the attempt to rise ...

My Dear Mother I think the chance for her life is next to nothing she dont suffer much pain which keeps up my spirits ... I am in an agony when I think of her dyeing and recover myself as hope comes to my Assistance – when she is bad I am so & as she is better my spirits mend but God Almighty will be done.

She conveys George's anguish in a single sentence and wishes for her mother's practical presence:

George is so Affected he neither eats or sleeps I am truly sorry to find you are poorly & heartily wish you better – and when you can come pray do I ... I am distress'd and want you to talk to somtimes – and it wo[u] relieve me for five minutes to sit with the dear child when I cannot. [24.03.1789 Tenn 2/5/47]

The poet's grandson writes of the adult Elizabeth that 'she had not her mother's serenity of temperament' and 'in times of crisis her nervous excitability caused her acute suffering'.[14] Mary's letters, written when she was 'in an agony' rather than serene, reveal that Elizabeth's 'nervous excitability' was recognized and caused her 'acute suffering' when she was a child of twelve.

She was still unwell three months later:

we arriv'd all safe and well and better than I expected from Bessys complaint she continues still the same weakness in her body and yesterday had sixteen stools tho she had taken twice of a bottle to stop the Violence of it but as it had not the desir'd Effect she has taken somthing more powerful to day and tho she is greatly better in this respect she is constantly sick and Grip'd and is never able to take the least nourishment – I fear from other Symtoms that she is not likely to get well soon. [26.06.1789 Tenn 2/6/28]

Her health is fully restored as she turns eighteen. Writing to George in London in April 1794, Mary concludes, 'Bessy never was so well as at this time she is quite fat' [27.04.1794 4TdE/H/2/7].

'The amiable Person & Manner of your eldest Daughter': August and September 1796

Elizabeth received her first, albeit indirect, proposal of marriage in August 1796 when she was twenty years old. A. R. Robinson, a Grimsby solicitor who became George's business partner when the Tennysons moved to Lincoln in 1791–92, wrote to Mary expressing his unnamed son's admiration for Elizabeth. Late-eighteenth-century England was a patriarchal society and Mrs Robinson's wishes are not mentioned, but Mr Robinson does not hesitate to enlist Mary's help on behalf of his son:

> Dear Madam
>
> I flatter myself you will excuse the Liberty I am now taking in addressing myself to you on a subject to me of the greatest Moment as it involves in it no less than the Felicity of a Child of whom I flatter myself I have some Reason to be proud. My Son previous to his coming to Town last Winter spent some time with you at Lincoln where the amiable Person & Manner of your eldest Daughter made (what I have every reason to be or believe will be) an indelible Impression. Anxious for the Happiness of my Son when M^r. Tennyson came to Town I made overtures to him on the subject who very handsomely acknowledged that he c^d have no objections to the Connection at a <u>proper</u> Time but that his Daughter was too young to marry at present … When he came down to Lincoln on the Partnership being concluded I find he was well recv^d by the Lady & Family … then of my surprize when in a Letter from my Son dated 23rd Inst: I find that in a Conversation with M^r. T he … requests him to behave exactly the same to her as to everyone else. He very properly adds that he sho^d not think of any Connection untill he saw him properly establish'd in Life … & in the mean time he was to be as a common Acquaintance.

Mr Robinson wishes George to reflect on his happy courtship of Mary and reconsider his decision:

> All I ask or wish is that he may be permitted in those Hours <u>necessary</u> & <u>proper</u> for <u>Relaxation from Business</u> [to] spend them as he wo^d wish with your amiable Daughter that he may be recv^d as <u>heretofore</u> not merely as a <u>common Acquaintance</u> & this I trust he has a Chance unless he forfeits that indulgence by any impropriety in his Conduct which I hope will never be the Case. I assure you on my Honor he knows nothing of this Letter …
>
> Your most obed^t Srv^t A. R. Robinson [29.08.1796 TRC 4606]

Mary's carefully conciliatory reply is at times repetitive because, as she states, 'this is a delicate subject':

> Dear S^r,
>
> I have had the Honour of receiving y^{rs} of the 29th of August … & am sorry that I have not had any an [*sic*] opportunity of answering it sooner & that your Son sho^d think he has had reason to complain of any inattention of mine or Mr

Tennysons. I can assure you what ever has been said to him by either of us was really a view of serving him, Mr Tennyson admits you are perfectly correct in your quotation of what pass^{d} personally betwixt you & him so far as you have gone & I heartily join him in the sentiments he then expressed he begs you will recollect that he at the same time told you he did not know or think that his Daughter had any attachment to your Son.

Mary repeats her belief that Elizabeth did not have an 'attachment' to Mr Robinson's son. By doing so and by emphasizing 'her sincerity & honourable feelings' Mary strives to protect her daughter's reputation. For Elizabeth and her genteel female contemporaries, any perceived impropriety would jeopardize the successful negotiation of a future marriage contract. (As revealed in Chapter 5, the investigation of Frances Mary Hutton's previous attachment delayed her marriage to Charles.)

> I must add that I do not know or believe that she had any [attachment] at present, ... this I believe because I know her sincerity & honourable feelings & I do not think she has yet formed any attachm^{t} of this sort this is a delicate subject ... for me to write upon however I co^{d} not omit answering your [? ...] & in assuring you we both Mr T & myself will always be [? friends] to your Son & shall be happy to see you at Lincoln ... for as long a time as you can make it convenient Our Girls join us in respectful comp^{ts} & I am Dr Sr Yrs. [07.09.1796 TRC 4681]

Mary's formal salutation closes the correspondence with A. R. Robinson.

'The prospect before her in being happy with the choice she has made': September 1797 to January 1798

Until Elizabeth is twenty-one we learn of her life and character from the letters of other people. We read her own words for the first time in a letter to Mary Turner dated September 1797. She rejects the diminutive Bessy and signs her conversational, occasionally waspish and rather self-satisfied letter Eliza:

> I have asked leave to answer my dear Grandmothers Letter which my Mother has just received it is a long time since we regularly corresponded but I hope it is needless to make assurances that it did not proceed from a coldness of affection, though was you merely to estimate it by the frequency of our Letters it would be greatly under value, but I cannot account for it, when we are gadding about why we do not write except that our minds are forced into activity about the little

occurrences which of course always happen in a life of gaiety & then things of greater importance are neglected.

After her long excuse for not writing she turns to news of family and friends. Like her mother when younger, Elizabeth has decided views on the character of her neighbours:

> You will be surprised to hear that my Father has sold his House to M[r] Burton for £1500 & we quit next May day,[15] we shall be at Grimsby for some time which we are all glad of as it is much nearer you, my Father thinks of building a House from the old foundations at Tealby, we none of us regret quitting Lincoln every body agreeable seems tired of the place & talk of leaving, M[r] Field is not at home but when he returns & is informed of this resolution of my Fathers I think he will be sorry, indeed we shall be as much hurt to leave them for no one who is thoroughly acquainted with M[r] or M[rs] F- but must respect & esteem them … but we must own that the Generality of Lincoln people are not pleasant.
>
> I hope my dear Grandmother you remain well we are all so excepting Colds how are my Uncles We often have opportunitys of hearing of you from people we see – we have not yet heard what Physician takes Dr Fellowes's House I think Byron will not find it answers he has rather too good an opinion of himself – we have no news stirring which will entertain you or be worth penning I am ashamed to send this scrawl but a bad Letter is better than none.

Perhaps because Elizabeth writes on her mother's behalf she signs herself 'your very affectionate daughter Eliza Tennyson' [22.09.1797 Tenn 2/1/31].

Three months later George approves a 'Connection' for Elizabeth. She is to marry Matthew Russell (1765–1822) a captain, later a major, in the Durham Militia, who inherited a mining fortune and several houses, including Brancepeth Castle and Hardwick Hall in County Durham, when his father died. William Russell (1735–1817) was a banker and one of the 'Grand Allies' who controlled the late-eighteenth-century coal trade in north-east England.[16] Mary writes at length to her mother about 'the Major' and 'the Wedding':

> I'm sorry to say in reply to yours respecting the Major that Illness was the principal cause of his staying so long at Hull he did not return till last Night 7 o'C was confin'd to the House the whole of the time he was away by a Violent cold and cough … he has yet the remains of a cough and looks thiner, but he hopes to have no further occasion to visit Hull till March he therefore has settld all his affairs & given up his Lodgings – to take up his residence with us – 'till the Wedding takes place which I believe will be accomplish'd about the 3[d] or last week in next month

I flatter myself my dear Mother that the dear girl may [? contemplate] the prospect before her in being happy with the choice she has made and, so approv'd by all who know him – when he is mention'd from what ever quarter we hear nothing but his praises resounded – ... I have only to add that I hope you will not delay in coming in time to settle yourself that is at Least 10 days or a fortnight before and so to give me the comfort of your company after they are gone as well as before

I am very busy preparing, as she will have everything new from Head to foot, and a complete assortment. [15.12.1797 Tenn 2/6/31]

Mary's reference to 'the choice she has made' indirectly reflects the fact that since Hardwicke's 1753 Marriage Act, which limited the requirement for parental consent to those under twenty-one, Elizabeth and her contemporaries had greater freedom to choose a potential husband. Roy Porter notes that parents settled 'only for the right of veto, and the eloquence of the purse'[17] and Matthew Russell's 'purse' was particularly eloquent.

Elizabeth and Matthew were married on 23 January 1798 at the thirteenth-century Church of St Mary Magdalene, close to Lincoln Cathedral. Elizabeth's uncle, Samuel Turner, conducted the ceremony, and the witnesses were Robert Burton and Frances Brown. Few details of the marriage settlement survive, but George's later and possibly draft letter to Mary's 'Brother John' mentions that 'Mrs Russell has received her £5000' [[1808/1809] TdE/H/63/75].

'May she live to be a Blessing to the Family': September 1798 to Summer 1800

Robert Burton, writing to George in September 1798, asks 'how Mrs Russell goes on & when M^{rs} T goes there'. Mary's impending visit to the Russells suggests that Elizabeth is pregnant and in due course Mary's brother John confirms the birth of the Tennysons' first grandchild. The congratulations sent to George and the assumed preference for a boy reflect the male/female power imbalance of the time:

I sincerely congratulate you on having a fine Hardwick Grand Daughter. May she live to be a Blessing to the Family. Above all, is my great Pleasure to find dear Eliza doing so well after such severe Bouts

But the Brancepeth Gran.Dad would have wish'd it a Lad

Excuse haste ... I remain Dr Sr Yours sincerely John Turner. [[late 1798] TRC 2685]

The letter reveals that family correspondence cannot always be trusted. In his 'haste' John Turner had misread or misheard the birth announcement, and research revealed that the Russells' first child was indeed 'a Lad'. William Russell, named for his paternal grandfather, was born on 9 November 1798, baptized at St Michael's Church in York the following day and his baptism entered in the register at Sedgefield St Edmund Parish Church in County Durham. The Russells were in Yorkshire because Matthew was stationed with his regiment when the Durham Militia moved from Hull to Burstwick Camp, near Hedon, in 1798.[18]

Mary soon fears that the Russells' social obligations are affecting Elizabeth's health:

> she is well at present I hope but says in her first that she had been attack^u with most violent spasms such as neither Gin or Laudanum wou^u remove Mr Cox then gave her Senna & Jalap which by slow degrees remov^u the pain, yet she observes it did not quite leave her of some day[s] from her own account & her fears of what she has to go through the ensuing Summer, I have mine too … they are now never alone and so many amongst the great going to & giving dinners and sitting up till morning that I really fear it will cost her, her life – [01.06.1799 TRC 4682]

'Mr Cox' prescribes powerful remedies. 'Senna & Jalap' are purgatives; 'Laudanum' is made by using alcohol to extract morphine from raw opium.[19]

The Russells' lifestyle continues to concern Mary. 'The Major likes this life', she tells her mother, 'but I think poor Eliza would be more comfortable with her Child & Husband at home' [21.09.1799 Tenn 2/6/32]. Three months later George Clayton writes in relief to his father:

> How happy I am to hear that the Major has at last given up his commission – for without taking into consideration the uncomfortable Life my Sister & himself must have led, I think that the [? regiment] would inevitably have ruined his constitution … had he remained among such hardlivers as the Militia Regiments usually are. [30.12.1799 TRC 4670]

During the 1790s the Tennyson family began to disperse. On 8 October 1796 George Clayton went up to St John's College, Cambridge. (Michael Tennyson died at Hedon two days earlier.) In 1798 Charles moved from St Peter's to Louth Grammar School. The Tennysons had not settled in Lincoln and in May 1798 moved again to Clayton House, Grimsby, which George inherited from his uncle, Christopher Clayton. After Matthew resigned his commission, the

Russells divided their time between Hardwick Hall and Brancepeth Castle.[20] Brancepeth is a corruption of 'Brandon's Path', the path to St Brandon's shrine in the nearby parish church.[21] In February 1800 they were at Brancepeth where, as George Clayton reports to his father, young William is thriving:

> [Elizabeth] says, 'Little William is so much improved that you would not know him, he is grown quite loquacious & ... is thought here to be a prodigy' – I suppose that there will be now no hindrance to the Major & her visiting you in the Summer. [15.02.1800 TRC 4671]

But 'in the Summer' an anxious Mary writes to George from Hardwick:

> I wish this troublesome Durham Ball was over the weather is so very hot poor Eliza is quite overcome already ... Mary & Eliza will both write to fulfill their Promises & Acknowledge their Indolence.

Elizabeth fulfilled her promise by adding a note for 'dear Nedsir', the girls' affectionate nickname for their father:

> Seeing a piece of blank paper I have an inclination to say a few words though of little consequence ... We are all relaxed with the hot weather & long for a few cool dips in the Sea, where we hope you will make all the Haste possible to meet us farewell dear Nedsir / your affectionate Eliza. [[summer 1800] TRC 4684]

'How are all in the North?': November 1801 to August 1802

For several years Elizabeth had little apparent 'inclination to say a few words'. We hear of her only through the letters of other family members. In July 1801 Charles followed George Clayton to St John's College; writing to his father in November, he closed with a brief enquiry: 'How are all in the North' [11.11.1801 TdE/H/60/12]. Elizabeth's silence continued, and six months later Charles complained to his mother:

> I understand the Russells are in Town – Eliza and the Major I suppose are vegetating at Hardwicke. I should like to hear from her, and if I thought a Letter from me would draw one willingly from her I would write to her. [07.05.1802 TdE/H/61/20]

By 'the Russells' Charles means William and his second wife, Anne, née Millbanke (1752–1818): he remarried in 1790, three years after the death of Matthew's mother, Mary, née Harrison (1738–1787).[22]

George Clayton's letter to his father in August 1802 gives details of the Russells' busy social life:

> you seem to express some doubts as to the propriety of my accompanying my sister [Mary] to Scarbro'. Now as Mr [William] Russell himself particularly invited me, and I cannot put him possibly to any inconvenience, as he has taken a whole house and has a number of beds to spare, I cannot see any reason why I should refuse his offer. We are going to day to pay the first dinner visit to Dr & Mrs Cayley where we meet the Russells. At night we go to the County Election Ball – Mrs [Anne] Russell is constituted Lady Paramount, and my Sister [Elizabeth] expects to have the honour of leading off the first dance with Mr Burdon. We shall set forward to Scarbro' either on Friday or Monday. [09.08. [1802] TdE/H/61/15]

He adds a puzzling postscript:

> On Wednesday we shall be in Durham again on account of the Assize week when the annual visit which Mary well remembers is to be paid to the princess of the Palatinate.

Durham is a county palatine, 'ruled by a hereditary nobleman' who exercised a 'quasi-royal prerogative' within the area.[23] In Durham the hereditary noblemen were the bishops, whose autonomous power lasted until 1836. The bishop was also supreme judge of the Durham courts, ecclesiastical and temporal, so perhaps the 'annual visit' in 1802 was to the incumbent, Shute Barrington (1734–1826) and his possibly younger second wife, Jane, née Guise.[24] Or perhaps George Clayton simply liked the alliterative effect of 'princess' and 'Palatinate'. He was already an accomplished poet. Inspired by Elizabeth, his 'Muse', he marked her return to County Durham with *Verses Addressed to a Lady on Her Departure*, which concludes, 'Star of the North farewell – thy brilliant ray | Shall happier skies illumine – O restore | To us thy lustre, visit us once more | Our life, our light, our day'.[25]

'The grand trial of her strength': February 1804 to April 1809

By August 1802, when the Russells visited Durham, Mary Turner's health had begun to deteriorate. She died aged eighty-six and was buried in Caistor on 24 February 1804. Mary was confined to Caistor by bad weather, distress at her mother's death intensified by separation from her 'dear dear Husband' and 'dear Eliza' who were at Tealby.[26] Young Mary had been with her grandmother throughout her final illness:

> Now that my dear departed Mothers remains are consigned to the earth and the tumult of my mind is abated to a calm resignation to the will of the Almighty – it is a severe disappointment to me not to have it in my power to return to you … how unfortunate I am to be so situated with my dear Eliza – to have her under my roof and within 7 miles, and neither be able to get to her or she to me. [25.02.1804 TdE/H/62/3]

Writing again the following day, Mary includes for Elizabeth a discussion of fabric for mourning clothes. In the Georgian era, the mourning period for a parent was six months to a year.[27] Initially mourners dressed in black, to denote the 'privation of life', as black was considered the 'privation of light'; later they could wear colours such as grey, brown or mauve. Mourning etiquette would become stricter in Victoria's reign:

> As to the Cotton or Cambrick Muslin my dear Eliza we have but one piece left in the town … there is a Muslin to be got here yd & half wide thick, & fine & cheap – the reason I did not take it was because the black came off – therefore if you should determine upon any of these let me know. [26.02.1804 TdE/H/62/1]

Elizabeth is not mentioned again in family correspondence until October 1808. Between February 1804 and October 1808 the family began to increase in number. George Clayton had been ordained into the priesthood in December 1802. While waiting for the livings of Somersby and Bag Enderby he moved to Louth, where he met and in August 1805 married Elizabeth Fytche, known as Eliza. By October 1808 she had given birth to three children: George died in infancy, but Frederick and Charles survived. Alfred was born the following August and by 1819 there were eleven Somersby siblings. Charles was called to the Bar in 1806. On New Year's Day 1808 he married Frances Mary Hutton; by October she was pregnant with the first of their eight children, seven of whom survived, and the following June they moved to Caenby Hall.

In October 1808 Mary and her younger daughter were at Hardwick. Writing to George, Mary laments 'that our dear Elizas weakly state of health contracts me to make this melancholy separation from you' [27.10.1808 TdE/H/65/31]. Six days later her letter makes clear that, ten years after William's birth, Elizabeth is again pregnant:

> Indeed my dear Husband I most truly feel your lonely situation and grieve at the distance & time that is still to come before we meet again …

Our dear Eliza is much better the last 3 or 4 days and now gets large so that I trust we may now hope she will go on without mishap. [[02.11.1808] TdE/H/65/28]

She adds a rueful postscript: 'I was to have stay'd but 3 weeks'.

A week later Matthew writes at length to his brother-in-law Charles. His warm greeting and closing salutation reflect Elizabeth's later comment that her husband thought of Charles as 'his *own* brother':[28]

> My dear Charles
>
> We are all nearly as you left us. Eliza does not gain that strength we expected & having laid aside her fear I have long been desired to make her excuse to your Cara who I hope to hear is on the increase – was it the air of Hardwicke, or the Hermitage?[29] The latter the <u>Ladies</u> say has a very singular effect upon them.
>
> Your father will no doubt [be] closely interrogated on his arrival concerning existing Circumstances which I trust will turn out to your happiness & comfort – Why would you follow a Womans Advice about Inns & Post Houses? You were much better served at the Tontine than I could have expected – Since I lost my playfellow Still I have laid aside my fun & have been fully occupied in altering my Grounds which when I next show you them I have no doubt of your approval. I am my Dear Charles Yours ever very sincerely M Russell. [09.11.1808 TdE/H/66/19]

The letter epitomizes the writer's patriarchal society. Women's advice about 'Inns & Post Houses' is to be disregarded ('the Tontine' is presumably an inn, not a life assurance scheme[30]), female sexuality invites salacious comment, married men may have playfellows and 'fun', while married women are hoped to be 'on the increase'. Frances, Charles's *cara sposa* or dear wife, was indeed pregnant; their first child, George Hildyard, was born in July 1809.

Mary's letters from Hardwick relate the progress of Elizabeth's difficult second pregnancy. In December 1808 she writes to congratulate her 'dear Brother' Samuel, recently married to Barbara, née Bullock, the widow of Robert Haddelsey:

> I wish it was in my power to give you a more favorable account of dear Eliza [she continues] when I came here I found her weak and debilitated – insomuch that I fear'd she would not reach the end of her now approved tedious pilgrimage – she still remains feeble yet without mishap, and likely to go on – to the grand trial of her strength. [10.12.1808 T2/9/8]

A month later she tells Charles that Elizabeth 'goes on with all her complaints hanging on her' [14.01.1809 TdE/H/149/4]. In February 'her complaints' continue:

great weakness still pervades her whole frame & which I fear will still increase upon her owing to her natural rest being impeded from spasmodic pains ... she sometimes observes that a miracle must be effected to escape out of the conflict.

As so often when family health is concerned, Mary is supported by her faith:

I look up to the God of all mercy to grant us the grace of his Holy Spirit ... if he sees fit to spare to us the precious life of this dear creature and that she may be raised from her Bed with renewed health I trust through his aid I shall be ever grateful. [04.02.1809 TdE/H/67/22]

Mary shares her fears with George:

you already know the state of my mind that is agitated by a thousand fears for her safety ... She said to me the other day that she thought 'it might be possible for her to bear the Child – because the instance was rare when any one died undelivered – but that to support the shake it would give to her constitution was scarcely to be expected' ... I parried what she said by everything I could suggest to give her hopes advising her to commit herself to the Almighty that if human aid failed he could and would interpose to save her. [18.02.1809 TdE/H/67/5]

Her concern was not unfounded: 'perinatal complication was probably the single most common cause of death in women aged twenty-five to thirty-four, accounting for one in five of all deaths in this age group'.[31] Elizabeth would be thirty-three in April.

But Mary's next bulletin was more cheerful. Her empathy with Elizabeth allows her 'Spirits' to lift with her daughter's:

our dear Eliza has been so much better in health & Spirits the last two days that I cannot but feel my Spirits buoyant at this sudden and favourable change ...

she has an uncommon desire to drink new brew'd Liquor I fear'd to gratifye her but she was so urgent and said she should she thought *be* better of the pain in her side if she might be permitted to have a spoonfull or two of new Yeast ... when she took the Glass to her head we expected she would sip but off it went this was new brew'd beer as thick literally with Yeast as mud since which she has been better of her side and in her general feelings. [21.02.1809 TdE/H/67/6]

Perhaps helped by the 'new brew'd beer', Elizabeth survived 'the grand trial of her strength'. Emma Maria Russell was born on 8 March 1809 and baptized on 1 April. Her given names symbolize her parents' marriage. Mary, the English form of Maria, is the name of Elizabeth's grandmother, mother and sister. Emma de Bulmer, the Brancepeth heiress, married Geoffrey de Neville in 1174 and the resulting empire, 'ruled' from Brancepeth, lasted for almost four hundred years.[32]

'London was never more disagreeable': December 1810

Before Elizabeth's wedding Mary told her mother that Matthew is 'so approv'd by all who know him' [15.12.1798 Tenn 2/6/31]. He would not be 'so approv'd' today. His letter to Charles in December 1810 reveals his active engagement in contemporary politics and colonial exploitation:

> Your Letter is in my Port-folio to be attended to the next time I go to London – the fact is I had not time after the receipt of it & the unexpected report of H.M. Physicians ... London was never more disagreeable & nothing new but a hottentot Venus with a most enormous Bum – the broad bottoms are tools to her There is a good caricature of Sheridan with a Compass measuring Ld Grenville & her derrière a derrière – as a bit of a grazier I had a decent feel to ascertain whether it was real. It was my intention (had I stayed to have sent it to you knowing your taste for pictures)

> it was generally understood that in the event of the king not getting better the prince would be appointed Regent & that he would continue the present men (at least till all hopes were given up of H.M. recovery) but whether they will saddle him with restrictions (such as not to make new Peers &c) was not divulged before I left – his RH has so far conducted himself very satisfactorily to the public. [10.12.1810 4TdE/H/7/27]

In 1802 Matthew had become MP for Saltash, one of his father's 'pocket boroughs',[33] hence his receipt of the physicians' report. George III had 'collapsed once more into madness' in October 1810.[34] Parliament was recalled and the Prime Minister, Spencer Perceval, 'put forward a provisional Bill to name the Prince of Wales as Regent, carefully limiting his powers'.[35] Despite the Prince's objections, the Bill was steered through Parliament and on 6 February 1811 he was named as Prince Regent.

The 'hottentot Venus' refers to the deeply disturbing case of Saartjie, later Sara or Sarah Baartman (1789–1815), a young South African Khoisan woman. Born in the Eastern Cape, formerly a Dutch and from 1806 a British colony, at sixteen she was sold into slavery to a Dutch trader who, with an English ship's surgeon, brought her to England to be displayed 'for entertainment purposes'.[36] From autumn 1810 to spring 1811 she was 'exhibited at 225 Piccadilly' as the 'hottentot Venus'; wearing 'a skin-coloured body stocking and apron' she 'sang, danced and played a guitar'.[37] (At the same time Jane Austen was in London seeing *Sense and Sensibility* through the press.) Matthew's letter confirms that the performance 'encouraged salacious interest' and 'the "keeper" allowed visitors to touch her'. A legal challenge launched on her behalf by Zachary Macaulay (1768–1838) was unsuccessful, and she died in Paris in 1815 having been sold to an animal show. Her mutilated remains were displayed in the *Musée de l'Homme* until 1974. In 2002 she was repatriated at President Mandela's request and buried near her birthplace. Six years earlier, on 28 March 1996, *Venus* – a play based on the life of Saartjie Baartman by the American dramatist Suzan-Lori Parks – received its first performance in New York. Interspersed with lines of dialogue are 'Historical Extract[s]' taken from contemporary publications including an 'Autopsy report', which reveal how her body was abused and anatomized during her life and after her death. But as one character comments: 'The things they noticed were quite various | but no one ever noticed that her face was streamed with tears'.[38]

'The death and burial of an infant': December 1810 to September 1819

Matthew's letter closes with family news: 'and (so Eliza tells me) your sister is at last going to be married' [10.12.1810 4TdE/H/7/27]. Young Mary and John Bourne were married at Tealby on 13 August 1811. After this brief reference to 'Eliza' until her compassionate letter to Charles in 1819 we again hear of Elizabeth only through the letters of other family members. In October 1813 young William writes to his 'dearest Grandpapa' Tennyson:

> I have now undergone the awfull ceremony of being confirmed – and my Mama wrote to me very seriously on that subject to turn from all my wicked habits which I am affraid it is impossible for me intirely to do at Eton as there are so many temptations to wickedness. [15.10.1813 TdE/H/71/26]

Elizabeth is mentioned most often, usually with regard to health, in her mother's letters. In a postscript to Charles in December 1814 Mary notes: 'Poor Eliza is no better – I am grieved on her account' [13.12.[1814] TdE/H/72/14]. A year later she writes from Hardwick: 'in my letter to Fanny [Frances] Elizas answer is anticipated respecting your wishes of seeing her in Town and adds now another wish That she would most willingly sleep in a Dog Kennel provided it was near you' [12.12.1815 TdE/H/72/10]. 'Elizas answer' makes clear that Charles, Mary's favourite son, is also Elizabeth's favourite brother.

In April 1816 Mary tells Frances that Elizabeth's visit to Tealby may be postponed as her father-in-law, William Russell, is 'very ill':

[Eliza] wishes much to get here as the poor old man may not continue long – but from her husbands account ill as he is he wishes to get home. Should that be the case … she will not get here, much less her Husband.

Mary refers to the weather:

We have dreadful cold weather here and which I conclude is general throughout the kingdom experiencing one day the most heavy Rains – another Snow and cold Sleet, with sharp frost agreeing very ill with Mr Tennyson. [15.04.1816 4TdE/H/11c]

Despite her doubts Mary did see Elizabeth: 'Eliza came to us the 30 of April, and returned with her Husband to Hardwick the 3^d of June – we met them at Harrogate the 20th' [13.07.1816 TdE/H/96/3]. She and George are still affected by the weather: 'such an overbearing lassitude prevails, the effect I conclude of this Winterly summer on my nerves'.

Mary's reference to 'this Winterly summer' is apposite. The year 1816 is 'the year without a summer'.[39] Mount Tambora on Sumbawa Island in the Dutch East Indies, now Indonesia, erupted on 10 April 1815 causing immense loss of life, both immediately and subsequently through famine. Although much of the discharged debris fell onto surrounding islands, a significant amount entered the atmosphere 'spreading around the world and partially blotting out the sun for months'.[40] As Byron wrote in July 1816: 'The bright sun was extinguish'd, and the stars | Did wander darkling in the eternal space, | Rayless, and pathless, and the icy earth | Swung blind and blackening in the moonless air;' *Darkness*, 2–5.[41]

Writing to Charles from Hardwick a year later, Mary again refers to the 'rapid transaction from heat to cold and contrary-wise which in short had a sombrous effect on us all'. 'To day', she adds, 'the Rain, Thunder & Lightening being withheld we are more ourselves'. William Russell, 'the poor old man', had died aged eighty-two and was buried at St Brandon's Church by Brancepeth Castle on 13 June 1817.[42] Mary, George and Elizabeth visited his widow, Anne:

we all went on Saturday to pay a complimentary visit to the Solitary inhabitant of ye castle – whom we found in bed of the gout – where she had been confined some days Eliza on viewing her immaciated face – was excited to feelings of compassion – which I told her I was convinced could only be skin deep. [07.07.1817 TdE/H/76/14a]

Mary's unusually sharp comment suggests that she may resent Elizabeth's 'feelings' for her stepmother-in-law.

Anne Russell's solitary widowhood was short-lived. She died on 19 May 1818 at the age of sixty-six. As George later commented to Charles, Matthew became 'Mastʳ of the Castle' [20.02.1819 TdE/H/83/38] and began rebuilding Brancepeth. Although he engaged John Paterson, a Scottish architect who had worked with Robert Adam, Charles was the driving force behind and supervisor of the project that inspired his eventual transformation of Bayons Manor.

Mary's letter to Barbara Turner gives a vivid impression of the building work:

> Eliza inquired most kindly after my Brother [Samuel] & you, and said how much it would delight her Heart to see you both when the Castle is ready to receive her friends ... at present it is such a scene of bustle and as you can scarcely imagine no less than 300 people at work ... in short it will be a Palace – the family quitted it the day we left, to admit the workmen to the Old Interior ... Eliza wrote me that the workmen find old coins almost every day – on digging into fresh places apart from foundation walls – one she says, she values most is a Copper coin – of the reign of Charles the 1st – having my Broʳ in mind at the time of writing – she adds 'I woo na' give it up for a <u>farthing near</u>'. [20.04.1819 T2/9/9]

Elizabeth treasures both the coin and the uncle whose Lincolnshire accent she mimics.

Four months later, on 29 August, Charles and Frances's eighth and last child, William Henry, was born. His condition soon deteriorated, and he died in early September. Elizabeth's love for her brother and sister-in-law is clearly revealed in her moving letter to Charles:

> I did weep, my ever dear Charles, and found my eyes repeatedly filled with tears during the whole of yesterday and even when I laid awake in the night. There is something in the death and burial of an infant which touches the tenderest chord in our hearts, especially when it has belonged to those who are inexpressibly dear to us – dear Fanny could weep for it as yours, you would regret it as hers and I feel that it belonged to you both – I think Tasso speaks of an infant's death beautifully.[43] I cannot recollect the words but it sipped the cup of life and perceiving its bitterness turned its head and refused the draught. I can so well imagine from your own expression all you have felt and it is so happily expressed that I shall treasure your letter as a bit of your mind and heart embodied. Write a line and tell me how poor dear Fanny recovers. I would tell her how much consolation there is in the loss of an infant, but she knows this and will feel it, and that she ought to be happy in the thought that it has (if there be truth in revelation) gone to God; 'for I say unto you' are Christ's words 'that in Heaven their angels do always behold the face of my Father who is in Heaven'.[44]

Elizabeth offers but qualifies the language of religious belief as 'consolation', suggesting that her faith is less firm than her mother's.

'The unhappy death of poor Mr Russell': March 1820 to June 1822

Elizabeth's letter to Charles the following March is very different. With Matthew's backing Charles became MP for Great Grimsby in 1818. When George III died on 29 January 1820 Parliament was dissolved, an election held and he was re-elected. Elizabeth's letter of congratulation reflects her devotion to Charles and a new and 'constant alarm' for their mother's health:

> I did not imagine that <u>any</u> event could have given me so much delight as my beloved Charles's victory has done – After receiving the final state of the poll, the sun of happiness gilded all things & persons, & I viewed them through a kindlier medium – philanthropy blooms best, I am persuaded, in the hour of prosperity but I have neither time nor head, nor heart for Metaphysics, & alas by your Letter of yesterday the fine gold is become dim, for the <u>best</u> of <u>brothers</u> & of <u>Men</u> (truth) is ill from over-exertions.

> Our dear Mother too to whom I wrote on 13th, respecting whom I am in constant alarm, is, you say, far from stout; am I to interpret by this, that she is weaker than usual? God forbid! for if the strength of her constitution shows signs of failure, we may mourn under the expectation of consequences which would overcast the remainder of my Life …

> Thank dear Fanny repeatedly for her treaty with Mrs [? Heaslop], with whom I am charmed; her manners & voice are mild & gentle, & her mind seems delicate with regard to all that is intrusive; in short she knows her situation … she is defective in her pronunciation of the English Language … but she is so good humoured that in due time I may remark to her, her mistakes.

Elizabeth is still judgemental – in 1787 she believed 'the Generality of Lincoln people are not pleasant' [22.09.1797 Tenn 2/1/31] – and her class consciousness has developed. Although 'defective in her pronunciation', Mrs Heaslop is approved because 'she knows her situation'.

> I am still weakly & a little return of asthma alarms me, this fine weather however will do wonders, I only wish we were <u>en Castle</u>. … My Husband is so occupied with Electioneers & Architects that he cannot write <u>so much</u> as he wishes to you today, but … he is much delighted at your triumph.

After the closing salutation – 'yor ever affectionate Liz' – she adds a postscript:

> is Fanny glad that the mourning expires on the 30th of next Month. I expected to dissolve under the influence of bombesine ... the people here believing it was to be worn 6 months'.[45] [15.03.1820 4TdE/H/23[20]]

Dissolution under the weight of mourning dress is a humorous image, but one that diminishes local people who believe it must 'be worn 6 months'. As she notes, national mourning for George III expired at the end of April. Elizabeth's wit has a sharp edge.

In July 1821 news of Elizabeth comes from her mother's letters to Charles, who is with the Russells in Cheltenham: 'I am sorry there should exist a cause for her declining to the waters – she may be perfectly right they may cause an irritability on the nerves' [03.07.1821 TdE/H/86/22]. Ten days later Elizabeth's nervous irritability recurs: 'to have no relief either Summer or Winter is appalling, the overpowering excitability of the nervous system seems distroying her by Hair's breadths' [13.07.1821 TdE/H/86/4]. A postscript suggests that Elizabeth's temperament makes her a demanding house guest:

> I wish you were here [Tealby] all of you – you say nothing of any view Eliza ever had or may have of coming at the same time – If you think she could consent and Mr Russell so disposed till their house is ready your Father will write without delay ... I fear poor dear Lizzy is too unwell to bear our small house with any bustle. She told me if I had no one but ourselves the place was unquiet from callers, and threw cold water upon coming. [[1821] TdE/H/86/36]

The Russells did not visit Tealby. In April 1822 George Clayton and his wife Eliza were in Cheltenham and reported to Mary: 'We found the Russells here' [15.04.1822 TdE/H/144/148]. Two weeks later Matthew was in London, gravely ill, and George Clayton shared with Charles the family's 'heartfelt concern' for Elizabeth:

> Your distressing & unwelcome intelligence of this morning gave us all the most heartfelt concern. Eliza has shown me the letter she wrote to her husband which I think is so worded as not to be likely to give him any alarm. She there states that it is her intention to go up to London. But I am much afraid she will not be able to accomplish this. She is in such a dreadful state of anxiety & almost of derangement since the receipt of your letter to her this morning that I very much fear should she attempt the journey she would become delirious on the road. Fanny ... thought it advisable not to conceal the statement of poor Russell's health made in your first private letter to her & ... it has been so managed that her husband's critical state should be communicated to her by degrees

You must be in a state of very great Anxiety & so are we all – And with all our united love & prayers for the recovery of poor R[usse]ll. [30.04.1822 TdE/H/144/152]

Despite their 'love & prayers' Matthew did not recover. He died on 8 May aged fifty-seven and was buried in St Brandon's churchyard near Brancepeth Castle on 23 May 1822, five years after his father's interment.[46] He probably died 'from thrombosis':[47] he is described as a 'jovial giant',[48] implying obesity, and during the 'Winterly summer' of 1816 Mary noted that Matthew was 'not to be cast about with every Wind – his spirits and digestive powers never receiving a check' [07.07.1817 TdE/H/76/14a].

After twenty-four years of marriage Elizabeth, now forty-six, has become a widow. As with other life events, we learn how she responds to her sudden bereavement from family letters, not from her own. George Clayton reports to Charles in May: 'Eliza is somewhat more composed & slept better last Night. My father is also something better & they both follow us tomorrow to Bognor. I hope Eliza will consent to go with you into France as soon as you return from Brancepeth' [15.05.[1822] TdE/H/144/153].

Mary writes to Charles the same day:

your dear Sister has not had those frightful horrors we fear'd so much that her nights are pass'd as not most miserable with perhaps an interest of an <u>hours sleep</u> ... may it please Heaven to soften the Affliction of my dear Child so that peace may again visit her and be permanent. [15.05.1822 4TdE/H/87/6]

She tells Samuel in June that Matthew's death affected George's health:

The Gout of which I think I apprised you, made efforts in various forms, and alarmingly inflamatory ... and a continued cough without mitigation this follow'd close upon the mourning caused by the unhappy death of poor Mr Russell – and had not a kind providence interposed I should have lost my dear Husband ... however it pleased God to enable him to leave London for Bognor whither our dear Mourning Eliza had gone the preceding day as a place of quiet and retirement.

[After some weeks] we left our dear Eliza after enduring this heavy stroke settled into a more softened sorrow.

'<u>Time</u> and <u>religion</u>' as you justly observed 'usually ameliorate the most acute affliction' and [I] am happy to perceive the favorable effect although she will I believe go mourning through the remainder of her life. [24.06.1822 T2/10/20]

Elizabeth's letter to Charles after William Henry's death suggests she may not have the consolation of 'religion' in her bereavement.

'Paris is now cold, & as foggy as London': November 1822 to March 1823

As George Clayton hoped, Elizabeth did 'go into France' with her children, thirteen-year-old Emma and William who turned twenty-four on 9 November. Two days later Emma wrote on black-edged paper to her 'dear Uncle Charles' in London:

> Mamma desires me to say that she received yours of the 3rd last Saturday, & being confined to her bed with a bad cold & cough commissions me to answer it …
>
> Paris is now cold, & as foggy as London; as to this Hotel there are so many conveniences in it to balance against a few objections, that Mamma does not feel inclined to be troubled with moving. [11.11.1822 4TdE/H/28/52]

In mid-December Charles arrived in Paris after a 'perilous Passage'. Writing in relief at his safe arrival, Mary 'grieve[s] at the lingering Colds that have attacked our dear Eliza and Emma' [15.12.1822 4TdE/H/28/52]. A week later her concern for Elizabeth deepens:

> I feel much harrass'd with fearful apprehensions concerning her ultimate safety – surely she has not got any ulceration on her lungs? Tell me truly my dearest Charles for I am all but insensible about her She has been and I fear yet remains a severe sufferer for I knew not the commencement of this dreadful Cold & Cough … much as I wish to behold her dear face again – I am fearful of her taking fresh cold or crossing the Channel yet; [22.12.1822 4TdE/H/28/58]

Elizabeth and her children remained in Paris until the end of March 1823 despite the threat of war between France and Spain. In April France invaded Spain to restore the absolutist King Ferdinand VII, distant cousin of the Bourbon French King Louis XVIII. Turmoil in Spain posed a threat to Europe as Russia wished to intervene. England eventually remained neutral.[49]

By early March Mary's fears for Elizabeth's 'troubled mind' had intensified. She writes movingly to 'My ever dear Eliza' urging her not to '"desire" death', which was irreconcilable with Mary's religious faith:

> Had I been blessed with a discovery that your Health and Spirits were improved by your long continuance in France – I should have cause for less unhappiness at your later decision to procrastinate your return ... as it is, with your peculiarly delicate state of health – situated in a country that may be at War with us in a week – and your immediate friends away, there is no supporting the thought of what straits you might be driven to to get away ...
>
> The postscript you inserted in <u>that joint letter</u> (begun by darling Emma) is uppermost, and prescent, to my every waking hour, day, & night, it was a brief but very painful history of the [? travail] of your mental sufferings this, added to all which I am convinced you corporeally endure as the consequence of that decided & continual grief of Heart that I fear will be distructive to your better health ... how my beloved Child do you reconcile yourself to your God to 'desire' death if he does not will it, or, rather approve it? or how as I once before observed do you reconcile the giving pain to that dear departed spirit? wait (my too sensible creature to the evils of this life) and in patience 'passes your Soul'; but wait the Lord's own time and you will yet reap blessings in this Life as your reward ... and I may pray that it may please the wise disposer of all good, that he will restore you to your former self, for your own sake and all to whom you are dear. [02.03.1823 TdE/H/90/6]

Mary's reference to her 'mental sufferings' and 'continual grief of Heart' implies that Elizabeth was happy in her marriage.

Writing to Barbara Turner the following day, Mary 'report[s] well of both my dear Husband and myself':

> I wish it was in my power to say that the different branches of my family were going on <u>as well</u>. ... my poor dear Eliza has never yet known a days convalescence since she left England – her habitual complaint, spasmodic asthma, scarcely ever leaves her – this added to her continued depression of spirits, with a perpetual suffering from cold upon Cold – has had a most lowering effect upon her strength – Charles, & Willm Russell, with Emma – are waiting fair winds to bring themselves and Eliza back to england – War between France & Spain seems nearly decided – this, with the probable event of a rupture between France and England in consequence – will operate as a spur to their movements – Charles writes that he thinks the French king, and all the Bourbons are Mad & their Crown lost to them for ever. [03.03.1823 T2/9/10]

Charles's anti-French sentiments recur in his nephew Alfred's poems, most notably in the bellicose 'National Songs for Englishmen' written during the invasion panic that followed Louis Napoleon's *coup d'état* in December 1851.

Elizabeth and the Court of Chancery: August 1822 to July 1823

Emma's letter to Charles, written from Paris on Elizabeth's behalf while she was 'confined to bed with a bad cold', contains the only apparent reference in family letters to the litigation that closely followed Matthew Russell's death and which biographers seem to have overlooked:

> Mamma told you of my summons to the 'Palais de Justice' as Mamma was not able to go with me my Brother & Mr Thornton were my escorts. We waited an hour in the passage as each Witness is admitted in turn; At length I was rather appalled to find that no one was admitted with me & the [? Examiner] flew into a violent passion because William wished to accompany me, saying that no one was ever allowed to be present at the statement of the witnesses. He then ushered me in, questioning & cross-questioning me very sternly ... in came a Gendarme with a great sword & sat down opposite me accompanied by another old man in spectacles who was to write down my answers, he then cross questioned me again appearing as if he wished to puzzle me. However in half an hour he grew into better humour & I left this awful Tribunal safely. [11.11.1822 4TdE/H/28/52]

Chancery Court records confirm that within three months of Matthew's death Elizabeth began an equity suit to question the executors' administration of his will.[50] The suit was proceeding while the Russells were in Paris. The short title is Russell v Russell; the full title gives the executors' names: 'In Chancery Between Elizabeth Russell Widow and Emma Maria Russell an Infant by the said Elizabeth Russell her Mother and next Friend – Plaintiffs [and] William Russell Sir Gordon Drummond Thomas Robinson Grey and Charles Tennyson – Defendants'.[51] Emma is 'an Infant' because she is under twenty-one. With the exception of Thomas Robinson Grey, perhaps related to the Gray family of York, long-standing friends of the Tennysons,[52] Matthew's executors were family members. Elizabeth was challenging her son, brother and brother-in-law; Sir Gordon Drummond was married to Matthew's sister Margaret.

The Court of Chancery was an equity court, presided over by the Lord Chancellor.[53] Between 1558 and 1875 it was used by people from all walks of life and dealt with a wide range of civil cases relating to family inheritance and wills, land and property, and marriage settlements.[54] It was less inflexible than a common law court and had different procedures; as a reluctant Emma discovered, it gathered only written evidence.

To start an equity suit, a lawyer would submit a bill of complaint to the Lord Chancellor. When the disputed issues were defined, the Court would commission 'neutral men of substance' to examine an agreed list of people. During this examination detailed questions (Interrogatories) would be put to the defendants on the plaintiffs' behalf.

The examination in Russell v Russell was commissioned on 12 August 1822. The length and complexity of the five interrogatories confirm that Elizabeth was demanding a detailed analysis of the administration of Matthew's will. The defendants' equally complex answers can be summarized as follows: Charles had opened an executors' account with Matthew's London bankers, Roberts and Curtis. All transactions relating to the executorship passed through this account, or from money collected by John Shaw, Matthew's steward at Brancepeth. Matthew's assets – defined in detail – were sold and used, together with collected rent arrears, to pay his debts, legacies and funeral expenses. Detailed statements of expenditure are attached to the legal documents.[55]

No final decree has been found, which suggests that, as often happened, the suit was withdrawn. Although the documents confirm that Charles, regarded by Matthew as his '*own* brother',[56] was the most active executor, Elizabeth's close relationship with her favourite brother was unaffected. In July 1823 she wrote from Bayons, 'I grieve my dear Charles to hear of your being so unwell, but I comfort myself in the belief that you are renewing some active care of yourself' [07.07.1823 4TdE/H/27/11]. Why therefore did Elizabeth resort to prolonged and expensive litigation so soon after Matthew's death? Her 'dreadful state of anxiety & almost of derangement' [30.04.1822 TdE/H/144/52] on hearing of Matthew's illness, and the 'mental sufferings' and 'grief of heart' [02.03.1823 TdE/H/90/6] she endured after his death, indicate that she was 'happy with the choice she ha[d] made' [15.12.1797 Tenn 2/6/31]. Elizabeth's only surviving written reference to Matthew closes a hasty note to Charles and reflects a teasingly affectionate relationship: 'Matt hurries me & we shall get to a squabble or a bickering if I don't conclude' [02.02.1809 4TdE/H/7/26]. Perhaps, in her grief, Elizabeth needed to ascertain that Matthew's estate was being administered as he had wished.

'Locomotion is the only thing … for spirits like ours when depressed': July 1823 to July 1835

Elizabeth's health did not improve on returning to England. At the beginning of July she was too ill to travel to Brancepeth; as Mary told the Turners, 'the nearer the day approaches – the more unequal she appear'd to encounter the journey' [01.07.1823 T2/9/11]. In November she moved to Brighton and Mary 'had the consolation to see our dear Eliza in rather better health & spirits' [10.11.1823 T2/9/2].

The following March Elizabeth wrote to console Charles on the death of his aristocratic and possibly influential friend, Lord Titchfield (1796–1824).[57]

> After the first sentence of my dearest Brother's Letter of this morning, I could not for some moments proceed, his youth & amiable disposition could have occasioned regret & deep interest, but knowing him to be your friend & one whom you could Love for his heart & mind (without a consideration of his nobility being thrown into the scale) drew tears & a succession of them from my eyes – Life as we advance casts up more & more of its bitter sediment & if the cup ever sparkles it is only at the brim. [07.03.1824 4TdE/H/32/[1]]

The image of the cup of life, which Elizabeth used to comfort Charles on the death of William Henry in September 1819, is perhaps drawn from Tasso's allusion to the custom of sweetening the rim of a cup containing medicine for a sick child.[58]

Advancing 'Life' was to cast up more of its 'bitter sediment' for Elizabeth and the Tennysons. While expressing her concern for the family, Mary was understating the decline of her own health. In January 1824 she began a letter to Charles 'I have written myself tired', but turned immediately to Elizabeth: 'Poor Eliza has been very ill of a Tremendous Cold & Cough' [18.01.1824 4TdE/H/52/27].

Mary's fears for Elizabeth intensified. Writing to Samuel from Leamington in August 1824 she refers to 'her nerves':

> She was rejoiced to see us but I grieve to add that, her nerves were visibly shaken by the excitement our appearance produced … in short agitation of every kind she cannot combat. It is impossible to describe a state of nerves so affected – and so <u>severely</u>. [20.08.1824 T2/9/3]

Elizabeth's 'nerves' affect her physical condition, as Mary reports to George from Brighton the following May:

> she cannot sit up in a carriage to go a quarter of a Mile – but every effort is to be now exerted, so that a means may be devised – that she may lye at length in the Coach to obtain fresh air – which she has not breathed of nearly 3 Months – and for which she incessantly longs … may it please Heaven to grant that our dear Eliza may experience renovated health and finish this hitherto troubled life, at a more mature age in peace & joy. [05.05.1825 4TdE/H/33]

But in July 1825 Mary's letters to Charles and the Turners give details of her own deteriorating health:

> I know not how scarcely to convey, my asthma or <u>short breathing</u> – you will be sorry to hear – I am perpetually combating i.e. I cannot move even from Chair to Chair without heaving or rather palpitation of Heart. [07.07.1825 4TdE/H/33/-]

She adds, 'At present do not show this letter to poor Eliza as I would not have her for a moment roused to think worse of my case'.

A week later Mary confirms to the Turners that their golden wedding celebration is cancelled:

> It is the continuance of asthma day & night that has been so heavy upon me with an effusion of blood to my Head The lack of strength – is owing to sleepless nights, 4 out of 7 in the week ... but remember we shall always rejoice to see <u>you both any day</u> ... you may have it in your power to fix when you can both come to stop with us, as this will be even more comfortable to yourselves to be <u>quiet – I covet quietness</u> – of late the more particularly. [15.07.1825 T2/9/4]

At the end of July Elizabeth is anxiously in touch with Charles:

> This morning I have received the enclosed ... I try to catch a little hope & comfort from it ... I am <u>very glad</u> indeed, to find you are better; locomotion is the only thing I believe for spirits like ours when depressed & fixing exclusively upon one subject. [[28.07.1825] TdE/H/144/182]

Her nephew Alfred agreed that 'constant variation of scene and ideas should operate as an infallible restorative'. With Emily's encouragement, he maintained 'a belief in that family solution for the rest of his life'.[59]

In mid-August Elizabeth wrote to her 'dearest Mother' from London:

> I am afraid that you are not so well as I had hoped, my dearest Father writing that your appetite & rest are both bad, this account makes me very anxious to be at Tealby, & should Dr Armstrong say that I may travel with safety, I will lose no time ... God grant that nothing may prevent the <u>earnest wish</u> of <u>my Heart.</u>

To be closer to her mother during the autumn, Elizabeth proposed moving into the house of William Cooper (George's agent at Tealby) and his wife Sarah. She does not suggest where the Coopers might live:

> I have thought whether it were possible ... to occupy the House or part of the House for the 3 Autumnal Months, that Cooper now inhabits, I might then see

you whenever occasion required, at all events I should be happier than when Miles seperate us. [15.08.1825 4TdE/H/33/b]

Elizabeth's wish to be closer to her mother was not fulfilled. Mary died on 20 August 1825 aged seventy-two, gaining the eternal 'quietness' she coveted. Elizabeth's incoherent letter to Charles is evidence of her renewed distress, just '3 years' after Matthew's death:

> I need not tell you my most beloved of brothers what are my feelings, they are almost too [? ...] to [? bear] with sanity, it seems as if she were the only Mother who ever existed & for us it was so, all other Relatives may be multiplied excepting a Father or a Mother – The blow 3 years ago, seems to leave her no effect in lessening the receipt of this. I had begun to look about me & am again stunned – ... Thank you my dearest Charles, for your beautiful descriptions of her last hours, they are, & will always be my first treasures while life is continued in me – If ever an innocent Life (so protracted) attained a happier, she has done so, her pure-intentioned, upright, humble & Charitable Heart, have seldom been equalled, but these recollections are not likely to make us Weep the less recollect every word our sainted Mother uttered, to tell to me; ... it is a comfort to pour out some of my feelings, but do not believe me selfishly engrossed with the sorrow of my own heart, I weep for you my Bro^r but no words are sufficient to express my Sympathy for the Parent yet preserved to us ... may you be blessed & our beloved Father! but our angelic Mother's blessings will descend upon us all, I feel they will & surely she is only gone a little before us. [August/September 1825 4TdE/H/33L]

She adds a brief but telling postscript: 'Emma mourns much'.

By 1831 Elizabeth's relationship with her 'beloved Father' had deteriorated. Charles, writing to George from Dalby in May, concludes, 'Nothing has passed here as to any difference between you and my Sister [Elizabeth], except the deep expression of her *sincere regret* at what she was carried away to say'. He adds, 'Mr. Bourne is all kindness and hospitality as well as my Sister [Mary]'.[60]

Four years later, learning of her 'poor dear Father's' increasing physical weakness, Elizabeth does not rush to his side:

> I received your [Dr Barton] kind letter while on a visit to Stoke ... it is painful to read of my poor dear Father's increased debility, but the strongest individuals must suffer from this almost unparalleled weather, I am almost exhausted by it ... in consequence of your letter I intend setting off on Wednesday 24th ... & expect to reach Usselby the next day. [13.06.[1835] TdE/H/13/6]

George died at Usselby on 9 July 1835 aged eighty-five. Perhaps overwhelmed by sadness or ill health, Elizabeth and her children did not attend the funeral.

Afterword: 'Ever yours affectionately A. Tennyson': April 1827 to September 1865

Alfred's elegy for his 'Grandmamma Tennyson'[61] was published in *Poems, by Two Brothers* in April 1827. A small volume by unknown young poets was unlikely to cover its costs and Elizabeth may have paid for the publication. In November 1827 Alfred followed his brothers to Cambridge 'where he proposes to stay until the 100£ you kindly promised him is exhausted' [23.11.1827 TdE/H/148/12]. Elizabeth's generous gift, equivalent to more than £10,000 today,[62] became an annual allowance that continued for years, at least until 10 April 1854 when the Poet Laureate reported, 'One half of your cheque has been missing ever since the day it came'. Three days later he acknowledged its replacement: 'Dearest Aunt – received!'[63]

The affectionate correspondence between Elizabeth and Alfred continued. It survived Elizabeth's justified suspicion that the 'old grandfather' of *Maud* (1855), 'Master of half a servile shire, | And left his coal all turned into gold' (X, 334–47), was based on her father-in-law, William Russell, whose fortune Matthew inherited. Alfred rejected the suggestion: '(Assure yourself that you utterly mistake)'.[64]

His affection is clearly apparent after Elizabeth's 'terrible fall' in May 1856:

> I now write to ask whether you *are* going on well ... pray, dearest Aunt, let me know, for though I write seldom I have not the less affection for you, do not the less joy in your joy, and grieve with your grief –, though I may be somewhat undemonstrative.
>
> Ever yours affectionately A. Tennyson[65]

Throughout her widowhood Elizabeth continued the 'locomotion' she recommended to Charles [[28.07.1825] TdE/H/144/182]. And her mother's wish was fulfilled. Elizabeth did 'finish this hitherto troubled life, at a more mature age', it is to be hoped 'in peace & joy' [05.05.1825 4TdE/H/33]. She died in Cheltenham on 30 September 1865 in her ninetieth year.[66]

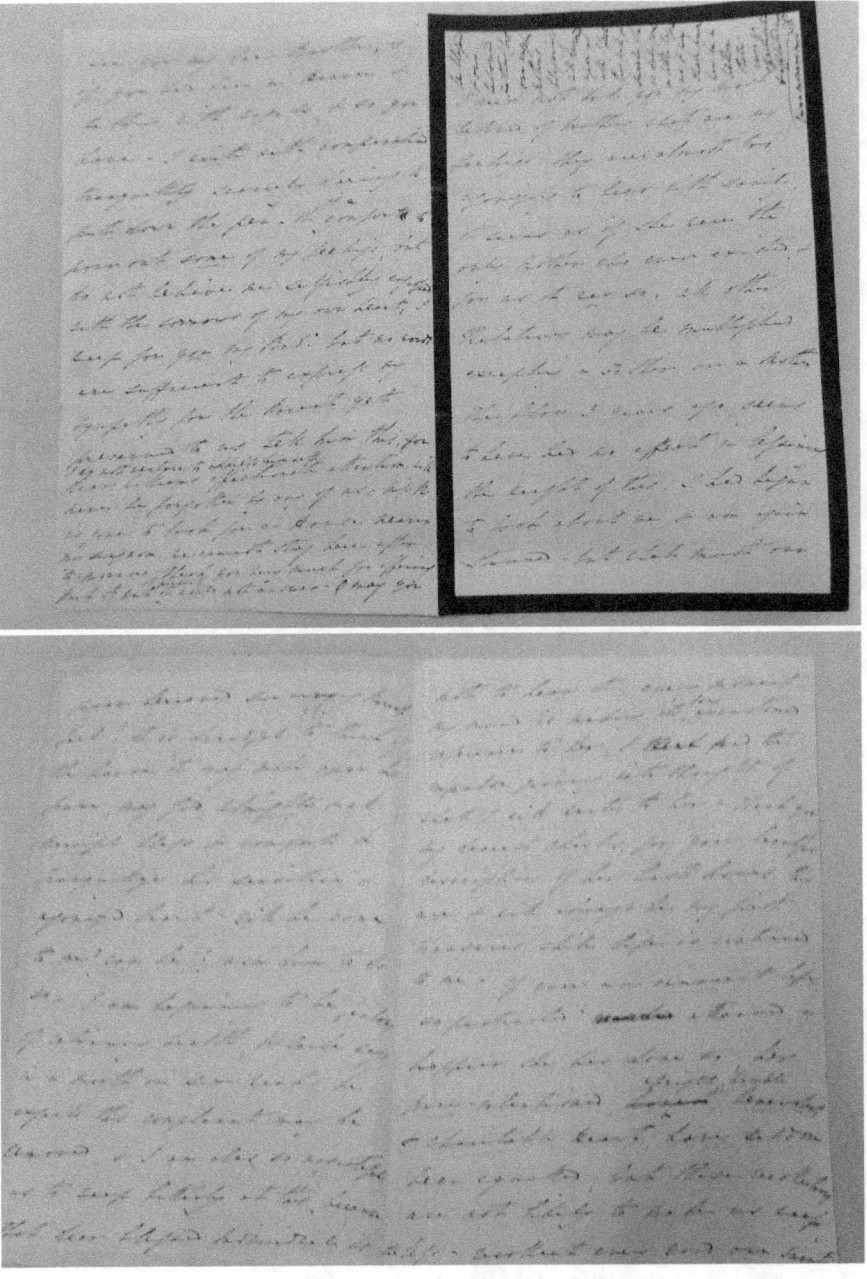

Figures 3A/3B Elizabeth Tennyson Russell to Charles Tennyson [August/September 1825 4TdE/H/33L].

Notes

1. Christopher Sturman and Valerie Purton, *Poems by Two Brothers: The Lives, Work and Influence of George Clayton Tennyson and Charles Tennyson d'Eyncourt* (Stamford: Watkins, 1993), p. 3.
2. Robert Bernard Martin, *Tennyson: The Unquiet Heart*, 2nd edn (London: Faber & Faber, 1983), p. 4.
3. *The Letters of Arthur Henry Hallam*, ed. by J. Kolb (Columbus: Ohio State University Press, 1981), p. 675 (30 October 1832).
4. John Markham, 'The Tennysons in Holderness', *Tennyson Research Bulletin*, 6:2 (1993), 130–7 (133).
5. Back teeth, which come through between sixteen and twenty-two months, are larger than first teeth and often more painful for the child. https://www.babycentre.co.uk/a558193/toddler-sleep-concerns-teething [accessed 2 June 2020].
6. Apothecaries, originally shopkeepers or warehousemen, later drug sellers, secured protection by statute in 1543 and gradually strengthened their right to practise medicine. Charles Tennyson and Hope Dyson, *The Tennysons: Background to Genius* (London: Macmillan, 1974), p. 15.
7. 'Mablethorpe' was written in 1837 and published in the *Manchester Athaenaum Album* in 1850.
8. Hannah Newton, 'The sick child in early modern England, 1580–1720', *Endeavour*, 38:2 (2014), 122–9, https://www.ncbi.nlm.nih.gov/pmc/articles/PMC4330552 [accessed 30 May 2020].
9. https://www.thornber.net/medicine/html/medgloss.html [accessed 1 June 2020].
10. Founded by St Paulinus of York in AD 627, St Peter's is the third oldest school in the UK. https://www.stpetersyork.org.uk [accessed 11 June 2020].
11. Susan Sked, 'Women teachers and the expansion of girls' schooling in England, c. 1760–1820', in *Gender in Eighteenth-Century England: Roles, Representations and Responsibilities*, ed. by Hannah Barker and Elaine Chalus (London: Longman, 1997), pp. 101–25 (101).
12. Amanda Vickery, *The Gentleman's Daughter: Women's Lives in Georgian England* (New Haven, CT: Yale Nota Bene, 2003), p. 117.
13. Thomas Morris, 'Weird and Wonderful Medicine in 17th and 18th Century England'. https://www.historic-uk.com/HistoryUK/HistoryofEngland/Weird-Wonderful-17th-18th-Century-Medicine [accessed 11 June 2020].
14. Charles Tennyson, *Alfred Tennyson* (London: Macmillan, 1950), p. 7.
15. George sold the remainder of the lease to Mr Burton. £1,500 in 1797 is equivalent to £189,883 in 2019. https://www.bankofengland.co.uk/monetary-policy/inflation [accessed 11 November 2020].

16 *In Step with History: 'Alfred and Aunt Elizabeth' Brancepeth & the Tennysons* (Brancepeth: Brancepeth Archives & History Group, 2011), p. 1.
17 Roy Porter, *English Society in the Eighteenth Century* (Harmondsworth: Penguin, 1982), pp. 42–3.
18 I am grateful to Liz Bregazzi, County Archivist DCRO, for copies of baptism entries for William Russell in 1798 and Emma Maria Russell (also at Sedgefield) in 1809.
19 Elizabeth A. Martin, ed., *Concise Medical Dictionary*, 3rd edn (Oxford: Oxford University Press, 1991), p. 382.
20 Hardwick Hall near Sedgefield, County Durham, now a luxury hotel; not to be confused with Hardwick Hall in Derbyshire, owned by the National Trust.
21 http://www.brancepeth-parish-council.org.uk/html/history_group.html [accessed 5 July 2020].
22 I am grateful to Vivienne Lowe of Brancepeth Archives and History Group for information on the Russell family.
23 https://en.wikipedia.org/wiki/County_palatine [accessed 11 July 2020].
24 https://en.wikipedia.org/wiki/Bishop_Durham [accessed 11 July 2020].
25 Sturman and Purton, pp. 69–70.
26 The Tennysons moved to Tealby Lodge in 1801. Later renamed Bayons Manor, it was eventually transformed by Charles.
27 https://www.geriwalton.com/mourning-in-the-georgian-period [accessed 13 July 2020].
28 Tennyson and Dyson, pp. 179–80. Italics in the original.
29 The 'Hermitage' may be one of the public pleasure gardens, inspired by but smaller than London's Vauxhall Gardens opened in 1661. https://www.18thcenturycommon.org/english-pleasure-gardens [accessed 24 July 2020].
30 *Concise Oxford English Dictionary* defines a tontine as 'a scheme for life assurance in which the beneficiaries are those who survive and maintain a policy to the end of a given period'; named after Lorenzo Tonti, an eighteenth-century Neapolitan banker.
31 Vickery, 2003, p. 98.
32 *Brancepeth & the Tennysons*, p. 10.
33 Charles Tennyson, p. 7. Matthew was MP for Saltash in Cornwall from 1802 to 19 February 1807 and 26 February 1808 until 8 May 1822. https://www.historyofparliamentonline.org [accessed 7 July 2020].
34 Jenny Uglow, *In These Times: Living in Britain through Napoleon's Wars, 1793–1815* (London: Faber & Faber, 2014), p. 511.
35 Two years later Spencer Perceval (1762–1812) was shot dead in the lobby of the Houses of Parliament by John Bellingham, who was later hanged. Magnus Magnusson, ed., *Chambers Biographical Dictionary*, 5th edn (Edinburgh: Chambers, 1990), p. 1143.
36 sahistory.org.za/people/sara-saartjie-baartman [accessed 27 July 2020].

37 E. J. Clery, 'What Jane saw: Exploring Austen's creative hinterland and recoverable influences', *Times Literary Supplement*, 9 February 2018, p. 28.
38 Suzan-Lori Parks, *Venus* (New York: Theatre Communications Group, 1997), p. 47.
39 '1816, the year without a summer', *In Our Time*, BBC Radio 4, 21 April 2016.
40 Dennis Mersereau, '15 Facts about "The Year without a Summer"', https://www.mentalfloss.com/article/73575/15-facts-about-year-without-summer [accessed 7 August 2020].
41 https://www.poetryfoundation.org/poems/43825/darkness-56d222aeeee1b [accessed 7 August 2020].
42 DCRO reference EP/Br 16.
43 Torquato Tasso (1544–1595).
44 Tennyson and Dyson, pp. 177–8.
45 Bombazine is a twilled dress fabric of worsted and silk or cotton, especially a black kind formerly used for mourning clothes.
46 DCRO EP/Br 16.
47 Sturman and Purton, p. 22.
48 Tennyson and Dyson, p. 59.
49 https://www.onwar.com/data/francespain1823.html [accessed 22 September 2020].
50 The will was dated 1 October 1818 and 'proved at London with 2 Codicils' on 22 June 1822. NA PROB 11/1658/309.
51 Russell v Russell NA C 13/2791/9; C13/1739/31.
52 See Chapter 1, n. 7. Also Almyra Gray, *Papers and Diaries of a York Family, 1764–1838* (London: Sheldon, 1927), p. 69.
53 John Scott, 1st Earl of Eldon (1751–1838) was office holder from 1801 to 1827.
54 In 1875 it was replaced by the Chancery Division of the High Court of Justice. https://www.britannica.com/topic/Chancery-Division [accessed 8 May 2020].
55 The huge parchment sheets are damaged and faded. DCRO have a copy of the 'answer and examination' (D/Br/F.301) and I am indebted to David Butler for help in interpreting the interrogatories (12655 02.12.2019; 12934 10.12.2019).
56 See note 28.
57 https://www.geni.com/people/William-Henry-Scott-Bentinck-Marquis-of-Titchfield [accessed 27 September 2018].
58 'So we, if children young diseased we find, | Anoint with sweets the vessel's foremost parts | To make them taste the potions sharp we give; | They drink deceived, and so deceived, they live'. Tasso, *Gerusalemme Liberata*, 1.3. http://www.italianverseread ing.ac.uk/liberata/translation/htm [accessed 28 September 2020].
59 Ann Thwaite, *Emily Tennyson: The Poet's Wife* (London: Faber & Faber, 1996), pp. 69–70.
60 *The Letters of Alfred Lord Tennyson*, ed. by Cecil Y. Lang and Edgar F. Shannon, Jr, 3 vols (Oxford: Clarendon Press, 1982–90), I, pp. 59–61 (18 May 1831). Italics in the original.

61 Lang and Shannon, I, p. 2 ([October 1821]).
62 https://www.bankofengland.co.uk/monetary-policy-inflation/inflation-calculator [accessed 19 October 2020].
63 Lang and Shannon, II, p. 88.
64 Lang and Shannon, II, p. 155 ([*c.* 16 July 1856]) and note 1.
65 Lang and Shannon, II, p. 149 (19 May 1856). Italics in the original.
66 Death registered 6 October 1865. GRO certified copy of entry of death reference DYE 478203. Cause of death 'Paralysis and Exhaustion'.

4

Mother and sons: Mary Turner Tennyson, George Clayton Tennyson and Charles Tennyson, 1778 to 1825

Rosalind Boyce

Mary Turner Tennyson, grandmother of the poet and wife of George Tennyson, was an inveterate letter writer, firstly to her mother, Mary Turner, until her death in 1804 and then to her younger son Charles. This chapter concerns her relationship with her two sons, George Clayton, born in 1778, and Charles, born in 1784, and shows that Charles was her favourite. The letters and lives of the two elder children, Elizabeth and Mary, are discussed in Chapters 3 and 6. The letters to Charles begin in 1808, the year of his marriage to Frances Hutton, and their numbers increase as their family grew. Significantly, there are no known letters from Mary to George Clayton although some are referred to, and only two known letters from George Clayton to his mother. The whereabouts of other letters, if they still exist, are not known.

George Clayton Tennyson, 1778 to 1831

'I think I never saw a child so rude and ungovernable'

Much of George Clayton's childhood was spent with his grandfather Michael Tennyson in Holderness, East Yorkshire, and possibly some of his troubles can be traced back to this period. He seems to have been a wayward, petulant child: 'I think I never saw a child so rude and ungovernable', wrote Mary to her mother after George Clayton had been visiting [17.05.1785 Tenn 2/7/23]. According to Robert Bernard Martin 'the child's position as eldest son … indicated that he was intended to inherit money and position and to enhance them'.[1]

In 1787, aged nine, George Clayton was sent to St. Peter's School, York, where his brother Charles joined him, also at the age of nine, in 1793. In a letter to the headmaster, the Reverend John Robinson, in June 1793, George wrote, 'My Boys are come home in very good health & spirits & I have to repeat my thanks to you & Mrs Robinson for your attention to them, George I am sorry to say speaks as bad or worse than ever' [30.06.1793 TRC 4657].

George Clayton went up to St John's College, Cambridge, in 1796 where, according to Patrick Waddington, his behaviour 'tended to be wild'.[2] On one occasion he apparently 'put a pistol-shot through a window of Trinity chapel', but the 'wildness' is not indicated in the letters.

He wrote many letters to his father from Cambridge, often requesting money: 'I really have not been extravagant and I hope you will not think so but every thing now is almost doubly as expensive as when I first came here' [07.05.1799 TRC 4667].

The tone of the following letter suggests that he was trying to gain his father's affection:

> I shall never be able sufficiently to thank you in that you have so kindly expressed yourself in your last letter and I should be inexcusable if after it I did not entirely rely upon you and give you the whole Amount of what I owe here – Had it been possible for me one moment to have doubted who was my best friend I needed but your last kind letter to assure me of it and therefore it shall always be my first duty [? …] to oblige you – The hesitation and backwardness I felt in disclosing to you what will certainly appear extravagance has been in a great measure dissipated by the assurance that by acting openly I shall not incur your blame … Pray inform my Mother that my Cravats & Stockings are in a tolerably good but that my Shirts are in a very deplorable Condition – Give my Duty to her & my best love to my Sister. [13.05.1799 TRC 4668]

George Clayton's health problems become apparent at about this time: 'I don't feel myself much better & find it quite impossible to apply to anything for any length of time but I trust I shall be better soon – I hope you are well' [21.05.1799 TRC 4669].

On one occasion when returning home to Grimsby from Cambridge, George Clayton showed some enterprise when doubtful about getting a place on the coach: 'I cannot be at Brigg till Wednesday night and, as the coach which passes thro' Alconbury hill may be full & is the only conveyance, I may be even in this be disappointed – I would rather therefore be left entirely at liberty, as I can very well walk from Brigg to Grimsby and should be sorry that the horses waited for me unnecessarily' [07.06.1801 TdE H/60/28]. Grimsby is twenty miles from Brigg.[3]

In 1801 he travelled to Russia. Apparently the purpose of this journey was to attend the coronation of the new Czar, Alexander I, but through some misunderstanding he arrived too late for the event.[4] Charles Tennyson and Hope Dyson suggest that he invented the story later in 'a pathetic attempt to create for his children the romance of George Clayton Tennyson, to which unkind fate had denied reality'.[5] Whatever the truth, he was back in England in February 1802 and was ordained priest on 19 December of that year.

He married Elizabeth Fytche (always known as Eliza) of Louth in 1805 and in the same year was awarded a Master of Arts degree. He was appointed to the livings of the Lincolnshire villages of Benniworth, South Willingham, Somersby, Bag Enderby and, later, Grimsby, all of which had been obtained for him by his father, who was providing security for him in this respectable position. It was customary at the time for a family's second son to enter the church. However, in this case his father may have felt that, despite George Clayton being the elder son, with his poor health and 'ungovernable' nature country parishes would be more appropriate for him.

Eliza and George Clayton's second surviving son, Charles (later Tennyson Turner), was christened on 23 August 1808. George Clayton invited his brother Charles and his wife Frances to the ceremony, hoping 'that Fanny and you will give us the pleasure of your Company' [23.08.1808 4TdE/H/67/18].

No mention is made of the grandparents, Mary and George, being invited.

The letters from the early years of George Clayton's marriage reveal a caring family man. This is reflected in a letter to his brother Charles concerning plans for the two families to spend a holiday together at Mablethorpe: 'About a mile from the sea at Mablethorpe there is a very nice cottage, with a very comfortable parlour also a good bedroom & good bed for yourselves with a fire place, another good room with bed, fire place for a Nursery' [19.08.1819 TdE/H/71/18].

At the time there were seventeen children in the two families.

The brothers were close. In later years George Clayton became fond of Charles's wife, Frances, née Hutton, later referring to her as 'my mesmate [mess mate]' [01.02.1824 TdE/H/144/160]. Writing to Charles on one occasion Frances says, 'My love to your Brother; no more romps for me until I see him again, and do particularly give my love to his good wife and children' [10.10.1818 TdE/H/144/130].

George Clayton depended on Charles who, on at least one occasion, helped him to prepare a sermon he was to deliver at the opening of the Assizes, possibly in Cambridge:

> I am very much pressed for time & have not thought of an assize sermon. Can you write me one, or a part of one, as you did before, or choose a text & give me any thoughts of [? ...] upon it. It would help me mightily. [May 1813 TdE/H/71/25]

The following letter is one of only two from George Clayton to his mother:

> I fear you will think that I have treated you very unkindly in not having before this returned an answer to your very affectionate letter addressed to me at Mablethorpe, which owing to the neglect of the postmaster at Alford in not forwarding my letters, I did not receive till Yesterday on my return from London, where my Sister, Eliza, little Mary & myself have been for the last three weeks – Here [? ...] the oculist whom I consulted in town gives me just encouragement respecting my eyes & says that all the symptoms I have experienced are entirely nervous; that perhaps they may never become worse & may gradually grow better; but advised me at the same time to consult him again if I were again to suffer any deprivation of sight. [30.10.1813 TdE/H/71/28]

'Little Mary' is George Clayton's fourth surviving child and eldest daughter.

Mary's concern for George Clayton is reflected in her letters. She would probably have denied that Charles was her favourite son, but she never writes to George Clayton or Eliza as she does to Frances and Charles. He is 'poor George' or 'poor dear George', whereas Charles is always 'Dearest Charles'. He may not have had an appealing or affectionate nature, which Mary found difficult to understand. She may also have been influenced by his father's harsh attitude towards him:

> Poor George left us on Friday [she wrote] much better in his spirits and appetite but his complaint which does not exactly put on the appearance yours did – still returns upon him about once a week – on Thursday Even^g he sat with his Head on his Hand as though he was musing – when his Wife observed 'he is not well'. We spoke – he did not answer – we repeated he made no effort to speak & was insensible – when he open'd his eyes they rolled without meaning and then he spoke incoherently for a minute this wandering of the intellect is alarming when I described this affliction to Mr Barton he said he thought it indicated Catalepsy rather that [? than] Epilepsy be what it may he should be careful to indicate the cause as soon as possible – he has employ'd a Dr Bousefield of Spilsby who was a pupil of Harrisons – but his Pills he is careless about taking – for he knows not

how he has been affected – or that anything has been the matter. [31.03.1816 4TdE/H/11a]

Epilepsy is a neurological disorder possibly caused by genes affecting brain function. About one in three people with epilepsy have a family member suffering from it.[6]

By June 1819 George Clayton and Eliza had ten surviving children, six boys and four girls. An eleventh, which was to be the last, was expected. George Clayton was overwhelmed by all his responsibilities. As well as his poor health, his parish duties and the presence of so many boisterous children, he had taken it upon himself to educate his sons at home. In addition, the children were unwell and the household was in chaos:

> We have all got the Measles (I mean the Children) & one, (Matilda) is I fear dangerously ill. Think of having 8 Children down at once. The worst of all is, that Eliza has exerted herself so much in going up & down our abominable steep Staircase in attending upon them that she is confined to the Sofa & I much fear a miscarriage. Misfortunes I have heard never attack us singly.

Despite his troubles he had closely followed his brother's political career and adds a postscript: 'You have been dumb for some time in the house but I see you opened your Mouth on Friday last & as I understand it from the Times intend to dilate it still wider on Monday on the Bankrupts bill' [27.06.1819 TdE/H/144/136].

'House' is the House of Commons.

Throughout his life George Clayton was bitterly hurt by his father's attitude towards him and by August 1820 the rift between them was becoming apparent:

> With the sentiments you yet entertain and have entertained for more than twenty years, I cannot wonder you told Mr Bourne you had not a spark of affection for me. The rude and unprecedented manner in which you first address'd me at Hainton, after a long absence, on your return from York (I quote your own words 'Now you great awkward booby are you here') holding me up to utter derision before Mr Heneage, his son & Sir Robt Ainslie, & your language & conduct in innumerable other instances, many of which here made a deep impression upon my mind, sufficiently prove the truth of your own assertion – you have long injured me by your suspicions. I cannot avoid them for the fault is not mine … You may forget or pass off as a jest what penetrates & rankles in my heart; you may break what is already bent, but there is a tribunal before which you and I may speedily appear, more speedily perhaps than either of us desire or expect. [14.08 1820 TdE/H/144/142]

A rare letter to his mother is from Cheltenham where he and his wife, Eliza, were taking the waters:

> I fear you have been some time expecting an answer to your last kind letter. The fact is I was so very unwell before I set off from home, that I thought it would answer no purpose to send you a more unfavourable Account of myself than I had done before – Eliza & I are both here; she is by no means in a good state of health & I have consulted a Physician with respect to each of our cases. He gives me great hopes that the waters will reestablish my health. [15.04.1822 TdE/H/144/149]

Cheltenham has been a health resort since the discovery of mineral springs there in the eighteenth century. It became fashionable after a visit from George III and Queen Charlotte in 1788.[7]

But a few months afterwards Mary, in some distress, wrote to Charles about George Clayton:

> My mind and your poor Fathers is terribly torn and harass'd about your Brother. I wish things were all settled to his wish when I trust a happy change of mind may be productive of good effect on his dreadful disease – I would go tomorrow to Somersby but wish to know whether I might go without a hazard of great agitation to him ... O may it please the great dispenser of events to restore this dear afflicted Child to his former strength & health – as well also to a calm & quiet mind. [09.11.1822 4TdE/H/24/5]

Unable to understand the situation, she may have been afraid to go to Somersby and confront her son. A few days later she writes again to Charles:

> Although I write in seemingly good spirits my Heart is cruelly lacerated on account of our dear George poor fellow he has had not only to contend with his own mistaken impressions, but with most villainous incendiaries that have lost few opportunities of blowing him into a flame against both his Parents. May it please Heaven to restore him in all respects both of mind & body & spare you My dearest Charles a blessing most inestimable to us. [13.11.1822 4TdE/H/24/47]

The 'villainous incendiaries' may refer to the slander George Clayton was receiving from his Somersby parishioners who feared his erratic and violent behaviour.

Early in 1823 Frederick and Alfred, George Clayton's sons aged sixteen and fourteen, were staying at Bayons Manor. There is no mention of the other Somersby children although they were similar in age to Charles's children: 'Frederic & Alfred too have been with us a week last Tuesday and every thing goes on pretty smoothly – Geo [Hildyard] & Fred^c with Alfred very good friends – and really as happy a party as you can possibly see' [08.01.1823 4TdE/H/31/19].

Two weeks later there was more disquiet about George Clayton:

> It is greatly to be fear'd that a convalescent state is far from him – for he is fearfully circumstanced his Nerves and spirits so very weak, Medical aid he will not hear of – should you write to him dont mention his low state of spirits – this is the term Eliza his Wife gives it – & nervous to a high degree we will if we can get him here free from the Noise of his Children. [22.01.1823 4TdE/H/27/-]

George Clayton and Eliza now had eleven children, ranging in age from four to sixteen.

Early in February 1824 Charles invited his brother to accompany him to Paris, but George Clayton, his responsibilities weighing heavily upon him, declined the invitation:

> You speak of going to Paris – How happy should I be could I accompany you there.* I think it would give me something like health of which I cannot boast at present. Less Application & a Change of Climate & a removal from the harassing business of instruction would perhaps restore me. But I feel my powers of mind sensibly declining, & the attacks to which I am subject must necessarily injure the intellect
>
> * I am so netted by the instruction of my Family that I cannot. [01.02.1824 TdE/H/144/160]

'A severe sufferer': George Clayton, 1825 to 1831

By June 1825, there was increasing concern over George Clayton's health. Eliza wrote at length to Charles:

> We received your letter last night & which I answer without delay. I read it to poor George as he was too ill to see what it contained himself. He has never been free from his disorder since your Father left us he could not perform the service at his Churches last Sunday nor attend the Bishop's Visitation on the Friday following [? …] he had a violent Paroxysm yesterday in the afternoon & greatly alarmed us all as we really thought he would have lost his senses but thank God it abated in a few hours & tho he continued exceedingly ill until twelve o Clock at night he then got a little rest which enabled him to read prayers today [? …] he was scarcely able to walk to Church he got through with the Service better than I could have expected. He is indeed a severe sufferer & has such frequent

returns of his complaint that I fear ultimately, if he lives, it will deprive him of his intellects. He was pleased with your letter my dear Charles & bids me say he shall be happy to see you next Month when you are in Lincolnshire. I hope dear Fanny will accompany you. We shall be much gratified to see you both & to thank you for all your kindness to ourselves & Frederick. Your Nephews & Nieces desire their kind remembrance. George joins me in best love to yourself & Fanny. [21.06.1825 4TdE/H/36/5]

Two months after his mother's death in August 1825 George Clayton wrote to Charles from Cheltenham. The letter reveals his affection for his father despite the rift between them. Perhaps he hoped that their common grief over Mary's death would restore the relationship:

I am very sorry that I had not the opportunity of seeing my dear father & yourself when some time ago Charles, Alfred & myself went over to see you at Tealby. I am anxious to hear how my poor father does & whether he has in any degree recovered his spirits & peace of mind. The season was getting so late that I thought if I were to derive any benefit from the Waters here I could not delay any longer and that I could visit Tealby on my return – shall you be at Tealby in the course of about three weeks? I can take it on my return & shall be truly happy to find my poor father more tranquillized than when I left him. ... Let me have a line from you by return of Post stating how you all are & With best love to my dear Father Fanny & yourself. [22.10.1825 4TdE/H/33/m]

From 1826 George Clayton's condition worsened. In a letter to his father he says,

I fear you will think it long before you hear from me I only returned home from Cambridge last Night, having had there a violent Attack of the Cholera Morbus which obliged me to divide the journey into two days & which has rendered me so thin & Weak that I am scarcely able to stand. The Physician who attended me states that he never almost saw a more serious Attack ... If I am no better I shall send for Dr Bousfield tomorrow, for tho' I believe the danger is past the symptoms are very distressing – My wife is at Mablethorpe with Mrs Bourne. [27.10.1827 TdE/H/144/173]

'Mrs Bourne' is Mary Tennyson Bourne, Eliza's sister-in-law. 'Cholera morbus' is acute gastroenteritis.[8]

Dr Bousfield of Horncastle, George Clayton's doctor, had already visited him and wrote to Dr Barton:

I yesterday rode over to Somersby ... I found Dr Tennyson, except complaining more than the rest of the company of heat as well as I have usually seen him of late, and in an argument which took place after Dinner displaying the same acuteness of mind and playfulness of manner as when I first met with him more than thirteen [? thirty] years ago. A slight indisposition, however, of the eldest daughter, for which she wished to consult me, gave me an opportunity of seeing Mrs Tennyson alone, and I found that she really does labour under the apprehension at which our letter hinted, from the violent state of Nervous agitation which breaks out occasionally in her Husband. It is more however on her childrens' account than her own that her placid disposition appears so greatly unhinged ... A temporary removal from objects connected of late with so much distress and agitation would afford the finest chance of recovery. A Continental tour of a few months would, I confidently hope, return him to the bosom of his family restored in a great measure to both bodily and mental health, and capable of enjoying that happiness which a most promising and highly gifted set of children would naturally produce. [17.10.1827 4TdE/H/39/1]

Charles was doubtful about the suggested 'Continental tour' and wrote to Dr Barton:

This morning bro^t me yours and Dr B[ousefield]'s letter to you. The information it conveys much what I expected. I have long tho^t change of scene wo^d be of great use but how is that to be accomplished? He is not in a state of health to travel alone – neither wo^d it answer to him if (as he would not) he co^d be prevailed on to go. [21.10.1827 4TdE/H/39/3]

Meanwhile, in desperation, Mary Anne Fytche, Eliza's sister, wrote the following letter to George Clayton, now so changed from the 'caring family man' planning the holiday in Mablethorpe a few years earlier:

In consequence of the severe illness of my Brother, & the infirmities of my Mother, the painful task devolves upon me to remonstrate with you on the unparalleled barbarity of your conduct to dear Eliza. Surely it was sufficient misery to be subject to the caprices of so dreadful a temper as yours for twenty two years without having her character vilified where she has no means of justifying herself. You have deprived her of all authority in the family, & encouraged the servants to insult her, she is not allowed to have any Money, & if she asks for some for the necessary expences of the family, she is refused in such language as I should be ashamed to transcribe. [24.10.1827 4TdE/H/39/18]

Perhaps his unreasonable behaviour was caused by frustration at being unable to deal with his illness, overwork, many children, and the unsympathetic nature of his father. Whatever the cause, it had a lasting adverse effect on his wife and children. Dr Bousfield had described the children as 'highly gifted' but the only one who fulfilled this early promise was Alfred who became Poet Laureate.

A few weeks later, three years after a visit was first mooted, the brothers did eventually travel to France together. The rift having healed a little, George advised his father:

> As I am going abroad for some time I shall be much obliged by your taking the charge of my children and family concerns during my absence and I enclose you an order on Messrs Clayton Garfitt & Co to honor your Draft on my Account. I also request & authorize you to act generally in all my concerns as if you had a full & general power of attorney. [21.11.1827 TdE/H/148/10a]

Refreshed by the experience, George Clayton commented to his father: 'The Air of Paris agrees with me & I propose staying here some time after Charles's departure, having a Valet de Chambre whom you know who is very attentive & who would pay me the utmost Attention should I again be attacked with a spasm, of which however I have had no occurrence' [30.11.1827 TdE/H/148/17].

George Clayton was an erudite man, perhaps too erudite for his country parishes. There are many scholarly works in his library, now in the Tennyson Research Centre in Lincoln, including science, history, theology, literature and Latin and Greek texts. He was beset by many problems, not least his poor health, which may have been caused by epilepsy and alcohol addiction. At the time epilepsy was thought to be caused by masturbation and considered to be shameful. George Clayton's letters confirm that he wanted his father's affection, but instead, his father, who favoured his younger brother, despised and humiliated him. Martin argues that epilepsy 'would in part explain their father's decision to pass over the normal expectations of George, since a disposition to fits was no recommendation as head of the great family the elder George Tennyson hoped to found'.[9] George Clayton is remembered primarily as the father of Alfred Tennyson, Queen Victoria's Poet Laureate. If his health had been better and his father more sympathetic towards him, he might have fulfilled some of his early promise and led a more distinguished life.

After years of ill-health George Clayton died in March 1831, probably of alcoholic poisoning, although the official version was typhoid fever.[10] The only family members who attended his funeral at Somersby were his sister Mary Tennyson Bourne and his nephew George Hildyard, Charles's son.[11] The final humiliation came when his father would not attend his funeral, claiming ill-health, and not allowing him to be buried in the Tennyson family vault at Tealby. Alfred was deeply affected by his father's death and 'slept the night in his own father's bed ... hoping that his ghost would appear and confirm the continuity of life after death'.[12]

Charles Tennyson, 1784 to 1861

'Commit yourself to the healing hand of the Almighty'

Charles became Mary's favourite son, perhaps because he was the youngest child, born several years after the others. She had kept him at home as a child rather than sending him to live with grandparents as she had done with her daughter Mary, and George Clayton, and this may be another reason.

After school in York, and subsequently Lincoln School and Louth Grammar School, Charles went up to St John's College, Cambridge, and took his degree in 1805. He went on to study in a barrister's chambers in London at Boswell's Court, Lincoln's Inn Fields. He had a successful career in the law, setting up practice in Lincolnshire, and later had a long and distinguished political career, first entering Parliament in 1818 as Member for Great Grimsby.

Charles married Frances Hutton of Morton Hall near Gainsborough in 1808. Mary favoured their children, particularly the eldest, George Hildyard, over her Somersby grandchildren, referring to them affectionately as 'twigs' and 'chickens', although they were often rowdy – 'I hear my Chickens very merry below' [29.01.1823 4TdE/H/31/25].

Mary was perpetually anxious about all aspects of her family's lives. Health, or the lack of it, is a recurring theme throughout her letters. She had a deep religious faith and called upon it in times of difficulty. Faith in 'the great Physician of both soul and body' was the only comfort and relief available in an age when doctors could do little. Charles suffered from poor health throughout his life. Although the nature of his illness is not known, it may have been epilepsy. This caused great anxiety both to himself and to his mother, as shown in a letter of January 1809:

> The account of you my dear Charles has depress'd our spirits Your letter to me was evidently written much out of Spirits – we fear'd you was not well and Fannys letters confirm it – tell us the worst because suspense is less bearable, have you had a direct attack of your complaint or only symptoms? ...... You deplore the irritable state of your nerves – as having an Effect upon your temper I really with you believe it originates in your disease but dont let this or anything else prey upon your Spirits – for the health of the body will fall a sacrifice to the mind

if too much indulged ... Doc[r] Harrisons medicines I trust will have a blessing in them commit yourself to the healing hand of the Almighty – he is the great Physician of both soul and body. [14.01.1809 TdE/H/149/4]

Early in 1809 Charles Chaplin of Blankney invited Charles to join his militia as a Captain. Charles's preoccupation with his health is confirmed when he declined the invitation because, 'I almost think in my present State of health & long field day in w[h] I might have to <u>stand</u> sev[l] hours with wet Cloaths & with wet feet and to be motionless perhaps a considerable part of y[e] time might be too much for one' [01.02.1809 TdE/H/67/2].

The militia was the oldest reserve force. Organized in county regiments, it was recruited by ballot from able-bodied men on lists drawn up by parish constables, and its officers were local gentlemen.[13] Charles Chaplin was a major in the Lindsey Regiment of the Lincolnshire Militia in 1809, and MP for Stamford from 1809 to 1812.[14]

As so often, Charles's health was causing problems and took precedence over everything else, as shown when replying to a request from his mother to obtain George's gout medicine in London:

> I almost fear being able to procure any Gout Medicine before I leave Town but Angerstein says that he will contrive to favor one with 2 or 3 Bottles if any sho[d] arrive before I go. There can be no necessity for our remaining in Town beyond two or three days longer and in truth I never felt more anxious to get out of it. The first two or three days I was absolutely overpowered by the heat which conspiring with a fortnights predisposition to be unwell has made me very much [? ...] the last 2 or 3 days. Last night however I slept tolerably but I find myself obliged to eat almost nothing my Stomach is in so weak a State. [13.06.1810 TdE/H/68/7]

John Julius Angerstein, a family friend, was a landowner of Stainton-le-Vale, Lincolnshire, a marine underwriter and sometime Chairman of Lloyd's. He was involved in the development of the National Gallery.[15] The Tennysons would have enjoyed having such a distinguished friend.

Caenby is a small village approximately halfway between Tealby and Morton. Frances and Charles moved to Caenby Hall in June 1809, and by February 1811 they had two children. Something of a social climber, Charles was making improvements to the house, no doubt to make it more 'gentrified', and asked his father: 'If you c[d] meet with two <u>genteel</u> classical <u>white</u> figures on brackets for y[r] spaces above my new book cases you w[d] oblige me by purchasing them at a moderate rate' [02.1811 TdE/H/69/6]. But later he changed his mind and cancelled them [10.03.1811 TdE/H/69/7]. Perhaps they did not meet his high standards.

'God only knows whether we ever Meet again on such a day': December 1814 to March 1816

Frances and Charles moved to London in December 1814 and took up residence at 23 Lincoln's Inn Field where Charles continued his law practice. Perhaps he felt that in London he would be in a better position to pursue a career in politics. Mary's immediate reaction to the news of the move is not known. She may have hidden her disappointment from her son. The children stayed with Mary and George while the move was taking place, but she was hoping for a visit from the whole family before they left:

> As your Affection led you my dear Charles to say before you left us that if we did not come to Morton you would certainly come home again In that case would it not be made conveniently practicable for yourself & Fanny to make your final departure from hence with your children to Town – we trust you will so determine and when you think you can fix a day for coming let us know and our Carriage & Horses shall meet you at Spittal – I am happy to say the Children are all particularly well and have been ever since you left us – The Baby [Louis] tell Fanny is quite handsome & blooming. [13.12.1814 TdE/H/72/14]

'Spittal' is Spital in the Street, a small settlement astride Ermine Street (the present day A15 road) close to Caenby.

Mary eagerly awaited visits from Charles and family. Despite the move to London, they often returned to Lincolnshire, but she realized that it would not be possible for them to meet so often.

> I have only to say we are sorry you cannot come to us tomorrow – fearing that your visit and Fanny's will necessarily be shorten'd to us – however excepting we hear again from you to the contrary, you will meet our Horses at Spittal on Monday we have not any engagement to prevent us sending them for you any day ... the dear Children are well and happy – and it will be a satisfaction to you to know that George – seems to acquiesce perfectly in your wish of taking him to Town – showing not the least disappointment. I confess I had reckon'd much of seeing you both here Christmas day – for God only knows whether we ever Meet again on such a day. [22.12.1814 TdE/H/72/6]

George is George Hildyard, eldest son of Frances and Charles, and Mary's favourite grandchild. Frances had told her widowed mother Mary Hutton: 'We shall always come down to the country for two months every year' [28.04.1814 4TdE/H/6/55].

There are no known letters from Mary to Eliza, George Clayton's wife, but many to her other daughter-in-law, Frances, including the following, sent after returning from a visit to the family in London: 'After sleeping at Sleaford on Friday Night we reached home on Saturday about half after four O'Clock and very thankful to be set down in safety after the hurry scurry of nearly a seven weeks <u>perpetual</u> motion.'

But there was no rest for Mary, as visitors were arriving straightaway. The letter continues:

> In the midst of unpacking – I was call'd down stairs to Mr Barton who show'd particular interest in most minute enquiries respecting yourself and Charles and your family – he is a friendly creature and I believe laments very sincerely the loss of that friendly society he was in habit of enjoying at Caenby, totally independent of pecuniary interest – afterwards came the Robinsons viz: Mrs Robinson and Miss Alington with their Carriage and Horses driven by young Abram Stephen and I much fear some accident will happen them for they by no means understand what belongs to the nice fitting of Harness – the poor creatures are gall'd and raw to the flesh all round, their hocks owing to the lightness of the collars which makes them frisk, and prance and fret and fume – till they are almost worn out with fatigue. [16.05.1815 4TdE/H/50/17]

The Robinson and Alington families from Louth were related to each other and were friends of the Tennysons. Zephaniah Barton, also a family friend, was a well-known and respected doctor in the Market Rasen area.

The health of Frances and Charles living in the noxious atmosphere of London was a worry for Mary. She was preoccupied with bowels and frequently reminded family members not to neglect them. 'Throughout human history, bowel irregularity has been considered dangerous to health'.[16] 'Bustling' is her favourite word for hurried activity.

> And now my dear Fanny let me know how you are going on respecting your health how is your Throat? & how is the stitch in your side? for I trust since you look so bustling people your nerves will be in a better state and all your little complaints subside and how goes on my dear Charles? his nerves a little quieter may be a help to his amendment for he certainly was much shook – but I charge him not to neglect the proper state of his Bowels – no health can be expected – if the secretions do not go on correctly more particularly the intestinal canal ... I wish you could now both breathe and all your children the pure air.

Although Mary missed the family, she took advantage of their presence in London to request the purchase of generous gifts for friends:

> We have never given Mr Barton at any time, anything beyond his exact Bill – I should like to make him a little useful present, such as a Silver Snuffbox quite plain and thin, with a bend to wear in his waistcoat pocket. I saw Many the last morning when I went with your Father up the Strand and also in Holborn but he said we had no time then to shop and you would do it for us … Remember it is to have a bend to fit the pocket (waistcoat) – If the order round goes beyond the price of 2 guineas – or you think it is too large take the size of the inner round – it is to have no carving about it, or figure & gilt within – I wish if you could bring it, and y^r cream saucepan with you, when you come to Morton. [16.05.1815 4TdE/H/50/17]

Snuff boxes came in many different shapes so Mary would be sure to obtain one with a 'bend'.[17] Pre-decimalization, a guinea was worth one pound, one shilling.[18]

In November 1815 Mary was packing for a visit to her daughter and son-in-law, Elizabeth and Matthew Russell, at Hardwick, County Durham. Frances was expecting her fifth child the following March:

> My dear Fanny – I rec^d yours of the 4th for which I thank you, and rejoice at your renovation of health & spirits two most desirable blessings which I hope may now travel with you to the month of March – when the check I trust will be only for a short period when if upon drawing near this month you still wish to see me and I am in the land of the living & (all things considered) I fulfil my promise of being with you I am in the Midst of Packing – that is gathering all my Items for the great Trunk putting them in tomorrow in readiness for 8 O Clock the next morning – for I have been weary of home since you all left me and am sighing for another change. [15.11.1815 TdE/H/74/45]

Charles and Frances's fifth child, Eustace Alexander, was born in March 1816. A few days later Mary wrote to Frances:

> Your letter of dear Fannys safety and the birth of a fine Boy gave us great satisfaction and I waited Mr Barton's return before I sent off to you both our affectionate congratulations and he very kindly took his dinner with us yesterday.

Charles Tennyson MP, 1818 to 1826

Sponsored by his brother-in-law Matthew Russell, Charles was elected MP for Great Grimsby in 1818, and held the seat for eight years. Mary wished to know more about his success: 'We hear little of Grimsby. The last report was a publication of <u>how well they all live</u> having Beef, and Coals – &c which they hoped would be followed by something to drink – this was in a Boston Gazzette a week or two since I hear' [05.02.1818 TdE/H/ 79/12].

George Clayton's reaction to his brother's success is not known.

George Hildyard, aged ten, and Frederick, George Clayton and Eliza's eldest surviving son, aged twelve, were staying with George and Mary in August 1819. Like his father at a similar age, Frederick seems to have been 'ungovernable', which Mary and George hoped to rectify:

> I thank God he [George Hildyard] is in good health – regular in his Bowels & yesterday we thought his swelled Lip was somewhat gone down – indeed I perceive it is always better in the afternoon – Mr Barton advises Sea Bathing – & your Father intends taking him to Cleathorpe or Grimsby soon … am glad to have it in my power to add that although Frederic is an older Boy there is a perfect agreement and his manners we think will be corrected during his stay for your father & myself endeavor to make him ashamed on his [? …] – otherwise in speaking a sentence – George will not be in danger of any disadvantage for it is a southern pronunciation … I have time for no more than to say that dear George is not tempted to eat anything (or drink Coffee) that he believes you & his mama would disapprove so that for prudence you may at present trust him the world over … for although such different children I do not know but I could love Julia as much as George she is truly amiable he is the same as ever. [15.08.1819 TdE/H/81/20]

This is a rare reference to George Clayton's children. Frederick, Charles and Alfred are occasionally mentioned in Mary's letters, but not his other children. Perhaps the Somersby children were boisterous and less affectionate than their cousins. The 'southern pronunciation' suggests that a Lincolnshire accent is not considered an advantage.

Charles and his family moved from Lincolns Inn Fields to 4 Park Street, Westminster, in 1819. Martin states that there were difficulties in the marriage and that Frances and Charles divided the house so that they could be in London at the same time without living together. However, this cannot be confirmed:[19]

> 'All health attend you my dearest Ch^s in that Babylon [wrote Mary] to which you are hastening as well as a safe Asylum in your dwelling, will be the prayer of your Affectionate Mo^r'. At the end of the letter is a list of items needed for the Park Street house: 'Bell Pulls / Stair Carpet / Parlor Carpet / qu [? query] lamps'. [14.11.1819, TdE/H/82/86]

Mary was comparing London to Babylon which in the Bible was a symbol for sin and rebellion.[20]

King George III died on 29 January 1820. He had reigned from 1760 and was the third Hanoverian king of Great Britain. During his reign, Britain lost its American colonies but emerged as a leading power in Europe. He suffered from what were thought to be 'fits of madness', and after 1810, his son acted as regent.[21] Charles attended his funeral at Windsor but had a poor opinion of the proceedings:

> I have just returned from the Kings Funeral at Windsor wch in [? point] of Pageant &c I tho^t ill got up ... I am much harried to day in / Consequence /So must conclude saying that I am really very well tho' the fatigue was considerable. [17.02.1820 TdE/H/85/8]

Mary was hoping that Charles would be re-elected as MP for Great Grimsby in 1820 following the death of the king: 'To read from under your own hand this morning – by Mr Brooks – your hopes after (all the fatigue you have encountered) of ultimate success both for Mr Duncombe and yourself – was most enlivening to your dear Fathers spirits as well as my own' [5.03.1820, TdE/H/23/ [15]. William Duncombe canvassed with Charles and came second to him in the poll.[22]

George Clayton reacted acidly to his brother's re-election: 'I do not think it worth my while to congratulate you on your success at Grimsby, as you never wrote me one word upon the subject; (not but that you sent me a printed circular) & I first learnt the event from the Lincoln paper' [28.03.1820 4TdE/H/23[42].

Mary, as always, was looking forward to a visit from Charles's family:

> We hope to have the happiness of seeing at Tealby yourself, dear Fanny and your three Elder Children – have you found friends returning from France to whom you can commit the care of your two sweet Girls? – or have you to go yourself? a most harassing thing it would be to you at this period – and besides France, <u>particularly Paris</u> – seems again in a state of wicked commotion – that you will find the going thither attended with some more than ordinary inconvenience – according to the report of the Papers – so that I feel very anxious about you on this score. [01.07.1820 TdE/H/85/44]

The 'wicked commotion' was an attempted insurrection in Paris, known as the French Bazaar.[23]

'Wherever you are may the Almighty be with you': 1822 to 1825

In February 1822 Charles was about to depart for Cheltenham for his health. Mary showed her superstitious nature: 'Wherever you are may the Almighty be with you and ... support you ... did you see an account of an Earthquake in Yorkshire I am looking to the portentions & signs of the times – what dreadful doings in Ireland How is dear George [Hildyard]?' [02.02.1822 4TdE/H/26/-] The 'doings in Ireland' refer to 'the 'Captain Rock' campaign of 1821-4, one in a series of outbreaks of agrarian unrest that began in the 1760s and continued until the eve of the Famine, when starvation finally made concerted action impossible and the landlords closed in to make the evictions and clearances they had long desired.[24] Her remarks foreshadow her grandson Alfred's suspicion of Irish politics and his opposition to the Irish Home Rule Bill in 1886, as described by John Batchelor.[25]

A few months later Charles was causing Mary more concern. He was staying with his sister Elizabeth after the death of her husband Matthew Russell:

> I long to hear how you reach'd Brancepeth – having very often thought of your dear sickly, White face since your departure & with tears of sorrow – are you better of your Head? – or has the traveling made it worse. [25.09.1822 4TdE/H/24/38]

The brothers were in Cheltenham in November 1822: 'We have been most anxious to know how our poor dear George has supported the journey [wrote Mary] ... I trust for the best news of him by a few lines this evening from your ready hand ... The invalids of my family very much occupy my mind but I can only pray for them' [20.11.1822 4TdE/H/24/60].

Charles returned home a few days later. Mary was hoping for a visit from twelve-year-old George Hildyard but 'I am fearful that Georges Mamma will as she has a just right put in her claim for George for the Holidays – If so, we submit as we ought – but it is so long since we beheld that dear fellow that we feel a natural yearning' [23. 11.1822 4TdE/H/24/62].

A letter sent shortly before Christmas confirms Mary's fondness for Charles's children:

> Make yourself happy my dearest C^{hs} about your dear children they are by no means too many for us – we consider them more happy together, and as they do every thing to please their Grannies we are happy and pleased with them

poor Edwin took cold soon after he came but is getting the better of it – Geo is well and well distinguished in diet not being disposed to err in either quality or quantity Julia is in high health & spirits and so are the youngsters … Julia really performs pleasingly on the Piano and improves dayley thank you – have no Tooth Ache. [22.12.1822 4TdE/H/28/58]

'Grannies' refers to both grandparents.

Charles made frequent visits to France. The reason is not known, but he may have been on government business. His daughters had been at school there but were now continuing their education in England. Mary was always worried about these visits:

> Our hearts yearn towards you and anxious about all belonging to you, is it really time that you leave home for France on Tuesday next – I wish not to take up your precious time unnecessarily at this moment – you will be sufficiently harried without me … how sorry we are to read in the paper of the precarious state of Lord Titchfield poor young Man – although we knew him not we are hurt because he was a <u>friend</u> of yours my dearest Charles. [6.03.1824 4TdE/H/52/26]

After living with Mary and George for several months, Charles's daughter Julia was about to return to her parents:

> I shall deliver her into your Hands … which parting will be very painful to your father & Myself – having been a most interesting Child to us during the long & dreary Winter …. It has been too very gratifying to see her always so very happy with us. [30.03.1823 4TdE/H/29]

'I am quite adrift': Charles, 1824

Charles's friend Lord Titchfield, William Henry Cavendish-Scott-Bentinck MP, heir to the Duke of Portland, died on 6 March 1824 at the age of twenty-seven possibly from a brain abscess, 'a pus-filled swelling in the brain'.[26] Charles may have felt flattered to be in the company of a member of the aristocracy. Although he was much affected by his friend's death, he appears to be more concerned for himself.[27]

> My amiable and excellent friend is no more! He expired last night at ¼ before 8 and I knew it immediately … This blow is to me <u>in various ways particularly severe</u> and scarcely any one but himself can know how much I miss him. … In

all my political arrangements I am quite adrift & shall at present dislike the sight of the House of Commons. [06.03.1824 4TdE/H/28/12]

A week later he attended the funeral:

Yesterday I saw my late kind & lamented friend deposited in the Tomb. I bore this scene but ill ... The loss I have sustained seems to me daily more & more heavy ... Tomorrow morning I go to Paris. The weather seems now settled & fine, but be assured that I shall not cross except with a perfect security as it is possible to reckon upon. ... I think change of scene will relieve my mind from a position of its present [? ...] & I hope to return to England another being. [14.03.1824 4TdE/H/28/14]

A few weeks later Mary was hoping that when Charles returned from France 'it will be to a fuller enjoyment of life than you have had for years':

We are much refresh'd by the improved and cheery accounts you give us of your own health and prospects, may it please God to realize them and that, not only for yourselves, but for your dear children that they may be blest with health & strength, and show themselves more equal to worldly combat than their Parents have hitherto experienced ... I am expecting to hear from Fanny in a day or two having written to her to know how she is going on since your having mention'd her suffering under Influenza – dear George [Hildyard] too has kindly written to me and I still owe him my thanks he wrote me a most excellent letter in a very superior hand, previous to which I had one from dear Fanny most friendly all they were quite well. [02.05.1824 TdE/H/92/79]

Charles seems to have been a connoisseur of wine, and this letter to his mother mainly concerns the purchase of wine, but as so often his health was causing problems:

I harried myself so much with my letters on Monday that <u>until this morning</u> I have been at a standstill ever since – thus obtaining further conviction how impossible it wo^d be for me to recover myself properly in Town. ... Yesterday I settled about the wine and have ordered a Cask of Burgundy the same as the last & a Casket of the very finest quality of Vin de Grave (for there are many qualities) to be sent for you to the care of Mr Power who will be instructed by me to forward them forthwith to the care of Plaskett by sea to Grimsby. [13.05.1824, 4TdE/H/28/69]

Mary was still anxious about Charles:

All we are anxious about is just to have a line of information that there is still a prospect of your complete convalescence when your return does take place – but alas, you seem born to be bustled – surely a time will arrive when you may be more equal to encounter such harrass for harrass it must be to you, <u>sick</u> or <u>well</u>. [16.05.1824 TdE/H/92/74]

The following letter concerns the arrangements for Charles's daughters' education in England and of course, his health. Julia was fourteen at the time, and Clara was twelve. 'Miss Kirby's' is probably a school:

This morning I rec^d your affectionate note of the 3^d. Fanny rode up from Blechingley the night before last and I expect dear Julia & Clara this afternoon. I am very anxious to have an opportunity of judging of their improvement at Miss Kirby's before I decide for their return to her, especially as I find it [? …] expensive, however the first half year is always the worst on acc of Entrances &c &c. … I have been rather bilious yesterday & to day – A Naughty Liver is I fear the root of Evil with me. Have you got your Wine? God bless you my dearest Mother. [05.07.1824 TdE/H/92/57]

The wine may be the cause of the 'Naughty liver'.
Mary replied:

Both Fanny, Geo. & your^s I hope are all better – I wonder not at your being bilious pray exactly say, what is to be done with the wine of both sorts? And are both to have a dose of Eggs & Water and how much for each – & how much of each ingredient for each Cask? & how long to remain afterwards before Bottled … with love to Fanny & all her Chickens. [07.07.1824 TdE/H/92/56]

'Eggs and water' are used to clarify wine in a process called 'fining'.[28]
A visit to Tealby was being planned:

This morning I rec^d your affectionate Letter enclosing one for Fanny by which she appeared much gratified. Yesterday also bro^t me one from my Dearest Father. I do not think Fanny cou^d well manage to accompany me to Tealby as our family <u>must necessarily</u> be divided & during the boys & Girls holidays we c^d not leave any of them without one of us. … we hope to be able to start on Friday the 10th & be with you Sat^y the 11th in the Evening. [26.11.1824 TdE/H/92/7]

Mary was eagerly looking forward to this visit and had no worries about the 'accommodation'. Seven grandchildren were expected:

We wish (for your Father) joins me cordially to see them all but without inconvenience to yourself you cannot bring with you at this Season more than four in your Carriage – then dear Edwin and Clara – we <u>think</u> of and <u>long</u> to see all – so dear Fanny gives up at this time – Those that you cannot bring with you now, I trust Fanny will continue to bring with her at the next vacation … – dont make any hesitation about the accommodation for Beds – I can manage comodiously for them. [02.12.1824 TdE/H/91/71]

'A short conflict between the Heart & Blood': 1821 to 1825

From 1821, Mary's letters reveal that her health was deteriorating:

The Chair … is the best thing of the kind I ever saw your father enjoys it much and you have my dear Ch^s our united thanks as you also calculated to <u>my</u> comfort of which I am sorry to say I cannot avail myself as you have since heard me say, that I must when I sleep lie my head on the top of the Chair & so obtain a temporary apoplexy – bad – bad – bad. [1821 TdE/H/86/36]

Apoplexy is unconsciousness or incapacity resulting from a cerebral haemorrhage or stroke.[29]

In 1823 Mary, almost seventy, was feeling the impact of a hard winter:

What <u>your weather</u> is we know not, we have had frost and snow a week – but pray be careful of a relapse both for yourself, dear Eliza & Emma – this winter the <u>Wise Men</u> prognosticated would be long & severe although it has begun late – there is time to have it long – it already has proved trying to the aged. [22.01.1823 4TdE/H/27/-]

'Emma' is Emma Russell, daughter of Elizabeth.

Mary mentions her health again in a letter of January 1823: 'I thank God keep tolerably well; only occasionally intimations of the tenacity of life by a short conflict between the Heart & Blood passing through it – an old complaint' [29.01.1823 4TdE/H/31/25].

Despite the 'short conflict between the heart and Blood' and the hard winter so 'trying to the aged', shortly afterwards Mary accompanied two grandsons, Charles's sons, on the first part of their journey to school in London:

On Monday I lost my dear little Boys L̶o̶u̶ Edwin & Louis – … I went with them to Wragby setting off at 9 in the Morning – intending that Humphrey should proceed with them from thence in a Chaise to the Sarisons Head but alack no Chaise to be had at Wragby – & so I had no alternative but to go on as fast as I could with 2 pr of Horses for Lincoln … as we were with our little charges going on from Wragby and had reached Langworth we overtook a Hack Carriage on looking out to see whom it contained the first face I beheld to my joy was Mr Caldecot we all stopt when he call'd out 'give me your little Boys' it rained hard, and he was in an instant out of the Carriage in the midst of muddy road and took my thunderstricken Children. [05.02.1823 4TdE/H/47/2]

By May 1825 Mary's health had deteriorated further, and on 20 August she died at the age of seventy-two. Her illness, death and funeral are described in Chapter 2.

George Tennyson died in 1835 aged eighty-five. In his will he left all that he had inherited to George Clayton's family, and to Charles he left all the money he had made in his lifetime. Although George Clayton's family were well provided for, they regarded the will as financial disinheritance and it was the cause of a subsequent rift between the two families.

Afterword: 1835 to 1861

After the death of his parents Charles continued to further his political career. After Great Grimsby he was subsequently MP for Bletchingly, Stamford, and finally Lambeth where he sat for twenty years, retiring in 1852. During his long career Charles gave his support to liberal measures, advocating parliamentary reform, and the repeal of the corn and navigation laws. He was involved with many Bills including the amendment of the Game Laws, and the Insurrection Act, 1822 (Ireland). He was a signatory to a meeting held 'to consider the means of protecting from slavery the future children born of [slaves] in the British colonies'.[30]

In a letter of April 1822, George wrote, 'I observe what you say about India, not all the wealth of India sho^d prevail upon us to part with you' [24.04.1822 TdE/H/144/150]. Perhaps Charles was being considered for a post in India, but there is no further evidence that this was the case.

Charles, like his father, was socially ambitious, but never quite reached the top of the social ladder. In the 1830s he rebuilt Bayons Manor as a vast mock-medieval castle, complete with crenellations, moat and drawbridge. At the same time, claiming descent from the Norman family of Aincourt, he added, by Royal Licence, the name of d'Eyncourt to his surname.[31] Tennyson and Dyson suggest he 'felt that this would give them [the Tennysons] an eminent position in the county'.[32]

Charles outlived his brother by thirty years. He died in London, aged seventy-seven, at the home of his daughter Clara and her husband John Hinde Palmer, MP, QC, on 21 July 1861.

He is buried in the family vault at Tealby.

Notes

1. Robert Bernard Martin, *Tennyson: The Unquiet Heart* (Oxford: Clarendon Press, 1980), p. 5.
2. Patrick Waddington, *Tennyson and Russia*, Tennyson Society Monographs, 11 (Lincoln: Tennyson Society, 1987), p. 1.
3. https://www.google.co.uk/maps [accessed 7 September 2020].
4. Waddington, 1987, pp. 1–2.
5. Charles Tennyson and Hope Dyson, *The Tennysons: Background to Genius* (London: Macmillan, 1974), p. 38.
6. https://www.nhs.uk/conditions/epilepsy [accessed 3 October 2021].
7. https://www.cheltenham.gov.uk/info/37/local_history_and_heritage/ [accessed 7 March 2022].
8. https://www.merriam-webster.com/dictionary [accessed 15 August 2021].
9. Martin, 1980, p. 11.
10. John Batchelor, *Tennyson: To Strive, to Seek, to Find* (London: Chatto & Windus, 2012), p. 58.
11. Tennyson and Dyson, p. 78.
12. Martin, 1980, p. 132.
13. http://www.bbc.co.uk/history [accessed 28 February 2019].
14. http://www.historyofparliamentonline.org [accessed 28 February 2019].
15. https://www.nationalgallery.org.ukhistory [accessed 25 May 2020].
16. https://www.ncbi.nlm.nih.gov [accessed 13 April 2020].
17. https://www.sellingantiques.co.uk [accessed 13 March 2021].
18. Two guineas in 1815 would be £182.00 in today's money, https://www.bankofengland.co.uk/monetary-policy/inflation [accessed 3 May 2021].
19. Martin, 1980, p. 43.
20. https://www.learnreligions.com/history-of-babylon-3867031 [accessed 5 March 2022].
21. http://www.bbc.co.uk/history [accessed 15 March 2020].
22. https://www.historyofparliamentonline.org [accessed 30 November 2019].
23. https://www.marxists.org [accessed 9 April 2020].
24. https://www.historyireland.com/captain-rock-the-irish-agrarian-rebellion-of-1821-1824 [accessed 7 March 2022].
25. Batchelor, 2012, p. 348.
26. https://www.nhs.uk [accessed 22 June 2021].
27. https://www.historyofparliamentonline.org/ [accessed 2 February 2019].
28. https://winemakermag.com [accessed 12 May 2021].

29 *Oxford English Dictionary* (Oxford: Oxford University Press, 2006).
30 Papers relating to Charles Tennyson's parliamentary career [2TdE/H/61/28-9].
31 https://www.houseofnames.com/d-eyncourt-family-crest [accessed 08 March 2022].
32 Tennyson and Dyson, p. 185.

5

'A delicate, pretty girl': Frances Mary Hutton Tennyson, 1787 to 1878

Rosalind Boyce

Frances Hutton was married to Charles Tennyson, later Tennyson d'Eyncourt, Alfred Tennyson's uncle, for fifty-three years, and was the mother of his eight children. Biographers have been unkind to her, mentioning her only in passing and dismissing her as a nonentity, no more than an appendage to Charles. The poet's grandson, Charles Tennyson, describes her as 'A pretty, lively girl, heiress to a considerable fortune, but without any great intelligence or interest outside the domestic round of life in a Lincolnshire village'.[1] But this chapter will show, using previously unpublished material, that she was educated and intelligent, and became a capable woman in her own right. There is no indication where she received her education. As a naïve young woman of twenty, she was plunged into marriage with a husband who was often away and expected her to manage the household and servants, entertain guests and raise their children. But with the help of her mother in the early years, she grew into this seemingly impossible task.

Frances was born on 22 September 1787, the only child of the Reverend John Hutton and his wife Mary, née Stones. The Hutton family were prominent landowners in the Gainsborough area and owned estates in the Trentside villages of Gate Burton, Morton and later Knaith.[2] John Hutton, the Rector of Lea (by Gainsborough),[3] was the fourth of the ten children of Thomas Hutton.[4] In 1780 John married Mary Stones, the only child of Francis Stones, an apothecary (sometimes 'surgeon') of Gainsborough. Francis died in 1776, four years before John's marriage. In his will he left everything to his wife and daughter, Mary Stones 'and her Heirs … my messuages, cottages, closes, lands … wherever they are in the Kingdom of Great Britain' [Stow Wills/ 1772-77/353]. A messuage is a house with outbuildings and land.[5]

Life could be difficult for widows as family wealth automatically passed down the male line. However, Francis Stones had left his daughter well-provided for, and as she was the only child she was able to be independent.[6]

John Hutton died in 1789 aged thirty-four, when Frances was two years old, 'of a paralytic stroke after a few days' illness … greatly respected and lamented'.[7] By the time of the marriage, Mary Stones's mother had also died and Mary became a very rich woman. The source of the 'considerable fortune', as Charles was to describe it, which Frances eventually inherited, probably came from Mrs Hutton's properties in Lincolnshire, Yorkshire and Leicestershire.[8]

Frances and her mother lived at Morton Hall near Gainsborough. The identity of the 'uncle' involved with the details of the marriage settlement is not clear. John Hutton had several brothers, but it is likely to have been either William Hutton, who resided in Lincoln, eldest brother of John, or his youngest brother, the Reverend George Hutton, Vicar of Sutterton near Boston.[9]

Charles, the fourth child of Mary and George Tennyson, was born several years after his siblings, and baptized at Market Rasen on 20 July 1784. His mother had not been pleased to find herself pregnant, but despite this, Charles became his parents' favourite son as the letters demonstrate. In contrast to his elder brother George Clayton, who had many problems, not least his poor health, Charles must have seemed much more amenable.

After taking a degree at St John's College, Cambridge, in 1805 or 1806 Charles was called to the Bar and entered chambers at 2 Boswell Court, Lincolns Inn Fields, London. 'By 1807 he was beginning to build up a practice for himself and able to think of marriage'.[10]

Charles's health problems are a constant feature throughout the letters, but their exact nature is not clear. They may derive from epileptic fits, which affected many family members, notably his brother George Clayton, and recurred throughout the family.

The Hutton and Tennyson families were friends, but it is not known when or where Frances and Charles were first introduced. According to Charles's diary of his courtship, in May 1807 a visit to the opera in London had been arranged with Frances and her mother. There seem to have been many awkward silences:

> When I arrived I found them anxious for tickets – sat next to F at dinner scarcely spoke. The tickets were brought. We went with Mr Drake except M^r & Mrs H. Sat next F at opera, handed her in. Je serrai sa main[11] once and it was returned sat next her at the opera & talked much. She said her mother had told her I said she was stupid. I denied it. When we left the opera I handed her out & <u>much</u>

passed silently. In ye coach Je mis ma main au tour de sa veste.¹² I went in then departed.¹³

Robert Bernard Martin states that Charles 'dwindled into an engaged man', and the diary suggests that might be the case.¹⁴
A few days later Charles wrote to Frances:

> I cannot I dare not mention it [the proposed betrothal] to your Mother until I have written to my father – which I will do immediately and as soon as ever I obtain his consent she shall hear from me. … were I to say anything to her until I hear from my Father I have <u>nothing to propose</u> – am completely dependent in everything upon him. I will urge things on as fast as possible and hope that in the Summer they may be brought to that conclusion which I most ardently desire. In the meantime rest confident of my most unalterable attachment. [c. 19.05.1807 TRC 4612]

Charles first mentioned Frances to his father George on 21 May:

> I have lately and more particularly since you left London been thrown very much into company with Miss Hutton of Morton and as frequent intercourse between two individuals of any description will produce intimacy and sometimes friendship, so, that intercourse carried on between two persons of our age and relative situations will frequently be productive of more tender sentiments. This has in fact been the case with Miss H. and I … but I am well satisfied that my attentions are not received with indifference, and what affords me great satisfaction is, that her family does not appear adverse to my wishes … it was necessary and proper to invite your approbation. Of this I am far from despairing.

Significantly, he continues, 'Miss H. being an only child possesses or will possess, as I understand, a very considerable fortune' [21.05.1807 TRC 4630].

Frances and Charles and the 'Mines of Peru': 1807 to 1808

The important matter of the marriage settlement was soon under discussion. Frances was under a great deal of scrutiny as to her character and reputation, and the negotiations were lengthy. Women at this time had no autonomy: before marriage they were subject to their fathers (in Frances's case, her uncle) and after marriage to their husbands.¹⁵ Before committing himself to any agreement, George wished to know more about her:

> I know the use and value of money and consequent independence, but I would not have you risque <u>your</u> whole earthly happiness for the Mines of Peru – Before

you go any further it is quite necessary I should obtain information respecting the Lady's temper, conduct and character, which I am a perfect stranger to and for this purpose I shall go on Thursday to Knaith and learn of our honorable and enlightened friend Mr. Dalton. If all answers to my wish and expectation I shall see Mr. Hutton and endeavour to glean from him what Mrs. H. would do at present and what they would expect from me – You know how I am at present circumstanced in my affairs and will do anything you yourself desire knowing I may safely trust myself in your hands. Mr Hutton is an honest man but he will be for making a close bargain and the more you are thought to wish for the event the worse terms will be made. [25.05.1807 TRC 4658]

Henry Dalton of Knaith near Gainsborough was a trusted friend of the Tennysons whose advice was often sought. He was High Sheriff of Lincolnshire from 1802 to 1803.[16]

On 29 May Charles replied to his father, not entirely sincerely regarding money matters, and perhaps reflecting a sense of superiority:

I feel as disinclined as yourself to risque my earthly happiness for the mines of Peru ... I speak sincerely when I say that were Miss H. were [sic] to become a beggar tomorrow she would still be the woman with whom I should wish to associate myself for life, tho' in that case motives of prudence would at present necessarily interfere to prevent me from yielding to inclination. [29.05.1807 TRC 4631]

The chief difficulty was that Frances had previously formed an 'attachment' with a young officer, George Dealtry, of whom her mother and uncle did not approve. No information has been discovered about George Dealtry, but presumably he was thought to be of a lower class in society and have his eye on 'the considerable fortune'. At the time of their first meeting Frances was just sixteen and living with her widowed mother. No doubt Mrs Hutton was anxious for her to marry someone of a higher social standing and hoped she would forget George Dealtry. On 30 May, George reported on his meeting with Henry Dalton:

I opened the business as far as was necessary to our friend Mr. Dalton. He said he did not know much himself of the young lady but that she was handsomely spoken of and he thought her a delicate pretty girl very unaffected etc. – but that he had understood she <u>had had</u> an attachment and formed some acquaintance with a young man, an officer in the North or South Lincolnshire Militia, that Mr. Hutton and her mother were of course very averse. ... Mr. Hutton should certainly have stated to me the circumstances of this attachment. Mr. Dalton really thinks highly of the young lady and says living as she does with such a woman as her mother and never having been addressed by a gentleman there can be no wonder at what has happened. [30.05.1807 TRC 4659]

Charles replied two days later:

Everything I observed of Miss Hutton forbids my mind to harbour for a moment any suspicion in the slightest degree affecting her delicacy or [? …] To be explicit I know that George Dealtry paid Miss H. a considerable degree of attention which was coolly received by her. [01.06.1807 TRC 4632]

The discussions continued. George had been generous:

Mr. Hutton said Mrs. H. would immediately settle £500 a year. I said I would then recon [sic] your business at £300 and settle £200 more to make it up equal at present and guarantee the business at 300 a year and at my death settle £300 more to make it up equal in actual property besides business. Mrs. Hutton said she expected I would settle £500 immediately exclusively of business.[17] … Not a word was hinted at concerning former attachment. [10.05.1807 TRC 4663]

Charles responded on 12 June:

You indeed offered to do much more than I hoped would be necessary. I had of course thought much upon the subject and supposed Mrs H. might be inclined to settle £600 per annum and that you would guarantee my business at £300 more, with a settlement to take place at your death.[18] More than this I certainly would not expect … This is no shew but my real sentiments … I cannot say more on this subject until I receive your next but my mind is made up for tho' I entertain for Miss H. the sincerest attachment nothing shall tempt me to purchase my happiness with your comforts. [12.06.1807 TRC 4635]

Frances and Charles corresponded frequently, but neither seemed happy. Charles was not convinced that Frances's affections lay with him rather than George Dealtry. Consequently Frances was unsure of Charles's feelings for her.

A letter to Mrs Hutton reveals his insecurity and expresses his hope that she will give her approval to the marriage:

My mind has been relieved from a load of anxiety by a letter from my father in which I am informed that he has recently communicated at Morton my sentiments on a subject most interesting to my warmest feelings. Since I parted with you at Cambridge I have been labouring under such uneasiness arising not only from a consciousness that my conduct towards Miss Hutton required the earliest explanation but likewise from the state of doubt concerning your approbation in which I necessarily remained ... Will you have the goodness to deliver the enclosed letter to Miss H. [16.06.1807 TRC 4620]

The 'enclosed letter' to Frances reveals Charles's further doubts that Mrs Hutton would approve the marriage:

> If you entertain for me that sincere regard I have perhaps vainly flattered myself you do, you will not only participate in such feelings but communicate the anxiety by which I have been continually oppressed since our seperation. Under the state of doubt in which I was respecting your Mother's approbation every succeeding day added acuteness to the reflexion that I was suffering in your good opinion and consequently by your affections. ... [I] have of course many things to say, which, as far from being quite sure <u>that mamma will not peruse this</u> I shall reserve until we meet which I hope will not be later than the beginning of next week. [16.06.1807 TRC 4615]

Frances replied: 'my Mother and myself will be extremely happy to see you at Morton on Sunday evening to take a bed and stay as long as agreeable to yourself' [18.06 [1807] TRC 4648].

On 20 June George sent the following affectionate letter to Charles. Perhaps Charles was unhappy because he was regretting the engagement:

> In my anxiety for your welfare and happiness my very dear Charles, I find I have given you great uneasiness, and it hurts me extremely to have done so, ... My happiness depends on yours, you know how much your Mother and myself love you and on so material a transaction of your life, we can but think, and think deeply ... I would not for the worlds wealth have you made unhappy, but be prepared for any circumstance that can <u>possibly</u> arise. [20.06.1807 TRC 4665]

The 'attachment' to George Dealtry still troubled Frances:

> I have hitherto I own been foolish without considering the consequences which would arise; and believe me when I say, without knowing what real regard was! I fancied then that I did. but how was it possible? my mind was not then formed, what had I seen or known of the world? nothing. I was allured by first appearances without seeking any farther. You perhaps then think this would be the case now? ... all I can say is, that my future conduct towards you will I trust prove how great my affection is and ever will be for you and will erase from your memory even the slightest suggestion of my fickleness.

Despite agreeing to the settlement, Mrs Hutton was still doubtful about the marriage and was delaying matters:

I am confident that my mother will not do any more, indeed she has told me so, and moreover than that says she will never give her consent to our marriage until we are possessed of everything that is comfortable.

Presumably 'everything comfortable' means having enough money and a house to live in.

Frances was sufficiently confident to ask Charles to obtain some special tooth powder for her, and more significantly to request 'a small brooch with your hair in it'.

The letter closes with Frances saying she intends writing letters in French to prevent her mother from reading them and advises Charles to do the same [29.06.1807 TRC 4649].

Still full of doubts, Charles replied the same day:

I am not happy; I think, nay I am sure of your present regard. I might look forward with rapture to flattering prospects of our speedy and indissoluble union and its consequent blessing – but yet I am not happy – Tell me Fanny if it be the same with you. If you have loved before you can tell me whether any great uneasiness is usual when our affections are returned as yours must have been – ... I love you my dearest fanny with an undescribable purity of affection – I feel it is impossible I can ever love any other, much less than love another with equal ardour ... And were you to be taken from me the world would be a desert. [29.06.1807 TRC 4617]

Frances replied in a highly emotional state:

Words are impossible, my ever dear Charles, to express the agitation of my mind last night, on the receipt of your letter; your most afflicting and cruel letter; suffice it when I say, you have made me most completely miserable and almost despaired of being able to address you this morning after so recent a shock as you must be convinced it has given me – altogether it has harrowed up my feelings to nearly a state of despair, but more particularly your very strong allusion to a want of confidence in me; your expression 'I have your present regard' is dreadful – and sorry as I am to say I see plainly the cause of all this, it is from your knowledge of a most unfortunate affair you suppose my affections are divided. ...

I have however one consolation, notwithstanding your distressing implications; and that is the locket, which nothing shall make me part with, and which I shall wear for your sake when perhaps I may be forgotten by you.

My mother is extremely unhappy at seeing my uneasiness, the cause of which I have not told her nor would I shew her the letter without permission. [01.07.1807 TRC 4650]

Negotiations continued throughout July. Eventually Charles wrote to his father suggesting a solution to Mrs Hutton's doubts:

> Miss H says her Mother has told her she will not do anything more and will never consent to our marriage until we are possessed of everything comfortable … With respect to a house – I really think the best way for us who want an immediate income if the Trent party [Hutton family] will consent would be to appropriate part of Miss H.'s money to the <u>purchase</u> of a house. [01.07.1807 TRC 4636]

Charles wrote in a similar vein to Frances on the following day:

> It gives me pain to learn from your letter that your mother should continue her disinclination to hasten our marriage. It is as little my wish as it can be hers that you should be placed in a situation to find the want of any of those comforts and conveniences you have been accustomed to. My regard for you would not suffer me to think of it. … For tho' in the very little conversation I had with my father upon the subject he seemed <u>quite determined</u> to do nothing beyond what he had agreed to do at [Gate] Burton namely to advance £500 yet I flatter myself your mother will on consideration be inclined to <u>contribute</u> … I called on Waite my dentist yesterday but he was from home. I will however call again and send you his tooth powder and some of his brushes which are all excellent with the next parcel of music from Birchalls. [02.07.1807 TRC 4613]

Frances was fond of music and enjoyed playing the piano. Charles obtained sheet music for her in London from Robert Birchall, a music seller, publisher and instrument dealer in Bond Street.[19] As the only child in a wealthy genteel family, she could afford to indulge in this expensive pastime. She had no qualms about spending money, in contrast to her mother-in-law who had a very frugal nature, and often mentions making, mending and altering clothes.

The 'courtship' letters between Frances and Charles continued until August when Charles returned to Lincolnshire.

Two months later, Mrs Hutton having given her approval to the marriage, Frances wrote a touching 'thank you' letter to her future mother-in-law after a visit to Tealby:

> The first leisure moment since my arrival at Home, I dedicate to you which from your kindness claimed the earliest acknowledgement; my feelings at my departure from Tealby would not allow me to express my grateful sense of

that attention and goodness I experienced both from you and Mr Tennyson ... indeed my thoughts will often revert to those happy days I spent under your hospitable roof, which I will always visit with the greatest pleasure. [22.10.1807 TdE/H/144/65]

Marriage and children: Frances's 'Little Brats': 1808 to 1861

After their protracted courtship Frances and Charles were married at All Saints church, Gainsborough, on 1 January 1808.[20].

After the marriage there are no more letters from Charles to Frances that are known about, but for the next twenty-five years Frances wrote often to Charles when he was away in London, continuing his career in the law and beginning to take an interest in politics.

In the early years of her marriage, Frances, lonely without Charles, was in constant communication with her mother. There are about eighty letters in Lincolnshire Archives, mostly concerning the children, the household, servants, clothes, food, recipes, friends, visitors and general local gossip. Many are edged with gold leaf, indicating that they come from a wealthy household.

By February 1809 Frances was pregnant with their first child: 'Fanny is I think better than usual & in tolerable Spirits. She evidently increases in size and therefore there can now be little doubt that she is en famille', wrote Charles [01.02.1809 TdE/H/67/2].

The family moved to Caenby Hall in June 1809. Caenby is at the junction of the modern A15 and A631 roads, approximately halfway between Tealby and Morton. The property was rented together with seventy acres of land from Sir Charles Monck, a client and friend of George. The house was demolished in the twentieth century, but a section of a wall is still visible.[21]

Frances was full of anticipation at the coming move and wrote to her mother:

We positively take possession of our house on Wednesday next as we before proposed ... so that we both hope to see you on Sunday next the 18th to dinner. Mrs Raines goes with me, and I believe intends staying till your arrival ... bring with you some Tea & sugar for ourselves what quantity and price you know best: but so much as will serve us for some time. ... – and do buy me at Miss Bowers another pair of black kid shoes, a size larger than your own for these I have, wear extremely well indeed, and I think them very cheap ...

I am not able to say when we can send to Morton for the sheets etc. but it will certainly be some day this week. Chas thought of their being sent by the Rasen carrier, but I think it a bad plan – you no doubt will have the things ready. [12.06.1809 4TdE/H/6/3]

Perhaps the 'Rasen carrier' was unreliable. Mrs Raines is George's sister Ann. As a well-to-do woman, Frances's opinion of what she considers 'very cheap' is not known.

George Hildyard Tennyson was born at Caenby Hall on 10 July 1809. The proud father informed his parents:

> I am sure that it will give you and my d^r Mother & Aunt [Raines] great pleasure to be informed that my dear Fanny after rather a lingering time at 5 O'clock this morning gave birth to a boy who according to immemorial custom is the finest which has been seen; and calculated to all appearance to reward the anxieties of his Papa & Mama. [10.07.1809 TdE/H/67/9]

This was the first of her many 'lingering times'.

Mary Turner Tennyson, the delighted grandmother, replied the following day:

> You was not mistaken in supposing the happiness your communication of yesterday would give to your Father, your Aunt [Raines], and myself, we write in congratulations to yourself, dear Fanny & Mrs Hutton on the safety of the late Sufferer and the Birth of your Sweet Boy – whom we long to behold and salute – but shall constrain ourselves to behave properly on this occasion in consideration – to poor Fannys Nerves and consequent weaken'd frame ... – I hope she will not attempt to nurse it at her breast her constitution would not support a continuance May this Child prove a blessing from Heaven a comfort to Father and Mother and a useful member / as well as an ornament to society – Bless him from me with a kiss – and Kiss Frances too. [11.07.1809 TdE/H/68/32]

On 21 June 1810, already pregnant with her second child, Frances, writing to Charles, was 'very much disappointed to find that I shall not see you tomorrow, having made myself so very certain of y^r return and I really believe I sh'd be completely low spirited, if y^r Father and Mother were not here who join their united efforts to cheer me' [[Stamped 23 June 1810] TdE/H/68/10].

Seven months into her second pregnancy, she was busy with guests, weary with no 'leisure moment[s]':

> I certainly intended answering your letter much sooner, but have been so engaged with company lately that I have not had a leisure moment. My cousins only left me yesterday, after spending ten days here, during which time we have had many passing visitors: and tomorrow I suppose you know my Uncle George

and his little Boy [from Sutterton] are to be here and on Wednesday we expect M^r & Mrs Tennyson on their return from the North.

She was distressed by a family dispute, the cause of which is not known:

> I wish my dear Mother it was in my power to convince you of my innocence, and you will surely believe me when I affirm that I was not positively the person who informed Mr Tennyson of what you say, nor do I know who it was and so far from my having been informed of any thing of the kind. I was almost thunderstruck when he mentioned it, and therefore I hope you will be quite satisfied and that you will tell me so in your next. ... Don't grieve my dear Mother, any longer for I will declare upon my honor that I am innocent – and if you don't tell me in your next that you are quite satisfied, I shall be miserable ... I am very well and also little George who begins to get upon his feet famously.

Dress and fashion were important to Frances. Coming from a well-to-do genteel family, she was able to afford these desirable items:

> Do you think that Swan has any pretty patterns of washing silks or colored muslins. If he has wo^d you contrive to send me a few in y^r next letter. I don't mind paying double postage – for I really want something colored for common and have met with nothing at Lincoln. [05.08.1810 4TdE/H/6/6]

Until the introduction of the Penny Black in 1840 recipients had to pay for postage and were charged by the number of sheets in the letter and the distance travelled.[22]

Frances and Charles's second child, Julia Frances, was born on 13 October 1810. The next day Charles informed his father (but not his mother):

> On my arrival home about Midnight I found that heaven had blessed me with a little Girl and that My dear Fanny had got through her labour very well – It was somewhat severe but she bore it with great patience I have seen her for one moment and have taken a considerable view of my daughter as she lay asleep – She is said to be a very fine healthy child; she strikes me how^r [however] rather small. [14.10.1810 TdE/H/68/18]

A few days after the birth Frances wrote to her mother:

> I have the same good account to give of myself, and little Julia who improves hourly. You may think how well I am for having eaten nearly half a Boiled fowl, (besides pudding) ... I had a very kind letter from Mary Hutton congratulating me on the acquisition of a little girl, and saying they sho^d be happy to come over and see me as soon as I wo^d inform them, but I don't mean

to have them till I get downstairs, which will be next Sunday. [28.10.1810 4TdE/H/6/7]

Mary Hutton was probably Frances's aunt, sister-in-law of John Hutton. Roy and Lesley Adkins say that 'during this period of "confinement" or "lying in" [women] were expected to stay indoors, preferably in bed, for up to six weeks after the birth'.[23] Frances must have felt strong enough to go downstairs after three weeks, rather earlier than was customary.

Servants were always a source of worry for genteel families: 'I have heard of a Dairy Maid here whom I think is very likely to suit' [12.06.1809 4TdE/H/6/3].

Six months later Frances wrote, 'My new House Maid came yesterday, and I hope she will suit. My little Baby [Julia] thrives extremely well, and grows very fast' [04.12.1810 4TdE/H/6/9].

In 1811 there were more difficulties as Frances explained:

We are terribly off in the cooking way and not one servant (except the House Maid) knowing how to boil a leg of Mutton, and this along with a Batter Pudding, is the utmost of her Knowledge. [07.04.1811 4TdE/H/6/12]

Three months later Frances, now with two children under two years old, was about to employ a new nursemaid:

I think I told you in my last letter there was that day a young woman coming to offer to me as Nurse Maid. She came that evening and from her appearance, and manner of [? ...] with respect to children, both Symes and myself liked her ... I signed with her for six Guineas a year, and to find her own sugar- she is extremely plain but very neat looking. [21.07.1811 4TdE/H/6/15]

Pre-decimalization, a guinea was worth one pound, one shilling.[24]

The following letter from Charles to Mrs Hutton includes information about the marriage settlement:

With respect to y^r payment which will be due from you the matter starts thus: 'According to the Terms of the Marriage Articles you are to pay me the yearly sum of 45£ until Fanny's share of her Aunt's [? ...] money sh^d be received ... The words of the Deed would as you perceive entitle me to £22.10 now in addition to half-yearly payment of the other Annuity'. [13.10.1811 4TdE/H/6/16][25]

George Hildyard, now aged two, was becoming a source of amusement and delight: 'George always calls my Mother when she is spoken of Gran'ma' Applum Pye', wrote Charles to his father [27.11.1811 TdE/H/69/20].

A few months later, Frances reported to Charles:

> He [George Hildyard] is stouter in the face, tho' I still have my fears respecting him, he appears nervous, and delicate – on the night you left Caenby, he ingratiated himself in a wonderful manner into your father's and Mother's good opinion by his innocent but as your father termed it 'noble conversation' – Mr Barton says scarcely a day passes but he goes to his house to enquire after him.
>
> I was disappointed last night on inspecting the Bag to find no letter from you indeed I now begin to be so impatient to see you that when I don't hear from you I suspect your stay in London is delayed by unforeseen business. [12.05.1812 TdE/H/154/5]

Zephaniah Barton was a well-known and respected doctor in the Market Rasen area.

Eighteen months after Julia was born, Frances, now aged twenty-five, was close to giving birth to her third child and was:

> Tormented by the pain in my face, which I rather fear proceeds from a tooth that is very much decayed: nothing of any service to me but laudanum, which tho' used externally makes me very sick ... otherwise I am very well and active, and my legs don't swell in the least, which they did of Julia. [05.06.1812 4TdE/H/6/20]

Laudanum was an alcoholic herbal mixture containing 10 per cent opium. Called the 'aspirin of the nineteenth century, it was a popular painkiller and relaxant, recommended for many ailments'.[26]

On Saturday 27 June, Mary Turner Tennyson received good news from Charles:

> I feel well assured that you and my Dear Father will heartily sympathise in the pleasure with which I announce to you that about 1 o'clock this morning my dearest Fanny was (thanks to your old shoe) delivered of a <u>Fine Girl</u>. Both are doing exceedingly well. [27.06.1812 TdE/H/70/16]

The 'fine girl' was Clara Maria. Although there are many traditions regarding shoes, the significance of the 'old shoe' in connection with childbirth is not known.

Frances asked her mother on 12 August:

> Would you have the goodness to send me a loaf more of the sugar you got at Bowen's for preserving I think it was a shilling a p^d. It is very nice – I should like as large a loaf as you sent before. Would you be so good to send it by the carrier on Tuesday.[27] [12.08.1812 4/TdE/H/6/23]

Sugar was becoming popular, but it was expensive. 'It was the engine of the slave trade that brought millions of Africans to the Americas beginning in the early 16th century. Profit from the sugar trade was so significant that it may have even helped America achieve independence from Great Britain'.[28]

In September Frances hinted to her mother that she was pregnant again:

> You will I am sure with great justice accuse me of neglect, in not having written a single line to you since I left Morton (a week to day) but really the fact is I have been so busy, with company at home, and rambling about, that I literally have not had a moment to myself.
>
> On the day I left you, I was surprised to find when I arrived at home, that Charles was indispensably engaged to attend his Father at Tealby – and I was very sick, and poorly, with being in the Carriage, (and had been all the way) he pressed me, exceedingly to accompany him thinking the ride would be of service to me … We had a very pleasant, indeed I may say most delightful drive – and staid till the proceeding morning at Tealby, when we returned to Caenby with M^r & Mrs George Tennyson [George Clayton and family], a Nurse Maid, and 3 fine Lads [Frederick, Charles and Alfred] – who behaved themselves all the time with decorum, they are such stout merry fellows that they quite subdued my poor little George – but Miss Julia gave them a word for a blow in a moment – they staid with us till Saturday, when we again returned with them to Tealby … Chas is gone to Grimsby, and I think it not very unlikely, that he may receive a letter there from Dalby, desiring his presence there, as Mr Turner, is quite in a hopeless state, and may be gone in an instant … my dear Mother I ought to make my acknowledgement of your goodness to me and my <u>little Brats</u> which I shall always remember with heartfelt gratitude … I feel myself extremely well, and have within the last few days, had much better appetite, than when I was with you – but as yet no <u>other changes</u> has taken place – what do you think to me? [14.09.1812 4TdE/H/6/25]

Mr [John] Turner is Mary Turner Tennyson's brother.

Four months after the birth of Clara, Frances, feeling low-spirited, wrote somewhat formally to Charles: 'Many thanks for your kind considerations respecting my health. I am happy to say I have been better today, tho' I still feel weak and low which Mr Barton (who breakfasted here this morning) says I must expect & I must acknowledge' [02.10.1812 TRC 4654].

About three weeks later she seems to be improving despite the sad news of John Turner. Perhaps the muslin and the prospect of a good cook have lifted her spirits:

> I bought some muslin for my Gowns at Lincoln, but I shall not have them made up yet, for yesterday we heard that Mr Turner was expected to die at any moment

– so that I shall wait. I cannot say anything at present respecting our new Housekeeper, excepting that she appears to be a good cook. She is a withered old Maid of 46 or 7, I am sure, and rather cross looking. [27.10.1812 4TdE/H/6/28]

John Turner died on 12 November.

Both grandmothers were devoted to Frances and Charles's children, particularly Mary Turner Tennyson, who was more affectionate and indulgent towards them than she had been to her own children. She favoured Charles's children over those of George Clayton, although they were often rowdy. Mary Hutton, who died in 1814, would have known only the five eldest, George Hildyard, Julia, Clara, Edwin and Louis. As a wealthy widow, she seems to have been independent and strong and was very supportive to Frances.

Despite their frequent correspondence, Frances and her mother often visited each other:

Chas is just returned from Brigg, and he says he shall be very happy to accompany me to Morton on Thursday – we shall be with you in good time, and bring you a pig & Hare and a brace of partridges – we shall stay all night with you. [9.11.1812 4TdE/H/6/29]

With Charles so often away, Frances was pleased to have found a suitable person to keep her company:

You have heard me mention Mr^s Frankish a farmer's wife, who lives close by here – she has been with me, and is a nice woman. She is a clergyman's daughter, and has been well brought up. I never saw so much of her before, but I find her to be such a person – as I can at any time send for her to tea when Chas is out. [09.02.1813 4TdE/H/6/32]

On 7 April 1813 Frances was with Mary and George at Tealby where George Clayton's lively boys were also staying. Again, she was requesting fashionable items from London:

You will be surprised to find we are here – it has been to me An unexpected visit, as I knew nothing of it when I last wrote to you – but soon after we received an invitation from Mrs Tennyson saying she wished we would come and spend a little time with her ... she also invited little George, but we begged to have him excused, thinking it too early for him to leave home and particularly as there are two of Mr George [Clayton] Tennyson's little boys here, we feared they might be too riotous for him so soon after having broken his leg ... Chas says he shall go to London about the 20th or 21st of this month. I have quite give up the thought of accompanying for I think he will be so completely engaged in business that

I shall have but a dull time of it – he begs his best remembrances, and desires I will say if you want any thing from London he will be happy to get it for you. – I intend sending by him to Miss Brown for some things – she is nothing of a milliner but I am waiting to get an address to a person from whose hands I have seen some very pretty Caps and Bonnets when I hear I will let you know. Is there any thing you wo^d like Miss Brown to make up for you … I am in want of some cambric muslin, for little Clara some frocks. Am told it is very much raised [? in price], that I dare not trust my own judgement to buy any- therefore when you are at leisure will you have the goodness to get me some at Swann's. I think I shall want about a dozen yards, if it is a good width – but perhaps the cheapest way is to take a whole piece.

I think I never was better suited in the nursery. I am very well suited with Anne. … Since she has been here she is <u>wonderfully</u> improved and above all, I have <u>reason</u> to think her very steady. You will recollect, at the first we thought her slow, but it was shyness – she takes very good care of the baby [Clara]. [07.04.1813 4TdE/H/6/37]

Despite being 'better suited in the nursery', it was still difficult to find servants. Frances hoped Charles might find someone suitable in London:

I find there is no chance of either [? Linnitt] or Mr^s Cross being able to produce me a cook and Housekeeper, and as Palmer leaves me next week I fear we shall be in great distress. I therefore hasten to write a letter to you to say if you wo^d hear of such a servant as we want in London I really think the best plan wo^d be for you to hire, and in case you purchase a carriage, she might come down in it – I have now lost all hope of getting one here, as May-Day is close at Hand – poor Mary is going off very rapidly in a decline, that I shall have no cook to resort to.

May Day was the time when brides were chosen, servants hired out, and tenants took land.[29] 'Men and women hoping to be hired would stand around in the Market Place in twos and threes with tickets in their caps to show that they were looking for work'.[30]

Frances still had time to enjoy music and in the same letter she asked Charles, who was in London, to pay her music subscription and to investigate a suitable milliner. Although she was heiress to the 'considerable fortune', her money was her husband's:

I rec^d a letter last night from Mr^s Dale in consequence of my having returned my Music at present not knowing whether I meant to continue my subscription … so good to pay two guineas for me … She has sent me a Bill for carriage of Music which amounts to two guineas therefore in the whole four guineas are due.[31]

I last night recd a very kind letter from Mr^s Yorke giving me the address to the Milliner who supplies Mr^s John [? ...] with Hats Caps &c. ... now if you sho^d be able to find time to go there for me a Bonnet, I sho^d like it very much, as you wo^d then be able to give me your opinion whether she wo^d be a proper person for me to employ in the future. [07.05.1813 TdE/H/154/4]

More food was being sent from Morton to Caenby: 'What a Basket full of good things you sent me. It was a most excellent lobster, very fresh and I shall partake of it again to day. The gooseberries were also a high treat'. [20.05.1813 4TdE/H/6/38]

Hannah Glasse includes recipes for lobster in *The Art of Cookery*.[32]

In May 1813, the health of George Hildyard, now aged four, was causing concern, He may have inherited the epilepsy, or else the family feared that he had: 'Our little boy continues tolerably well but he is very nervous & subject to constant periods of languor. The other day Fanny was apprehensive for an appearance wch he suddenly [? assured] that ano^r fit was coming on. For myself I am <u>very well</u>' [28.05.1813 TdE/H/71/54].

This word cannot be deciphered, but the sense suggests that George Hildyard was assuring his parents that another fit was not coming on. Although Charles does not miss an opportunity to mention his own health, on this occasion he is feeling better.

On 4 July 1813 Frances gave birth to her fourth child, Edwin Clayton. Two weeks later Mary wrote to Charles about a suitable wet nurse:

This Morning brought the letter from Mrs Yorke on the other side [of the page] Mr Barton has just call'd & says that it is possible he may tomorrow be in your Neighbourhood & I take the opportunity by him of acquainting you of the result of my enquiries through Mrs Yorke who seems to have taken great pains to succeed – you will now be enabled to make your choice of a Wet nurse for dear Edwin ... I cannot now make any comments either on the propriety or otherwise of taking this young Woman knowing nothing more of her than what you hear in the report. [21.07.1813 2TdE/H/101/11]

Mrs Yorke was a friend from Louth. 'On the other side' is her letter:

Immediately on the receipt of Mr Tennyson's Letter. I walked down to Mrs Paupins [? ...] & found her in great distress of Mind; she was desirous for her Daughter to take the situation in your family; but the Father of the Child objected to it, he declared his intention to Marry the Girl; but did not say at what time ... & she has so far succeeded that he has promised to Marry her at this time three weeks, I have made every other enquiry without effect. [02.08.1813 TdE/H/71/17]

The solution to this difficulty is not known, but obviously Edwin came to no harm.

The employment of a wet nurse, where a mother was unable or unwilling to breast feed her baby, was commonplace amongst well-to-do families at this time.[33]

Charles, seemingly more concerned for his career than for Frances, spent a considerable amount of time away from home, leaving her alone except for the children and servants: 'I shall not I fear, be able to come to you on that day, <u>unless you c^d conveniently send your carriage and horses</u> for me, otherwise I must remain at home till Chas^s return which will not be until Monday week', wrote Frances to her mother on one occasion [03.12.1813 4TdE/H/6/46].

Like all Frances's letters to her mother, this one on 21 April 1814 not only concerns the household, children and servants but also describes going to a ball. She does not say where it was held, but as 'Miss Pelham opened the Ball', it may have been at Brocklesby near Grimsby, the seat of Lord Yarborough.[34] Frances obviously enjoyed herself, although she was six months pregnant, but the matter of servants was still a problem:

> I have never experienced the least inconvenience from being so late at the Ball. Mrs T [Mary Turner Tennyson] wished me very much to have gone home sooner, but I was so much amused that I felt reluctant at leaving the party which was small and every body I knew that rendered it pleasant. ... we had a very elegant supper Lamb in plenty which was sent from London – Miss Pelham opened the Ball ... Mrs T. desires her best Comp^{ts} to you, and wo^d have been glad co^d she have helped you to a dairy-maid, as she says she thinks it must be a good place for a young woman first going out – but she says she will not give up the search ... before I left home Julia happened an accident ... She was climbing on a chair in my room fell down, and cut her under lip nearly thro' ... I think I never saw a girl so frightened; her teeth were certainly loosed but they are now quite fast – and she is quite well, indeed was before I left home, or I sho^d not have stirred ... Do you think you can come to me when I get home? [21.04.1814 4TdE/H/6/54]

In June 1814 Frances was close to giving birth to her fifth child: 'I think it would not be prudent to [? hazard] travelling in the carriage [to Morton], particularly as I am much increased in appearance since you saw me – I am sorry it has so happened ... I must content myself at home' [19.06.1814 4TdE/H/6/57].

Louis Charles was born 23 July 1814: his descendants were to deposit the Tennyson family papers in Lincolnshire Archives.

Although there are no letters surviving from Mrs Hutton to Frances, her diaries for 1813 and 1814 are kept in Lincolnshire Archives. Entries are sparse, but nevertheless indicate that there was much toing and froing between Morton and Caenby.[35] The entry for 6 January 1813 states, 'George [Hildyard] broak his leg'. On 16 January: 'Came home from Caenby having spent a month from yesterday'.

On 18 March 1813, Frances wrote, 'In the first place I must thank you for a very nice Pike, Sweet-Bread and ½ a Dozen snipes. The Fish we had yesterday, and the Sweet-Bread which I think was the finest I almost ever saw' [18.03.1813 4/TdE/H/6/36].

Mrs Hutton was clearly actively involved with the children. The entry in the diary for Friday 4 June 1813 states, 'Went to Caenby for the children', and on Sunday 6 June, 'Came home with Julia & Clara'. On Tuesday 7 December 1813, 'Carriage this day gone to Caenby for Mrs T and children. Fanny brought a Hare & a Brace of Partridges'.

In September 1814 important guests were expected at Caenby, including an MP who it was hoped might assist Charles in his ambition to enter Parliament. Frances needed her mother's help with the dinner menu:

> Many thanks for the Basket of fruit you sent us, which was most acceptable – I dare say the pears will be very good when they are sufficiently ripe as we are obliged to ask Sir Montague Cholmely and some few others for next week. I dare say they will then be right … Wednesday next we shall have our company, therefore do you think you c^d possibly get me some Fish for that day. I suppose it is possible to get salmon. [15.09.1814 4TdE/H/6/59]

Sir Montague Cholmely (1772–1831) was MP for Grantham.[36]

The family was about to move to London, where Charles was hoping to further his political ambitions. Understandably the news had upset Mrs Hutton, and Frances tried to mitigate her disappointment:

> Chas says he hopes you won't be very unhappy about it for we shall hope to see you in London and we shall always come down to the country for two months every year. [28.04.1814 4TdE/H/6/55]

But there were to be no visits to London for Mrs Hutton. The first indication that she was ill appears in a much longer letter from Frances amid all the household news:

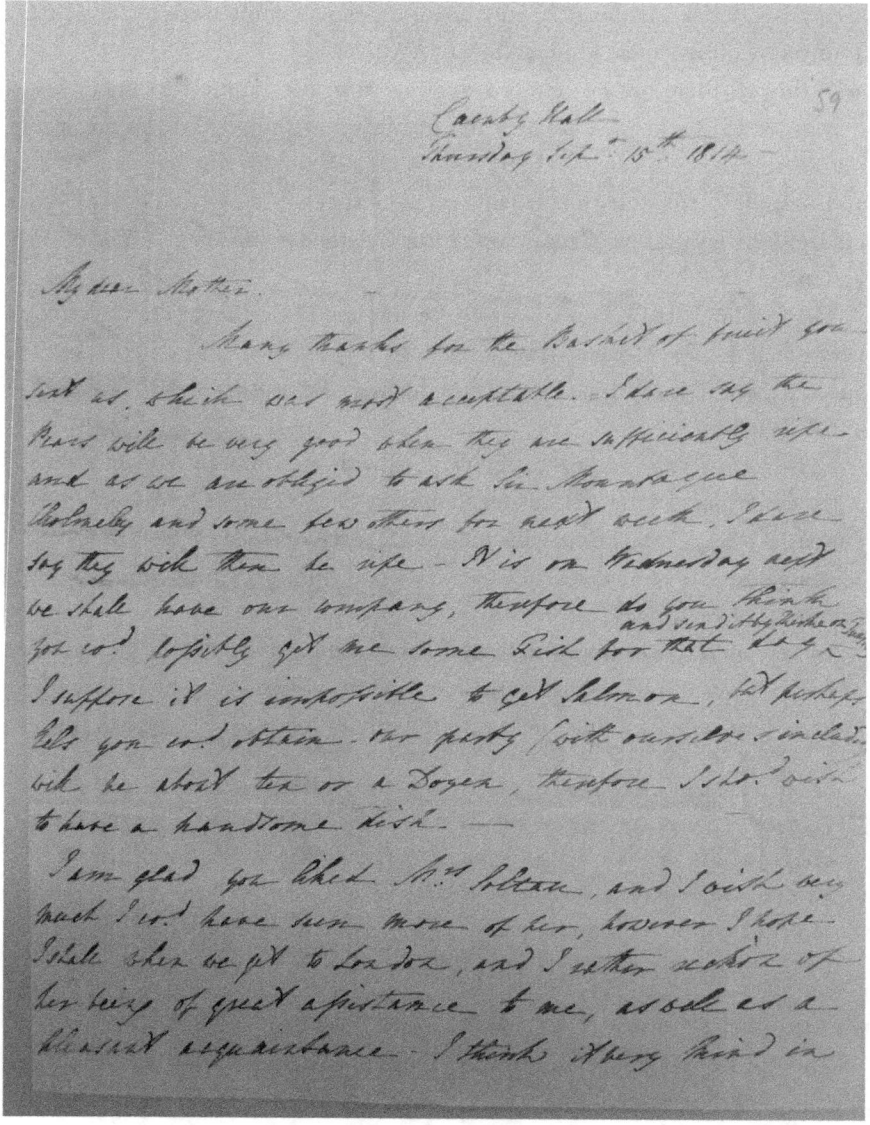

Figure 4 Frances Mary Hutton Tennyson to Mary Hutton [15.09.1814 4TdE/H/6/59].

I am glad to find your thoughts of consulting Dr Peacock, and I hope by now that you have done so, as I sh^d not like to rest entirely on Dr Barton's opinion, and I think very often things are neglected from not being taken in time. I shall be very anxious to hear his opinion – has he advised you to take advice [? in] London? [25.09.1814 4TdE/H/6/60]

Mrs Hutton herself does not mention her illness until about a month before her death when there are several references in her diary to Dr Peacock visiting.

The signature on the following letter to Mrs Hutton is illegible but is likely to be from her sister-in-law, Mary, the wife of John's brother William (therefore also 'Mary Hutton'). She was obviously a kind and compassionate woman:

> I only say on this sad subject, that I do feel in my heart for you & <u>at any time</u>, if you think I can be of <u>use</u> or <u>comfort</u> to you, I will be with you ... I've very lately heard of a Lady who lived 30 years in good health after going through what perhaps you must do – we have no fear you will do well ... Dr Peacock is the kindest hearted Man that can be, you will find him some comfort. [[1814] 4TdE/H/6/48]

The diary entry for Sunday 16 October is disturbing, considering the state of surgery at the time: 'Mrs Hutton submitted to an operation for cancer in her breast'. Sadly, but not surprisingly, 'Mrs Hutton died' is the entry for the following Saturday. This information has been added later.

Around the 1750s several surgeons, including Jean Louis Petit, Henri Le Dran, Claude-Nicolas Le Cat and Benjamin Bell, began performing breast cancer surgery.[37] By the mid-nineteenth century surgery was the available option for breast cancer. The development of antiseptics and blood transfusion during this time also made survival after surgery more possible.[38] Very little could be done to alleviate pain during surgery until nitrous oxide and ether were used later in the nineteenth century.[39]

William Cooper, George's and later Charles's agent at Tealby, sent a letter of condolence to Charles, but not Frances: 'Allow me to express to you the sincere concern I feel at the melancholy event, which has closely followed the operation which poor Mrs Hutton had undergone, with much fortitude' [31.10.1814 4TdE/H/6/61].

London: 1814 to 1816

Frances must have been bereft at the loss of her mother, especially as the family was about to move to London, away from the Tennyson grandparents and the familiar Lincolnshire surroundings.

The family's first residence in London was at 23 Lincolns Inn Fields. Mary Turner Tennyson, the concerned mother and doting grandmother, wrote to Frances:

> I hope your house has become progressively warmer since you have occupied it [? …] &c and that dear George [Hildyard] is become reconciled to the concourse of people walking in his Garden – the Children in general I fear will call all your watchfulness respecting the state of their Bowels – for being very variable when with me – a more immoveable state will naturally succeed to the change of <u>Bread</u> and <u>Air</u> – but you & dear Charles are alive to all this- I wish to know how you feel yourselves since all your fatigues of mind and body … Tell my dear sweet George I thank him for his [? …] and if I had time would answer his every line – tell him too I hope he will learn to write soon when he need not trouble his father – kiss him and all the dear Children. [11.01.1815 TdE/H/149/12]

At the time, the area around Lincolns Inn Fields was a public garden, which George Hildyard, being a country child, would have found unusual. The present layout dates from the early nineteenth century and has not changed significantly since.[40] The importance of 'Bowels' is of great concern to Mary, particularly regarding young George. The 'poor air and bread' in London was another worry.

In January 1816 George Hildyard, aged six, was about to start school. Anxious as always, Mary wrote to Charles:

> So the sweet dear Boy George has left you to enter a new world; may the blessing and protection of the Almighty preserve him from the grosse contamination of its wickedness … tell him when you see or write to him – that if I live I will make it a matter of business to see him – because I love him so much … tell my dear Fanny, if nothing unforeseen prevents me she will see me in March – but I wish her to say when she thinks she may expect to be confined. [03.01.1816 4TdE/H/11d]

Frances and Charles's sixth child, Eustace Alexander, was born on 24 March. A week later Mary wrote:

> It is a great pleasure to know (as by your last) that dear Fanny is going on well I trust as she never was a [? …] & that she is able by this time to [? …] up a Rump Steak or something as good I often wish I could peep at her and all of her – but at this distance no flying leaps of this sort – how goes dear George? tell me this in you[r] next & of what the Baby is like- and what is his name – something I suppose high sounding for this little General. [02.04.1816 4TdE/H/11b]

A few days later she advised Frances:

> As every account since your confinement has been favourable I am led to hope you are gaining strength daily by the best of all possible means viz: nourishing food taken with a good appetite – this together with a little exercise from room

to room, and afterwards without doors in your Carriage ... I have often wished for Wings that I might have the power of peeping at you sometimes but the greatest consolation to me previous to your confinement was the comfort you would desire from having your favourite good Man in that trying moment. I can only call such an event under such safety a Blessing from Heaven of which I doubt not you truly estimate. [31.03.1816 4TdE/H/11a]

The 'good Man' may be a 'man-midwife'. Although childbirth traditionally involved only female attendants: 'When educated surgeons became involved in obstetrics as "man-midwives" or "accoucheurs" they replaced some of the female midwives. ... They transformed childbirth, making use of the recently invented forceps, and scientifically researching, debating and publishing on aspects of pregnancy'.[41]

In July 1816 Charles took Julia, aged six, to her new school in Paris. It is not known why he chose to send his daughters to school in France. Martin believes it was to keep them away from their mother, but this has not been confirmed and seems unlikely.[42] Perhaps Charles thought that the French education system was superior to that in England: 'Napoleon felt that education was important for girls but did not generally expect them to have the same sort of education given to boys'.[43] By contrast, education for girls in England at this time was viewed as a luxury: 'girls were generally taught at home, if at all, by their governesses or their mother'.[44] Mary did not approve of her granddaughter being educated 'remotely placed from under your immediate observance and protection, amongst strangers, in a country where religion is little thought of' [13.07.1816 TdE/H/96/3].

This was shortly after the revolution in France when religion had been suppressed and the political power of the church passed to the state.

As an intelligent woman, Frances wished all her children to have a good education, but it is not known how she felt about her daughter being sent away. In early-nineteenth-century England's patriarchal society the mother's view probably would not have been considered.

Martin has suggested that Charles had a mistress from about this time, Mary Thornhill, daughter of the squire of Stanton near Bakewell in Derbyshire, and a friend of his sister Elizabeth Tennyson Russell.[45] Apparently she wrote many letters to him over a period of about twenty years, addressing him as 'Dear Beauty', and signing herself 'your affectionate Beast'. She is somewhat familiar: 'Don't be shocked at my familiarity – I know you by no other name & y^r profile looks so kindly & complacently at me that I feel intimately acquainted with you & I like you so much & your extravagant ways' [16.04.1816 4TdE/H/11/32].

However, only three letters have been found in Lincolnshire Archives; the whereabouts of others are not known, if they exist, and no further information has been found to confirm or refute such a liaison.

Frances gave birth to her seventh child, Ellen Elizabeth, on 17 July 1817. Research suggests the birth took place in Brighton, although there is no indication of this in the letters.[46]

By this time Charles, at the age of thirty-three, had been elected MP for Great Grimsby, thus beginning a distinguished political career.

Frances and Charles's eighth and last child, William Henry, was born on 29 August 1819.

> We thank you my dearest Charles [wrote Mary] for your prompt and ultimately happy information about which we have been most anxious – and after so trying and painful a period to dear Fanny – we heartily rejoice with and congratulate you both on her safety – and on the birth of another fine Boy ... on my informing him yesterday that his Mama had been very ill he [George Hildyard] appear'd with a genuine countenance immediately asking if she was better ... I told him he had got a new brother when his surprize was apparent as well as his knowledge as an 'O have I indeed, then that was it', which spoke a Volume – the subject was not continued – at that time. [02.09.1819 TdE/H/81/39]

But a few days later Baby William was causing concern. Mary called upon her strong religious faith at this sad time:

> Very anxious for a more favorable account of poor dear Fanny's state of health – and that of her suffering infant tell dear Fanny ... that she has my constant prayers for her return to health & good spirits ... our blessed Saviour has said 'Suffer little Children to come unto me, and forbid them not, for of such is the Kingdom of Heaven' ... he [George Hildyard] wishes much to write to [you] in reply to your long letter and particularly in reply to your question of a name for the Baby ... he yesterday said 'dont you think G-mama that Willm is a good name' & Henry too – but then all our children have two names well then, (recollecting himself 'why not William Henry' ... when I read to him that his Mama was not quite so well as she had been & that his little Bro^r was not likely to live till he saw him ... he was cast down very much & said he thought his Mama would fret and that would make her ill – but his surprize was great and it pleased him to hear of the combination of names such as he had suggested. [08.09.1819 TdE/H/81/40]

By the time Mary's letter was written William Henry had died.

'A tedious and suffering labour' – 'a separation'?

Frances and Charles had eight children in eleven years of marriage. Martin speculates that the marriage was not happy and that a separation had taken place.[47] This 'separation' may not be quite what it seems – Frances had given birth to the children with much 'pain and suffering'. Perhaps and unsurprisingly, they wanted no more children and decided on a physical separation, and it was not a complete marriage breakdown.

As late as 1825, six years after William's birth and death, Dr Richard Gooch, a much-admired general practitioner and obstetrician in London, sent the following letter to Charles.[48] It is surprising that it was written so long afterwards. Perhaps there had been more pregnancies in the intervening time resulting in miscarriages or stillbirths.

> The circumstances which formerly led Mr Clive and myself to advise a separation must continue unabated because it is the one which will not vary with the state of health. It is a permanent narrowing of that space between the bones of the Pelvis through which the Child has to pass at its birth – the narrowing may increase, but cannot diminish. It would almost certainly occasion a tedious and suffering labour, and one in some degree dangerous. I do not mean that the delivery would be impracticable, or that Mrs T. might not recover as she has done before, but the question is, (and it is one which you can decide on as well as we can) whether it is worth while for the sake of return of intercourse to encounter a process which almost certainly will be tedious and suffering and therefore in some degree attended by danger. [01.10.1825 TdE/H/33/(25)]

Several years earlier Charles had entered in his diary: 'Fanny & myself weighed at Whitehead Paper Mill – my weight 10st. 12lb, Fanny 7st. 4lb'.[49] Obviously Frances had a very slight figure, which bears out Dr Gooch's comment about 'a tedious and suffering labour'.

In April 1822 Frances wrote to Charles from Cheltenham where she was staying with Elizabeth Tennyson Russell. The two of them had become friends and spent a considerable amount of time together, which may confirm Martin's suggestion that there had been a separation. According to him, the house at 4 Park Street was divided so that Frances and Charles could be there at the same time without meeting.[50] Frances wrote to Charles with concerns about the children:

> Edwin has had neither measles nor Hooping-Cough – Geo [Hildyard] is well, but alarms me <u>exceedingly</u> by amusing himself constantly when he is out of

doors by jumping some height over a string, chain, rail or any thing he can find –
I am fully prepared for his being brought home senseless – myself, Eliza, and
Emma Russell have all mentioned it to him but it is of no avail, and therefore
I am compelled to inform you as a word from <u>you</u> is I know of great service – his
looks are much improved, his spirits very great, and not the <u>slightest</u> symptom
of his disorder [epilepsy] has appeared – the water agrees wonderfully well with
him. [17.04.1822 TdE/H/144/179]

George Hildyard, now aged thirteen, was suffering from what may have been epileptic fits:

It hurt us so much to hear of our dear little Georges late attack [wrote his
grandfather]. We love that child & fear for him, we think you did right to leave
him at Cheltenham, will he be made happy there? [24.04.1822 TdE/H/144/150]

In September he was about to attend Westminster School. Frances was concerned about his health and that he should have a good diet whilst there:

George [Hildyard] set off for Westminster last Monday and I have since heard
of his safe arrival in London from Mrs Smedley who promises to conform as
much as she ... can do, to the plan of diet I wished him to pursue. [26.09.1822
4TdE/H/28/]

Three months later Charles was fetching Julia from school in Paris. Frances, ever concerned for her children's education, wrote to him from Cheltenham:

We were all much amused to hear of your perils and dangers, but at the same
time most happy to hear you arrived so safe and well at Paris, after enduring so
much fatigue and discomfort as you must have done. I am astonished you were
not made quite ill by sitting so long in wet clothes ... when you see Mrs Forster
will you be so good to ask her, the number of the set of Clementis Lessons that
she is learning, as I am anxious for her to have them here. [51] I find you had not
time to look out an Italian Dictionary for her – I have written to Miss Anne
Smedley to ask if she can lend her one, for as you said you had <u>two</u>, it would be
folly to buy one here. [12.12.[1822] 4TdE/H/28/(60)]

On 15 December 1822 Charles and Julia arrived home. It should be remembered that this was before the advent of steam power, and everything depended on the wind and weather for a safe crossing. Mary Turner Tennyson, of course, had been anxious about the 'perilous passage on crossing the channel', but when the grandchildren arrived safely at Bayons Manor soon afterwards her tone was more cheerful:

They all say they are very happy this morning – George [Hildyard] said he would write to you to day, but so fine a morning with a most glorious Sun I deem'd would be more profitable to him out doors, than to sit writing … so the whole party have sallied forth – Julia too, happy enough – quite proud of her Bro^{rs} being Sunday George [Hildyard] is very spruce, with a brilliant pin he says his aunt Russell gave him at Paris – Julia too sports her watch dayly. She is look^g and is well as ever. George is really become a fine young Man – Edwin happy looking, but not much grown – Louis is craneing above him – they commenced being such Dandies on leaving Town. [15.12.1822 4TdE/H/24/70]

A few days later, Charles received the following letter from Frances in Cheltenham. George Clayton was there too. Frances seemed able to bring out the best in him. He was obviously fond of her referring to her as 'my mesmate [mess mate]' [01.02.1824 TdE/H/144/160].

I rec^d the enclosed my dearest Charles this morning [wrote Frances] along with a letter from Mr Gregson announcing the departure of our three boys from London on Friday evening last the 15th Septr in high health and spirits, well furnished with [? …], warm [? stockings] and night caps to protect them on the road, and I hope very soon to hear of their safe arrival at Tealby. We are all tolerably well here (your brother better every day. Ellen's cough much the same) … Your brother is not like the same man, his spirits are very good, and he kicks up such rows, that I expect Captn Matthews will turn us out of the house for rioting … How is your health? Have you consulted anyone at Paris? [16.12.1822 4TdE/H/28/[?...]]

As related in Chapter 2, Mary Turner Tennyson died in August 1825 from what may have been heart problems.

After her death, there are few letters from Frances to Charles. The following letter was sent from Worthing so it seems that she and Charles were not together. Despite the inheritance Frances was still dependent on Charles for money. Although she signs herself 'y^r truly affectionate', it is not an affectionate letter:

I Thank you for y^r letter and another £10 – I have calculated [? …] my bills, and fear I cannot do with less than a hundred pounds & which will finish all. You will be surprised, but I am furnishing the girls with entire new cloaths, which I get much cheaper here than in London, so that when they get there I shall have nothing to buy for them. … I have regular fits of pain in my face and head, every evening regularly at 9 o clock, which continues more or less during the greater part of the night. This, with the opium I am obliged to take makes me feel very weak and [? …] and were it not for a ride, I believe I sho^d be quite worn out, but the horse exercise invigorates me …[52]

The little girls send their love, poor Ellen is very far from well. Pray take care of yʳ self and ever believe me / yʳ truly affectionate F.M.T. ... Pray come if possible. [09.12 [? 1825] TRC 4646]

The tone of Frances's letter sent two years later indicates there are family problems, and possibly continuing difficulties in the marriage. She is at Bayons Manor, perhaps with the children. 'Your sister' is Elizabeth Tennyson Russell.

Your sister behaves kindly to me, and Emma has adopted a more agreeable tone and manner – all has been explained and yʳ Sister acknowledges that she has said many things, but in consequence of having been <u>goaded</u> and <u>irritated</u> to the <u>greatest</u> degree by the representations made by others of your abuse of <u>her</u>; and Emma also says that she has actually [? been] questioned and cross-questioned but that she has not spoken ill of you but the reverse, and that much has been [? hatched] by the head of the family, and a certain Lady not far distant from this place. Your Sister too corroborates this statement I should say <u>come</u> and let all be cleared. I enclose a paper in your father's hand-writing; since the letter business he has treated me with great coolness, and spends most of his time at home in abusing me to others ... Since writing the above your sister has declared that neither herself or Emma have ever said a <u>word</u> against you to your father. [24.10.[1827] 4TdE/H/39/5]

The following letter is the last known from Frances to Charles. She urgently needed Charles's help with managing Eustace and Louis. The tone again suggests that the marriage may be in difficulties:

The enclosed you will find from Mʳ Preston of whom I made the enquiry you wished concerning Eustace, and you will see the answer. If he continues here doing nothing, or worse than nothing the effect will be bad, and he will not only be idle but make Louis the same, who will not care to scramble over his school business anyway so that he may get home – to kick up a riot (and which has already commenced) with Eustace. It is really difficult to know what to do with the latter, and I know not how to advise. [05.11[1827] 4TdE/H/39/6]

Charles was now MP for Bletchingley, a seat he held until 1831. After a brief period as MP for Stamford, he was elected MP for Lambeth in 1832 where he remained until his retirement in 1852.

Afterword: 1825 to 1878

In the 1830s, after the death of his father, Charles rebuilt Bayons Manor as a vast mock-medieval castle. At the same time, claiming descent from the Norman family of Aincourt he added, by Royal Licence, the name of d'Eyncourt to his surname.[53] He died in 1861 at the age of seventy-seven and is buried in the family vault in All Saints church, Tealby.

Charles showed little sincere affection for Frances. His chief concern was for the 'considerable fortune', which would assist him to further his political ambitions. Anxiety over his poor health, which may have derived from epilepsy or the fear of it, is a recurring theme. Although Frances's eight pregnancies resulting in difficult births would have seriously affected her health, her feelings don't seem to have been considered. But despite the difficulties, the 'delicate pretty girl' developed into a capable mother and household manager, and became something of a force in the family.

She befriended George Clayton when others found him difficult. She defended Alfred's attitude to George's will and the perceived disinheritance of the Somersby family and 'maintained stoutly that he was quite incapable of the remarks attributed to him'.[54]

Frances outlived Charles by sixteen years, but little is known of her life during that time. She died in London, aged ninety, at the home of her daughter, Ellen Bunbury, on 26 January 1878.

Charles Tennyson, the poet's grandson, quotes from a letter from Alfred to her son Louis with the following tribute: 'Don't say "my poor mother," rather "my happy mother" … It is we, who have lost the familiar face, that should rather be called "poor".[55]

She too is buried in the family vault at Tealby. The epitaph on her memorial plaque, which reads 'by Nature diffident and with a humble sense of her own merits, the simplicity and modesty of character attached to her many friends' does not do justice to the capable wife and mother that she became.

Notes

1 Charles Tennyson, *Alfred Tennyson* (London: Macmillan, 1950), p. 17.
2 Arthur Wollaston Hutton, *Some Account of the History of the Family of Hutton of Gate Burton, Lincolnshire* (privately printed, 1898), p. 50.
3 http://theclergydatabase.org.uk [accessed 13 May 2019].
4 Wollaston Hutton, 1898, p. 17.
5 *Oxford English Dictionary* (Oxford: Oxford University Press, 2006).
6 Among the rich, family wealth automatically passed down the male line; if a daughter got anything it was a small percentage. Only if she had no brothers, came

from a very wealthy family, and remained unmarried, could a woman become independent, *British Women's Emancipation since the Renaissance*: http://historyofwomen.org/marriage.html [accessed 24 June 2019].
7 Wollaston Hutton, 1898, p. 51, quoted from *Gentleman's Magazine,* May 1789.
8 From 'Mrs Hutton's Appointment of Estates in the County of Lincoln, Leicester and York and several sums of Money pursuant to a power contained in her Marriage Settlement in favour of her only child Mrs Charles Tennyson, January 1809' [RED/1/3/10].
9 Rev. George Hutton (1764–1817), Vicar of Sutterton 1804–17, tenth child of William Hutton (Wollaston Hutton), p. 17.
10 Tennyson, 1950, p. 16.
11 'I squeezed her hand'. *Dictionnaire Francais Anglais*, nouvelle edition (Paris: Libraire Larousse, 1989).
12 'I put my hand around her jacket', *Dictionnaire Francais Anglais*, 1989.
13 Extract from 'Charles Tennyson's diary of his courtship', copied by Sir Charles Tennyson, who commented 'Written on the back of a sheet containing the draft of some legal document. Very difficult to read' [TRC/BC/7562].
14 Robert Bernard Martin, *Tennyson, the Unquiet Heart* (Oxford: Clarendon Press, 1980), p. 23.
15 Alexis Iniguez, *Gender Roles in the 1800s.* https://prezi.com/v2cx1naharo8/gender-roles-in-the-1800s [accessed 2 December 2020].
16 Justin Simpson, *Obituaries and Records for the Counties of Lincoln, Rutland and Northampton from the Commencement of the Present Century to the End of 1859* (Newcomb, 1861).
17 £500 in 1810 = £39,559 in today's money; £300 = £23,735; £200 = £15,823; https://www.bankofengland.co.uk/monetary-policy/inflation [accessed 2 December 2020].
18 £600 in 1810 = £47,470.83 in today's money; https://www.bankofengland.co.uk/monetary-policy/inflation [accessed 9 December 2020].
19 https://bookhistory.blogspot.com [accessed 7 March 2022].
20 Gainsborough All Saints PAR/1/9, Entry 707.
21 Terence R. Leach and Robert Pacey, *Lost Lincolnshire Country Houses*, 4 vols (Burgh le Marsh: Old Chapel Lane Books, 1990–3), 1, p. 19.
22 Five Hundred Years of Royal Mail: http://500years.royalmailgroup.com [accessed 25 May 2019].
23 Roy and Lesley Adkins, *Eavesdropping on Jane Austen's England* (London: Little, Brown, 2013), p. 22.
24 Six guineas in 1810 = £474 in today's money; https://www.bankofengland.co.uk/monetary-policy/inflation. [accessed 2 December 2020].
25 £45 in 1810 = £3560 in today's money; £22.10 = £1740; https://www.bankofengland.co.uk/monetary-policy/inflation [accessed 2 December 2020].

26 History Magazine. https://www.historic-uk.com/HistoryUK/HistoryofBritain/Opium-in-Victorian-Britain [accessed 22 December 2020].
27 A shilling a pound in 1812 would be £3.55 per pound in today's money; https://www.bankofengland.co.uk/monetary-policy/inflation [accessed 2 December 2020].
28 https://www.livescience.com [accessed 24 June 2019].
29 https://www.hardysociety.org [accessed 27 June 2019].
30 https://issuu.com/zerosixdesign/docs/deeping [accessed 6 August 2021].
31 Four guineas in 1813 equal £279 in today's money; https://www.bankofengland.co.uk/monetary-policy/inflation [accessed 2 December 2020].
32 Hannah Glasse, *The Art of Cookery Made Plain and Easy* (New York: Dover Publications, 2015 (1805)), p. 59.
33 Adkins, 2013, p. 30.
34 Charles Anderson-Pelham, first Earl of Yarborough (1781–1846).
35 The Daily Journal: The Diary and Accounts of Mrs Mary Hutton, 1813 and 1814 [2TdE/H/81 & 82].
36 https://www.historyofparliamentonline.org/research/members [accessed 10 July 2021].
37 https://www.maurerfoundation.org [accessed 13 May 2019].
38 https://www.news-medical.net [accessed 13 May 2019].
39 broughttolife.sciencemuseum.org.uk [accessed 13 May 2019].
40 https://www.parksandgardens.org/places/lincolns-inn-fields [accessed 7 March 2022].
41 Adkins, pp. 24–5.
42 Martin, 1980, p. 43.
43 https://www.napoleon-series.org/research/society/c_education.html [accessed 9 April 2020].
44 Roy Porter, *English Society in the Eighteenth Century* (London: Penguin, 1990), p. 164.
45 Martin, 1980, p. 33.
46 www.myheritage.com [accessed 8 June 2019].
47 Martin, 1980, p. 43.
48 http://blog.wellcomelibrary.org [accessed 10 May 2019].
49 Charles Tennyson's Daily Journal, Complete Annual Accompt-Book 1815 [2TdE/H/76].
50 Martin, 1980, p. 43.
51 Muzio Clementi (1752–1832), Italian-born English composer, teacher and promoter of the piano. http://www.clementisociety.com [accessed 13 May 2019].
52 £10 in 1825 = £941 in today's money; £100 = £9415 in today's money; https://www.bankofengland.co.uk/monetary-policy/inflation [accessed 16 January 2021].
53 https://www.houseofnames.com/d-eyncourt-family-crest [accessed 8 March 2022].
54 Tennyson, 1950, p. 158
55 Tennyson, 1950, p. 440.

6

'Your truly affectionate Old Aunt Bourne': Mary Tennyson Bourne, 1777 to 1864

Marion Sherwood

Mary was the Tennysons' younger daughter. Less favoured by her parents than her sister Elizabeth, she was sent to live with her maternal grandmother for much of her childhood. Unlike Elizabeth and her sister-in-law Frances, who both married young and immediately became pregnant, Mary did not marry until she was thirty-four and remained childless. But she fostered an abandoned young boy and remained close to her many nephews and nieces. For Alfred and his Somersby siblings, the Dalby residence of 'Aunt Bourne' was 'the *second home*' of their childhood.[1] Mary's religious faith deepened with time and she moved from Anglicanism to Nonconformism, 'to the Chapel instead of the Church' [26.08.1815 4TdE/H/55/33]. And from the late nineteenth century Tennyson biographers have continued to define Mary by her religion. In his 1897 *Memoir* Hallam Tennyson included an observation made by Mary to the poet: 'Alfred, when I look at you, I think of the words of Holy Scripture – "Depart from me, ye cursed, into everlasting fire".'[2] This anecdote – possibly apocryphal – has been repeated, apparently without question, by twentieth- and twenty-first-century biographers to create a caricature of Mary as 'a gloomy, pessimistic Calvinist'.[3] (Welcome exceptions to this chorus of disapproval are Roger Evans and Valerie Purton.[4]) Examining her letters, many of them unpublished, lead the reader to question this biographical judgement. Crucial to this study are the letters written by Mary herself; as the earliest of these are dated 1805, for insight into her early years we must consider her mother's letters.

'I never saw a finer child': May 1777 to summer 1780

Mary Turner Tennyson's letters to her mother, Mary Turner, do not support Robert Bernard Martin's claim that the Tennysons' 'second child, Mary, was always difficult'.[5] Young Mary was born a year after her sister Elizabeth and baptized at Market Rasen on 4 May 1777. Soon after the birth Mary wrote, 'the Children are become great Friends' [02.05.1777 Tenn 2/1/11]. Like her siblings, young Mary was placed with a wet nurse where she thrived:

> Yesterday ... we call'd to see Mary at Middle Raisin And I think without Partiallity I never saw a finer Child it is as fatt as it can [? be] – it's disposition being easy makes her Fatter so much. [24.06.1777 Tenn 2/1/12]

Mary noted in December: 'I went to Middle Raisin last Wednesday and found her very well' [09.12.1777 Tenn 2/4/13].

A year later, on 10 December 1778, the Tennysons' third child, George Clayton, was baptized at Market Rasen. As the poet's grandson records, 'Mary and George [Clayton] were sent away at a very early age – Mary to live with Mrs Turner, her maternal grandmother ... at Caistor' and George Clayton to his paternal grandfather 'Michael Tennyson in Holderness'.[6] *Mansfield Park* (1814) provides literary evidence that 'the "boarding out" practice was widespread';[7] the historical evidence of her mother's letters reveals just how much of Mary's young life was spent away from the family home. During 1778 and 1779 her clothes and belongings were transported by carrier to Caistor. Initially Mary tells her mother, 'I have just sent Mary a Cupple of Frocks 4 Shifts, 1 Skirt 1 Pr Stockings 1 Pr Old Shoes & shall have more things to send her on Tuesday' [*c.* 1778–1779 Tenn 2/8/22]. Later she writes, 'With this you will receive a Pair of shoes for Mary which were made for Bessy and are too little' [*c.* 1778–1779 Tenn 2/8/27]. A 'bedgown' [*c.* 1778–1779 Tenn 2/8/32] and messages follow: 'remember me to Mary' [*c.* 1778–1779 Tenn 2/8/26].

In August 1779 Mary is concerned for the health of 'poor Mary', now aged two years and three months:

> I rather expected my Dr Mother to have a Line from you About poor Mary ... I hope as you make no Mention of her she is mending fast and I shall be glad to hear gets her Appetite – If she dont I'm Afraid her complaint is Worms which will be more difficult to remove than the getting her teeth[8] – But if she is to suffer and at Last be taken Away we must Submit Patient as we are Able to the will of Heaven. [17.08.1779 Tenn 2/4/15]

This is the first of many occasions on which Mary submits 'to the will of Heaven' during family illness. Three days later she is 'happy to hear Mary Continues Mending' [20.08.1779 Tenn 2/5/24].

Mary makes few references to young Mary in the following months and they appear as an afterthought, placed just before the closing salutation or in a postscript. She hopes in December that 'Mary is not too Noisy for my Father' [07.12.1779 Tenn 2/7/7] and in January that 'Mary and all of you are well' [25.01.1780 Tenn 2/1/17].

During the summer of 1780 it was decided that young Mary should continue to live with her grandmother in Caistor. The decision concerning her daughter's future is not mentioned until the final paragraph of Mary's letter, after extended discussion of dressmaking fabric, which implies a lack of concern:

> I have enclos'd some Patterns of Silks … And as Miss Nainby is so kind as to say she will take the Trouble of Procuring me one I have sent two sorts of Browns an[d] shou'd like to have a Gown and Petticoat of one of 'em …

> You are very kind in offering to keep Mary it will I redily Accept your Offer it will Most certainly save me a great deal of Trouble and expence As I am sure if we had all three at home we cou'd not do without another servant 3 Children all together must be a Great Trouble and one Persons work to take care of 'em – I am sensible that Mary is better Care taken of her than we can do ['Pray' smudged out over 'than'] than she cou'd Possibly be here and I think both she and we are greatly Oblig'd to you – [*c*. summer 1780 Tenn 2/8/12]

By the summer of 1780 Mary had been married for five years and given birth to three children. However, 'all three' were rarely 'at home' together. Each child spent many months with a wet nurse. In April 1780 George Clayton had still not returned and Mary 'judg'd it as Propper to let my maids pay their Annual Visits before little George came home as I cou'd not so well spare either of 'em then' [25.04.1780 Tenn 2/2/9]. By September 1783 'little George' was living with his paternal grandfather in Holderness, where 'he has had the Hooping Cough' [16.09.1783 Tenn 2/4/23] and from where he returned in 1785 'rude and ungovernable' [17.05.1785 Tenn 2/7/23]. Young Mary had already spent much of her life in Caistor. As a baby her 'disposition' was 'easy' and it is unlikely that her grandmother – aged sixty-two and with a much older husband – would have 'offer[ed] to keep Mary' if she too had been 'rude and ungovernable'. Mary claims she would need another servant, but as a genteel household the Tennysons already employed several servants.

As suggested in Chapter 1, Mary's decision was perhaps influenced by her health, apparently undermined by three pregnancies in just over three years. During 1780 she refers to 'great weakness' [22.02.1780 Tenn 2/3/6] and 'Fainting' [21.11.1780 Tenn 2/5/27]. Mary usually writes fluently and clearly, but in the final paragraph of her letter, attempting to explain her belief that young Mary would be better looked after in Caistor than at home, she smudges words and her handwriting and syntax deteriorate: 'I am sensible that Mary is better Care taken of her than we can do than she cou'd Possibly be here'. Perhaps it is a painful decision to accept her mother's 'Offer'.

'Mary ... is a fine sensible child': summer 1780 to March 1786

Mary continued to send clothes to Caistor:

> I have sent you a few more things for Mary ... if the Frocks dont fit I have sent some Peices which will help to make 'em in case they will not & If you have any old frock that is worth sending it will do very well for George [Clayton]. [c. 1780 Tenn 2/8/30]

From the 1750s until the late nineteenth or early twentieth century young boys wore dresses until they were toilet trained and 'breeched', usually between the ages of two and eight.

In February 1781 Mary asks, 'If Mary wants anything before I see her I beg youll be kind enough to get her what she wants' [06.02.1781 Tenn 2/6/17]. Thereafter the child fades from view for a while as Mary's recurring concern with her parents' and her own health intensifies. In January 1782, suffering from constant sickness and afraid she may be 'breeding' again, she 'strive[s] to make myself as happy as I can' [29.01.1782 Tenn 2/7/10]. Two months later family friends learn that she is 'very Dangerously ill' after a miscarriage [18.03.1782 Tenn 2/1/22]. By April Mary is 'perfectly well in health' and visits to Caistor resume:

> I shall have the same Pleasure in coming to see my Dear Mother nay more satisfaction to me As I do not come for my Health sake ... I'm oblig'd to you for asking George [Clayton] but I doubt I must not Venture of both and I promis'd Bess to bring her with me. [23.04.1782 Tenn 2/7/12]

'Bessy', she writes in August 1783, 'is vastly pleased to think of seeing Mary and I dont doubt but Mary is equally so' [12.08.1783 Tenn 2/6/21]. Despite their separation, the sisters remain close.

By December 1783 Mary is definitely 'breeding' and she struggles to come to terms with 'what for my self and your sake I wish'd never wou'd have happen'd again' [10.12.1783 Tenn 2/3/10]. 'Faintness and weakness' throughout the pregnancy leave Mary 'so low I with difficulty hold my pen' [16.03.1784 Tenn 2/7/14]. Her father, John Turner, died in April.[9] Mary, 'much oppress'd with pain', waits for her mother to be 'with me at the last' [01.06.1784 Tenn 2/6/22].

Mary and George's fourth and last child, Charles, was baptized at Market Rasen on 20 July 1784 and placed with a wet nurse. Two months later Mary wants young Mary to visit her family in Market Rasen:

> As you are willing Mary shou'd for a little time I intend sending [a servant] for her tomorrow Bessy and George [Clayton] Talk continually of her coming and I doubt not of her desire to see <u>them</u> and her <u>little Bro</u>ʳ If you can prevail upon her to leave you but am Afraid she will undergo a Conflict for her Attachment to you is certainly very great. [21.09.1784 Tenn 2/7/18]

Four days later she reports:

> Mary got Exceedingly well here ... they seem all happy together so hope you will not wish to seperate 'em yet – my Sister and I have been very busy in Making Mary a Pair of Stays. [25.09.1784 Tenn 2/7/19]

Mary's 'Sister' is her sister-in-law Ann Tennyson, later Raines. Girls and boys wore 'Stays' from a young age to encourage good posture.

By early October Mary Turner, still mourning her husband, is missing her granddaughter. Mary writes in concern:

> If I can send Mary on Tuesday I will, but fear we cannot finish all for her ...
>
> I wish much for your sake that she was back again tho we shall all be sorry to part with her – she is certainly some company to you tho' a Child –

She concludes on a happier note: 'Mary made up her lost time and got the second Night to the Assembly and danced two dances with different Gentlemen and got great applause' [03.10.1784 Tenn 2/6/23]. Despite the 'Conflict' of past and pending separations, young Mary – now aged seven – has the social confidence to participate in an 'Assembly', the 'supreme arena of polite leisure', an 'evening gathering accommodating dancing, cards, tea and, perhaps above all, talk'.[10]

After young Mary's return to Caistor, Mary reassures her mother:

> You say you hope Mary behaves well and does you credit, indeed she does we are much pleas'd with her ... she is a fine sensible Child I wish her father cou'd have seen her but as you wish so much to have her I won't prolong her stay. [05.10.1784 Tenn 2/5/37]

Young Mary continued to be her grandmother's companion. In January 1785, Mary compares their situation:

> I am many hours alone in an Evening so make the same company of Bessy you do of Mary she reads exceeding well I hope Marys reading to you will improve her Spelling, as <u>there</u> she is deficient. [25.01.1785 Tenn 2/5/39]

Fourteen months later Mary is 'happy to find my Dear little Mary is some consolation to you – I hope she m[a]y continue yet with you and I wish you every Comfort <u>in my power</u> to accomplish' [08.03.1786 Tenn 2/5/41]. As she implies, the late-eighteenth-century household was a patriarchy. It was George who had the '<u>power</u>' to prolong or curtail her stay and in January 1788 he decided to bring young Mary 'home'.

'I am quite charm'd with her neither co'd I do without her': January 1788 to June 1789

Mary's letters to her mother in January 1788 confirm that Bessy, aged eleven, was at boarding school.[11] Family letters provide evidence of the boys' education; no details survive of the girls' schooling:

> Bess wrote another to me a Post or two since wherein she says she is almost well & mentions what a pleasure it will be to her the having Mary with her and is sure she will like school ...
>
> Talking of Marys going to school will serve as a preface to mentioning her coming home – but George a day or two since entirely of his own accord Mention'd it 'that he had forebore during the Holidays a desire to have her at home to oblige you and me', but hop'd you wou'd not think it unreasonable if he nam'd the first day or week of Feb^y ... believe me to take her home so immediately at this juncture is a force upon my inclination for tho' it is very agreeable to me to have the child, I feel sensibly how much the parting with her will hurt you ... her father says he begs you will take it in a proper light and put it upon the footing of what he always said, 'that he wishes her to <u>know</u> and be <u>Attach'd</u> to home' he

being too, totally ignorant of her disposition – & which he observes shou'd be all accomplish'd before she goes to school … I hope you will perfectly compose your Mind about parting with her she shall come often to see you before she goes to school. [08.01.1788 Tenn 2/1/29]

Three weeks later Mary returns to the subject:

George and I had some conversation about Mary's manner of traveling home he observ'd she had not been us'd to ride either double or single [on horseback] and there cou'd be no way but sending any other conveyance than A Post Chaise to bring her safe provided you wou'd accompany her. [29.01.[1788] Tenn 2/4/25]

As her mother relates, young Mary was taken 'home' to Market Rasen in April 1788, just before her eleventh birthday. She had lived with her grandmother in Caistor since she was two:

My Heart sympathize'd sincerely with yours at our parting as I cannot be ignorant of your attachment to this dear Child, consequently you suffer'd a pang at separation, it seem'd mutual, & I have not a doubt but as sincere on her part, she griev'd much after she turn'd her back of the Town where she had so pleasantly pass'd her early years, in all probability they may prove the happyest of her Life tho' (if she lives) those to come may not be unhappy – yet she will feel anxiety & disappointment more acutely – she was more cheerful when we got nearer home – but some involuntary tears trickle'd down her cheek at different times during the evening – she is now more compos'd, as I shall be glad to hear you are & with a little chearful company I hope time will assist you in ceasing to regret the loss of your little Girl –

Mary was perhaps unaware that her mother had lost her own 'little Girl', the daughter of her first marriage to Thomas Stovin, Susan, who was born and died in 1740:

She will [Mary continued] as I observ'd to my Sister at some future time I hope amply reward you in gratitude for all your kindness shown her – & that you must look forward to, I had not time to think, in our harry of spirits at the last, to thank you for everything I feel I owe you on her account but you wo^d excuse it then – & also to my Bro^{rs} I ought to have said I was oblig'd more particularly my Bro^r John, as she has liv'd with you at his & your expence jointly since my poor Father dyed …

My Father Tennyson sends best respects as does George who … desires me to thank you for him on Marys Accounts & assures me he is hurt that you are likely to feel the loss of Mary so much hopes you cannot think it cruel of him taking her away from you before the time nesecssary [sic] for her preparation for school. [22.04.1788 Tenn 2/7/29]

Young Mary did 'come often to see' her grandmother. She was in Caistor again two months later:

> you and Mary wou'd wonder you had heard nothing of us I sho'd have wrote on Tuesday but intended surprizing you early on Wednesday Morn'g by the coming of myself Bessy and George [Clayton] to see you but the Weather and my Toothach together prevented us. [28.06.1788 Tenn 2/6/25]

Mary's closing salutation reveals that young Mary returned to Caistor the following March: 'Bessy joins me in kindest remembrance to you my Bro^{rs} and Mary' [02.03.1789 Tenn 2/5/45]. In late March Bessy became extremely unwell. Her anguished mother wrote, 'I have from the beginning my dear Mother put my trust in that great Physician of all or I co^d not have been hitherto supported'. However, she was also 'supported' by her younger daughter:

> Mary thank God is in perfect health and never ails anything & she behaves so tenderly and is so affectionate to her Sister with such an anxiety for her being better that I am quite charm'd with her neither co^u I do without her. [20.03.1789 Tenn 2/6/26]

Despite Bessy's continuing weakness, Mary and her daughters were in Caistor again in June. On their return to Market Rasen Mary wrote belatedly to her mother: 'Tho the Girls scribble'd a few lines to you when we had got home I yet think it will be Acceptable to you to receive a few from me' [26.06.1789 Tenn 2/6/28]. After these 'few lines', young Mary is not mentioned in family letters, either by name or as one of 'the Girls', until June 1793.

'Mary of course I leave': June 1793 to February 1804

Between June 1789 and June 1793 the Tennysons moved to Lincoln and their growing family began to disperse. George Clayton and Charles were at St Peter's School in York in June 1793 and George thanked the headmaster, John Robinson '& Mrs Robinson for your attention to them', adding 'My Wife & Girls are returned from Bath' [30.06.1793 TRC 4657].

Young Mary did not become 'Attach'd' to home' as George wished. Following the visit to Bath in June 1793 she continued to travel. Writing to George in London ten months later, Mary comments, 'Before this I make no doubt but you have seen dear Mary I long to know where she has taken up her residence' [27.04.1794 4TdE/H/2/7]. But in October 1795 young Mary visited Caistor with her mother, who confirmed, 'At the time Mary wrote I did not think we sho^d be able to reach you by tomorrow dinner but I hope to see you by half Past one O C' [14.10.1795 Tenn 2/6/29].

As her siblings grow up and move away, references to young Mary appear in their letters, and in the correspondence of family friends, and we begin to see her through their eyes. On 23 January 1798 Elizabeth married Matthew Russell and moved to County Durham, giving birth to a son, William, ten months later. George Clayton wrote from St John's College, Cambridge, in May 1799 to send 'my best love to my Sister' [Elizabeth] [13.05.1799 TRC 4668] and thanks for 'my Sister Mary's very kind Letter' [01.03.1800 TRC 4672].[12]

The Tennysons moved again in May 1798, to Clayton House, Grimsby, which George inherited from his uncle. Writing to her mother in September 1799, Mary mentions young Mary's sociable week in 'Harrowgate': 'I need not give you a repetition of that gay week though the weather was unfavorable it did not spoil their Balls & I am much pleas'd with her account' [21.09.1799 Tenn 2/6/32].

Charles followed his brother to St John's College, Cambridge, on 6 July 1801. From Charles we have the first teasing reference to young Mary's religious faith. Apologizing to his mother for not writing, he adds, 'Mary I hope will forgive my neglect of her with Christian goodness' [07.05. 1802 TdE/H/61/20]. And we understand from Charles why the family thank young Mary for her letters: 'I hope she will excercise [sic] her finger ends now and then in my behalf, I need not require her to do any thing else since that is the seat of her wit' [19.02.1802 TdE/H/61/26].

Charles's hope for young Mary's forgiveness reflects the siblings' continuing closeness. She was also regarded with affection by family friends. When Robert Burton wished for 'the pleasure of waiting upon' the Tennysons 'very soon', young Mary 'is so obliging as to say she will accompany me' [20.08.1799 TRC 4585]. Edward Bromhead 'beg[s] my kind respects to Mrs Tennyson & Love to Miss Mary if she is returned from the Dissipation scenes of Enderby' [07.12.1801 TdE/H/60/7].

By April 1803 young Mary, soon to turn twenty-six, was again living in Caistor as her grandmother's health deteriorated. Mary had been worried about 'My poor Mother' for two years [04.04.1801 TdE/H/61/2]. In April 1803 she wrote to George:

> my poor Mother has yet bad nights – bad appetite & bad digestion attended with a slow Fever – & which I fear in the end will wear her down ... However

my dear husband rather than you shall be low or dispirited for want of society I will (except my poor Mother should be very considerably worse) fix Saturday for returning – Mary of course I leave. [03.04.[1803] TRC 4685]

Young Mary remained in Caistor until her grandmother died aged eighty-six. She was buried on 24 February 1804 at Caistor, where 'all here unite in best affection with dear Mary & myself' [26.02.1804 MTT TdE/H/62/1]. When young Mary was taken back to Market Rasen in April 1788 her mother 'observ'd': 'She will … at some future time I hope amply reward you in gratitude for all your kindness shown her' [22.04.1788 Tenn 2/7/29]. Perhaps Mary Turner's 'reward' was to have 'dear Mary' with her throughout her long final illness.

Before reading the family letters and the many references to young Mary we, like her father in 1788, were 'totally ignorant of her disposition'. In the letters there is no trace of the 'always difficult' child mentioned by Martin. She was an 'easy' baby, who became a 'fine sensible Child'. 'Dear Mary' was 'so tender and affectionate' to her ailing sister that her mother was 'quite charm'd by her', and her actions and emotions reveal her to be a loving and compassionate granddaughter. Eventually, in letters dated February and August 1805, we can read young Mary's own words for the first time.

'My ever lamented & beloved Grand Mother': February 1805

The earlier of young Mary's two surviving letters was written in February 1805, a year after her grandmother's death. She is twenty-seven, travelling with a group of friends and writing from Bath to the two uncles she knows and loves from her years in the Turner household.[13] She writes at length, vividly and with humour: as her brother Charles noted, the 'seat of her wit' is at 'her finger ends':

> Now my dear Uncles as a dutiful Niece I think it high time I gave you some account of myself, but in the first place I am very anxious to know how you both are going on, I had a letter the other day from my Mother where she says she has no[t] heard at all about either of you since I left Tealby which is now three weeks since, we were nearly a week on the road, Travelling Twelve in company & 4 of them Children; we made many visits on our journey to gratify curiosity. Warwick Castle is well worth two hours inspection … what pleased me most were the paintings, some of which are very fine, there is a most beautiful one of Catherine of Aragon & more than one of poor unfortunate king Charles which gave me a more strong Idea of what I picture our Saviour to be like than anything I ever saw, a painful wish spoil'd me here for my ever lamented & beloved Grand

Mother. We after this proceeded to the State bed Room where Queen Ann slept last,[14] which Royal [? ...] is to suffice for poor Charlotte should she happen to pass that way as the Housekeeper gave us to understand that subject limbs would be a kind of profanation,[15]

... we stop'd to see the Ruins of Kennelworth Castle (Lord Clarendon) which are amazingly extensive & fine – & there we saw the <u>Ground</u> of an Apartment where Queen Elizabeth had held <u>Solemn Dancing</u> – At Nottingham we stopped to purchase Silk Hose, (rather a <u>sinking</u> in poetry) & at Coventry we saw the Ribbons Manufactories & got some <u>pennyworth</u> for the first two or three days we came here we were in the York Hotel where we got some <u>Guinea</u> worth being the most <u>Gentlemanly</u> eating place in Bath ...

Bath has never known more full, at one of the Balls I was at I suppose there must have been 17 hundred people. I was <u>borne</u> into the Room about nine O'Clock – Luckily I had my Arms placed very orderly by my sides had they been above my head they must have remain'd so, for in one of these Squeezes, as you enter that is your position for the night – from nine to eleven this Mob were conveying me once round the Room when I took my leave much dissatisfied that I had neither opportunity to show of[f] my Cloaths or Airs or Graces the last night – I was There there was an <u>Harmonic Club</u> at the lower Rooms which ... gave an opportunity of being seen & asked to Dance – the partner that first asks you is kept for the Night, luckily mine was a pleasant one – I have had <u>many proposals</u> of <u>Marriage</u> which I will not trouble you with, when anything is made <u>conclusive</u> I will write for your <u>advice</u> I have been turn'd over in a Chair, of course I immediately got out & walk'd home, the night being very slipery I tumbled & entirely spoilt a pair of new white Shoes

Sir Sydney Smith is just gone from here all the Ladies are dying for love of him,[16] I think him very similar to other men ... I imagine my dear Uncles we shall stay here about a Month or five weeks longer I wish you would continue & visit Bath during that time ... the Pump Room is as usual the resort of all the fashionables I neither drink the water or bathe & I think it is too much a place of <u>Shew</u> & <u>gaze</u> to promenade there often

I have got the reduced profile of my beloved Gmother home this day & <u>hope it will</u> be thought like I think it is best kept as close to the one you thought the most pleasing as possible though they neither of them answer my wishes. I shall get it yet in Town with her dear hair at [t]he back My Mother does not know of it as I wish to produce it unexpectedly & if she immediately is struck with the resemblance it will prove doubly satisfactory

remember me most kindly to all the friends that valued her & value you & believe me my very dear Uncles your truly affc^{te} Niece Mary

> I shall be very anxious to hear from one of you about you both & let it be directly sent to 36 Milson Street. My Sister & her husband are by this time in Town – the old people are coming here. [February 1805 T2/9/5]

Mary is revealed to be a thoughtful and independent young woman, who enjoys travelling and the social life of Bath. Socially confident as a child of seven, applauded for dancing at a local assembly, she is now a poised woman of twenty-seven who welcomes the opportunity to show off her 'Airs or Graces', although her view that the Pump Room is 'a place of <u>Shew</u> & <u>gaze</u>' suggests a serious nature. She is unimpressed by celebrity, unfazed by being 'turn'd over in a Chair' and the instruction to her uncles – 'let it be directly sent' – indicates a strong will. Mary's faith and love for her grandmother are exemplified by images. A portrait of King Charles represents her 'strong Idea' of 'our Saviour' and, she hopes, a 'profile' portrait catches the likeness of her 'ever lamented & beloved Grand Mother'.

'The nuptials of our brother George': August 1805

Young Mary's second letter is dated August 1805 and written from 'Tealby'. Since 1801 the Tennysons had been living at Tealby Lodge, later renamed Bayons Manor and eventually transformed by Charles. In December 1801 George Clayton was ordained into the priesthood. While waiting for the livings of Somersby and Bag Enderby he moved to lodgings in Louth.[17] There he met and married Elizabeth Fytche, known as Eliza, and Mary describes the wedding for her sister in 'Harrowgate':

> Last Tuesday morning Charles & I turned our half rested limbs out of bed by 5 oclock to go to Louth & attend the nuptials of our brother George, he had a new coat on the occasion, together with a pair of the best silk hose. She had on a white beaver hat, & lily muslin gown. The happy pair proceeded to Church at 8 oclock teeming with chastened delight. They were attended by two Miss Greens, their cousins, Mary Ann Robinson, John Fytche their brother, Mary Ann Fytche & myself, one of the Miss Greens & Miss Robinson bridesmaids. The carriage convey'd back to Mr Fytche's the Bride & Groom, the rest of the party trampled it amidst the gaze of spectators. We found a very plentiful breakfast awaiting us, spice cake and coffee contending which should get the mastery. After breakfast we danced 'come haste to the wedding'. Cotillions & waltz's followed fandangos & minutettos closed the revels of the morning. Cake was eaten by the tun in short dancing & [? plumbs] were the order of the day. Mrs Heneage came for tea

to us at Mrs Fytche's – she had four horses to her coach, in which Charles, Mary Ann Fytche, myself & Mrs H returned to Tealby, preceeded by our carriage, enclosing the bride and groom. We had three outriders all of which together with postillions and every horse had good white satin favors at a shilling a yard, tyed up by the bridesmaids, but trouble was nothing, expense was all!!!!!!

Ah! how dear it is to marry! no prudent person would think fit. They now live at York House .... Eliza is really a sweet tempered creature and the very woman for George. She is as opposite to Mrs independent of Bath, as fire to water. I think you would like her, she is particularly fond of and tender to animals, and quadrupeds.

Conversation she enters with more interest with [sic] than any other – but I have never yet had a quiet half hour with her and therefore cannot with justice details [sic] the varieties of her mind & soul.

Everybody admires the pictures extremely & think yours very like me.[18] ... Write to me soon, for I picture you with a superfluity of health and activity. good morning, my love to all. if you do not write soon, may your unforgiving spirit and devilish fury discharge itself at the end of your nose in nauseous mucous and may [t]he stopping of the odious issue be sealed by scabs.

Your truly affec^{te} sister Mary. [August 1805 TRC 5052]

Mary, like her mother, has an acutely observant eye and a gift for vivid imagery. Again writing at length and with humour, she describes an early-nineteenth-century genteel wedding where 'trouble was nothing, expense was all'. She gives a touching glimpse of 'sweet tempered' Eliza, who would give birth to Alfred in 1809, while implying her own wish to understand 'the varieties' of the human 'mind & soul'. The closing wish for her sister, however, strangely prefigures the 'coughs, aches, stitches' that were to afflict *St Simeon Stylites* (1842) and suggests that Mary's 'wit', like Elizabeth's, could have a sharp edge.[19]

'Mary has mention'd ...... her wish to live with George': June 1807 to May 1810

Between August 1805 and June 1807 young Mary's relationship with her parents deteriorated; for the first time her 'conduct' was criticized. As a child George Clayton was considered 'rude and ungovernable' [17.05.1785 Tenn 2/7/24], but Mary escaped censure. In June 1807 George wrote to Charles during negotiations for his marriage to Frances Mary Hutton. His letter reflects paternal concern for 'my very dear Charles': it also reveals overt parental favouritism and the occasional disharmony that Arthur Hallam later defined as the family's 'unfortunate spell against concord'.[20]

> Mary's and George's [Clayton] conduct towards myself and your dear Mother have of late made both myself and her low and dispirited. You and our dear Eliza have been ever kind and dutiful to us, and were they so likewise we could love them equally. [20.06.1807 TRC 4665]

Young Mary and her mother were at Hardwick with the Russells from November 1808 until late April 1809. Elizabeth was enduring a difficult pregnancy with her second child, Emma Maria, who was born on 8 March 1809 and baptized on 1 April. Mary and George's letters give differing views of their daughters' health and 'spirits'. Mary writes in November: 'Our dear Eliza is much better the last 3 or 4 days', adding 'Mary has been very bad of the Toothach – but is now [? something] easier' [02.11.1808 TdE/H/65/28]. By December George was also at Hardwick, reporting to Charles that 'Eliza ... looks <u>uncommonly</u> well – Mary, much as usual Your dear Mothers feelings are very acute for Eliza & Mary does not assist to keep up her spirits' [24.12.1808 TdE/H/66/22].

A brief reference to young Mary in her mother's letter to Charles in January reveals the extent of family discord at the time:

> Mary has mention'd to [Elizabeth] her wish to live with George [Clayton] and has given Eliza's leave to mention it to your Father – he cannot have any objection and has acceded to it for the comfort of all parties. [14.01.1809 TdE/H/149/4]

Less than four years after the happy family wedding, young Mary is planning to leave Tealby to live at Somersby with George Clayton and Eliza – now pregnant with Alfred – and their two surviving children, Frederick and Charles.[21] Perhaps Mary felt a particular affinity with George Clayton. Both spent many childhood years with grandparents, while Elizabeth and Charles remained at home until their schooldays. Elizabeth married at the age of twenty-two and settled at Hardwick: young Mary, by contrast, now thirty-two, travels the country with friends and makes teasing references to '<u>many proposals</u>' to deflect possible criticism of her single state. George is particularly critical of her conduct. Almost twenty-one years after she was taken 'home' he still appears 'ignorant of her disposition', unwilling to accept that – unlike Eliza Fytche – young Mary *is* '<u>Mrs independent</u> of Bath'.

George returned to Tealby in mid-January 1809. Mary remained at Hardwick, believing that 'continued watchfulness is absolutely necessary on this beloved

Child [Elizabeth]'. 'Mary's spirits are recruited', she adds, 'so I hope we shall get on' [14.02.1809 TdE/H/67/3]. On 14 February she notes, 'Mary and we go on very well – she is very far from well & sleeps very little' [18.02.1809 TdE/H/67/5]. Although young Mary's relationship with her mother is improving, the letters reflect a more subtle lack of favouritism. Mary refers to Elizabeth as 'this beloved Child' or 'our dear Eliza'; she has no term of endearment for young Mary.

'I am Dearest Molly for ever thine': December 1810 to 1816

As with other Tennyson events, we learn of young Mary's forthcoming marriage from another family member. In December 1810 Elizabeth's husband, Matthew Russell, wrote to his brother-in-law Charles. He mentions his son William, and his own visit to London,[22] adding:

> and (so Eliza tells me) your sister is at last going to be married when such a thing is mentioned in our parish Church our Clerk always cries 'God speed them well' so say I. [10.12.1810 4TdE/H/7/27]

Mary married John Bourne of Dalby at the eleventh-century 'parish Church' of All Saints, Tealby, on 13 August 1811.[23] Tennyson biographers define Mary's husband as 'a dissenting squire'[24] and for the poet's grandson 'land-ownership and dissent' were an unusual combination in nineteenth-century Lincolnshire. However, membership of dissenting churches 'increased steeply and consistently' from the 1750s, particularly in 'areas in which the Church of England ... was weak', and these included 'Lincolnshire'.[25] Jenny Uglow adds that evangelicalism appealed to the 'lesser gentry' because 'it gave them a status set by faith rather than lineage or wealth'.[26]

John Bourne (1768–1850) was a widower. On 16 March 1801 he married 'his Lancashire cousin' Mary Mather,[27] who was buried at St Lawrence Church, Dalby, on 24 May 1803,[28] nine months after giving birth to a daughter. The child, also named Mary, was baptized on 30 August 1802.[29] She was brought up by the Mather family and is not mentioned in the Bournes' letters, although a later document indicates that the Bournes were in touch with the Mathers.[30]

After their marriage Mary and John lived at Dalby Hall, near Somersby, until it was destroyed by fire in January 1841, although they travelled constantly before and after the fire. Martin believes the marriage was 'held together by their shared faith',[31] but the Bournes' letters confirm that it was 'held together' by mutual love and understanding. Twenty years after their wedding Mary wrote to her 'dearest

Husband' that 'I am gasping for your letter today' and closes 'Adieu longing to see you' [1831–1832 4TdE/H/42/[15]]. He assures 'My Dearest Mary' that 'My best love rests with you' and concludes 'I am Dearest Molly for ever thine' [1831–1832 4TdE/H/42/[37]]. The marriage lasted until John died at Cleethorpes on 15 December 1850 at the age of eighty-two.

When they married John was forty-three. Mary was thirty-four, still of childbearing age but, perhaps intentionally, the Bournes had no children of their own. Both had reason to be wary of pregnancy and childbirth. John's first wife died and their young child was sent to live with distant relatives. Mary was at Hardwick throughout Elizabeth's difficult second pregnancy. When her mother noted that young Mary 'sleeps very little', she added, 'this I do not wonder at after all that is now left her to ruminate upon' [18.02.1809 TdE/H/67/5]. Perhaps Mary's insomnia was caused by reflecting on the imminent birth of Elizabeth's child and her own possible future motherhood. Many contemporary genteel women 'tried to space their confinements, by delaying weaning their previous infant' (which suppressed ovulation), 'by coitus interruptus', or by abstinence.[32] But by August 1811 Mary had the contrasting example of her brothers' rapidly increasing families. George Clayton and Eliza had six children in the first six years of their marriage: five survived and they would have five more. Frances and Charles already had two children and were to have six more, five of whom survived.

The Bournes' life was not childless. They had frequent and fond contact with their nephews and nieces and Mary's unpublished letters reveal that they fostered – taking financial and personal responsibility for – a young boy called Hugh. In 1815 and 1816 Mary corresponded with Sarah Cooper, whose husband William was George's agent at Tealby. Sarah Cooper's only surviving letter shows that she was aware of the Bournes' different social status. Her language is formal and she addresses Mary as 'Madam'. Mary, who unlike Elizabeth is not class conscious, writes to 'My dear Mrs Cooper' and concludes 'your very sincere & Affec[te] friend' or 'your Affectionate friend'.

Sarah Cooper writes from Tealby in March 1815:

> Cooper desires me to unite with my own his sincere thanks for your present as well as past favours sincerely hoping they will at all times be gratefully remembered by us both who can only one wish [sic] and one Interest at heart, he also desires me to say that he is perfectly satisfied in every respect as to the Child assures me it shall never in your absence want from him the protection an unnatural parent has denied it and is really hurt to find there are such beings

existing in a Civilized and Christian Country. I did not recollect if the child has had the Smallpox or Cowpox may I beg to know your wish on that subject. [10.03.1815 TdE/H/55/34]

The letter confirms that Mary and John are to foster the unwanted, possibly illegitimate, child of 'an unnatural parent'. During their frequent absences from Dalby, the Coopers will take care of 'little Hugh' at the Bournes' expense.

Five months later Mary writes to Sarah Cooper:

I was so engaged when the hamper was sent to you last Thursday that I could not give you a line, I hope before this you have got it without any break – & that my poor little Hugh will like his plum cakes & Gingerbread – I have no doubt but he will give your little Baby some, I hear he is very fond of her. I shall like very much to hear occasionally how you all go on for I must ever be interested about you, & all that concerns you. We leave Dalby tomorrow Morning early when we settle for a Month anywhere. I will let you know, & I will trouble you to write to me. – I have forgot from time to time to tell you that little Hugh has never yet been inoculated, I would have him now vaccinated by Mr Barton – & I hope you will keep an account of any expenses you may be at for the Child, & Mr Stainton will repay you – I likewise wish to give you two Guineas annually fr washing him – Therefore you will receive fourteen per annum of Mr Stainton – You can draw it as you like out of his hands – I don't know whether I requested of you to let the Child go to the Chapel instead of the Church I do not wish him ever to be a Church Bigot or ever to go into one where the Gospel is not preached.

I sincerely wish you every happiness & that the blessing of God may go with you through life. – I am very busy as you may suppose & have not time to write anyone but yourself – I hope your Husband & little Girl keep well – as well as yourself – Mr Bourne has suffered much lately with the Ague – [26.08.1815 4TdE/H/55/33]

Zephaniah Barton was a local doctor and friend of the Tennyson family; Mr Stainton is not known. Fourteen 'Guineas' (fourteen pounds and fourteen shillings) in 1815 is approximately equivalent to £1,466.00 today,[33] so the Bournes' expenses were considerable.

We last read Mary's own words in her vividly humorous description of George Clayton's wedding in August 1805. Ten years later she is a married woman of thirty-eight, concerned for the welfare of a neglected child. Accordingly, although her letter is friendly the tone is serious. Yet she still writes directly, as if speaking to her correspondent and, as with the earlier reference to Eliza Fytche, conveys the same sense of wishing to know 'the varieties of her mind & soul'. Mary's faith is again apparent but, perhaps influenced by her husband – or by having encountered Anglican 'Bigot[ry]' in her sponsorship of 'little Hugh' – now inclining to Nonconformism and wanting the child to 'go to the Chapel instead of the Church'.[34]

The Bournes were 'leaving Dalby' again in June 1816. Mary writes to Sarah Cooper with details of the rather casual arrangements for 'sending little Hugh' to Tealby:

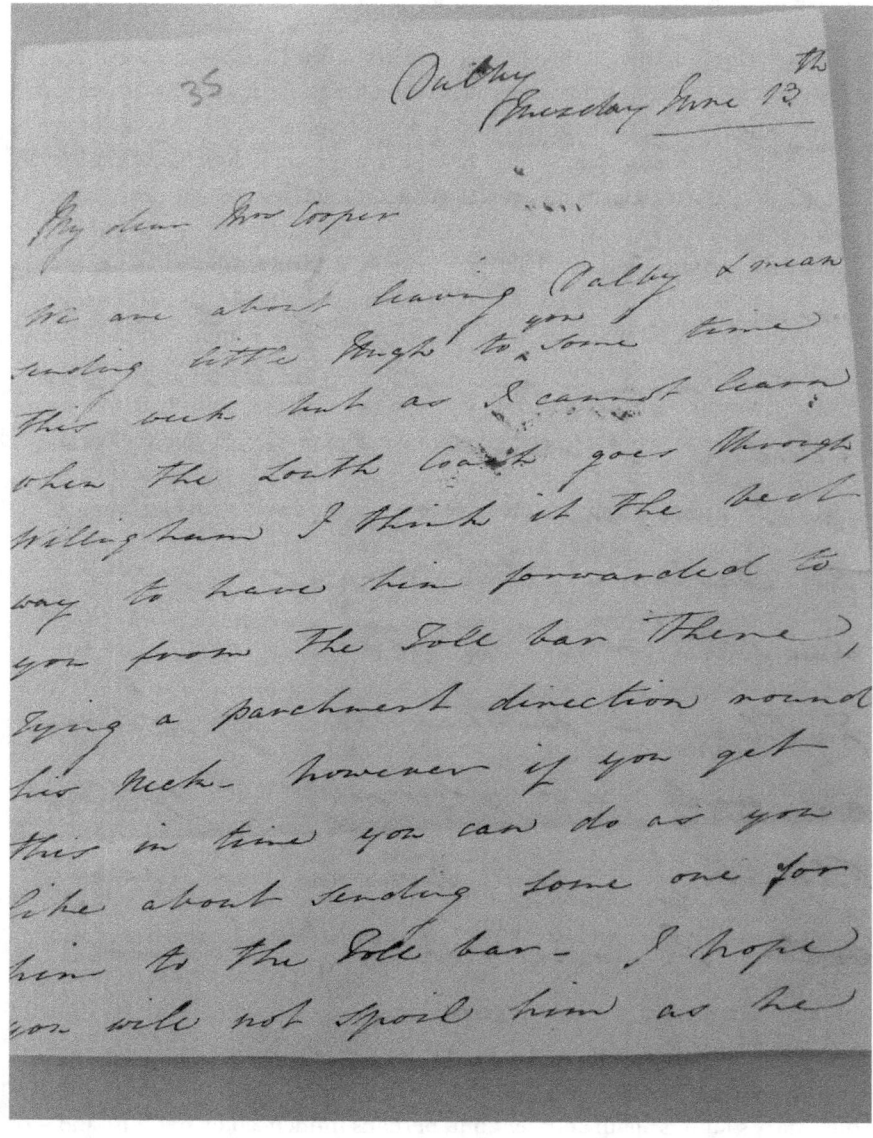

Figure 5 Mary Tennyson Bourne to Sarah Cooper [13.06.1816 4TdE/H/55/35].

We are about leaving Dalby & mean sending little Hugh to you some time this week but as I cannot learn when the Louth Coach goes through Willingham I think it the best way to have him forwarded to you from the Toll bar there tying a parchment direction round his neck – however if you get this in time you can do as you like about sending some one for him to the Toll bar – I hope you will not spoil him as he will not bear much indulgence he is an affectionate child & I hope may be a little amusement & comfort to you

As soon as he arrives at Tealby I shall be glad you will write to me & direct it to Dalby – tel[l] me how your health is – & also how my Father & Mother do, of whom as well as yourself I often think – Mr Bourne is very well I hope your husband is so. [13.06.[1816] 4TdE/H/55/35]

Mary's last surviving letter to Sarah Cooper is undated, but has a pencilled note, 'watermark "1816"':

I hope you have not been put to inconvenience owing to my delay in answering your letter. I now enclose the balance of your account for Hugh amounting to £7:13:6 the extra shilling is for postage[35] – I should have written to you long ago respecting Hugh & had I determined sooner you keeping him at Dalby, everything considered I think it best so to do, he has now learned to read tolerably well & I should wish him to retain what he has got by sending him to the Sunday School at Partney.[36] I think your hands are beginning to be full enough, and this plan will be a relief to you.

I am glad to hear you are so well, and getting on so comfortably in regard to Money Matters ... we talk of going in a month or Six Weeks time, should you have an opportunity of visiting us before that time, I need not assure you how very glad I shall be to see you with any part of your family that you m[a]y bring along with you. I should like much to have a peep at your little ones – Hugh talks of little <u>Bessy</u> with great affection. I hope poor Hugh will turn out well, but his temper we find to be extremely obstinate, and I much fear his disposition towards animals is cruel. I am confidant you gave him very good instruction, and was I ever to board him out again, I know of no hands I should like so well to place him as yours & shall offer you the refusal of him ... any cloaths you have of his at Tealby I will thank you to let us have if they are worth sending, and I will also trouble you to acknowledge the enclosed Draft for my own satisfaction – I am glad to hear of the health of my Father and Mother Mr Bourne and myself have been very well this winter – I shall at all times be glad to hear of the welfare of yourself, your Husband & Family – [[1816] 4TdE/H/55/31]

The arrangement for 'boarding out' Hugh has ended and he will remain at Dalby. The Coopers now have more than one child and Mary writes affectionately of wanting 'a peep at your little ones'. They are also comfortable 'in regard to Money Matters' and no longer need the 'account for Hugh'. Perhaps because Mary lived happily with her grandmother for years, she can refer with apparent ease to 'board[ing] him out again'. By doing so, however, she is recreating a cycle of separation and reunion that caused Mary herself to 'undergo a Conflict' as a child [21.09.1784 Tenn 2/7/18].

Mary's letters contain only one later reference to 'Hugh'. Like many genteel households, the Bournes had recurring problems with servants. Writing to her 'dearest Husband' in 1831–2, Mary adds:

> Brant, I believe leaves me next week why particularly just now I know not, but I should be very glad if you can bring a <u>Cook</u> with you – Hugh is my kitchen Maid & a good one. [[1831–2] 4TdE/H/42/[15]]

If this is 'little Hugh', grown to adulthood, the reference confirms that he is still in close contact with the Bournes twelve years after the 'boarding out' arrangement ended. And he did 'turn out well', in the sense that Mary praises or teases him as a good 'kitchen Maid'.

'Our vasillating movements after people places & things': December 1818 to August 1824

Mary told Sarah Cooper in 1816 that 'Mr Bourne and myself have been very well this winter'. From December 1818, however, Mary's health appears to deteriorate. Biographers accuse her of hypochondria,[37] but family letters provide evidence of 'Influenza', 'Mumps' and recurring debilitating 'Headaches' that affect her 'Spirits'. Despite Mary's ill health, the Bournes continue to 'leave Dalby' on many occasions. In December 1818 they visit Mary's mother in York where, as she explains to Charles, she is 'an inmate of our friends the Grays':

> I expect them every minute – so will hasten to conclude She said she could no longer hold on a denial of coming to us – as we might never meet again – I find she is often very low in Spirits she enquired after you & all yours she looks ill – has dreadful Headaches. [28.12.1818 TdE/H/80/15]

Mary's low 'Spirits' are reflected in her fear that 'we might never meet again'.

During 1819 the Bournes were invited to the Turners at Tealby, where Samuel, a clergyman and one of the 'dear Uncles' to whom young Mary wrote so warmly in February 1805,[38] is in 'returning health'. Writing to Mary's mother, Barbara adds, 'We are very sorry such a very indifferent account of dear Mrs Bourne I think Tealby agrees with her and we hope will be of service to her' [c.1819 T/2/9/16].³⁹ Tealby did agree with her; when the Bournes visited the Tennysons in November 1819 'everything … went smoothly on' [14.11.1819 TdE/H/82/86].

By 1819 Mary had acquired many nephews and nieces. Her three siblings had twenty surviving children between them and John's brother Titus had at least two daughters, thought to be the inspiration for Alfred's poems 'Adeline' (1830) and 'Margaret' (1832).⁴⁰ Mary's affectionate letter from Worthing to Frances and Charles's eldest son George Hildyard, soon to turn ten, reveals that despite ill health she was an attentive aunt who enjoyed her nephew's company:

My Dearest George

I see good judgement in attending to your humble request of two lines when two hundred could not explain the why's or the wherefore's respecting our vasillating movements after people places & things – Suffice it however at present to say that we do most certainly propose to go hence for Brighton on Tuesday next the 22ᵈ therefore you may direct for us continually to the post office there till forbidden so to do – we have much pleasure at the thought of receiving you soon at the Sea & of giving you a good ducking, the shore here is too flat for the purpose but Worthing is a quiet pretty healthy little place & plenty of Fish – and were I less nervous could be content possibly to remain a fortnight longer –

Within the last three days my Influenza has taken an unwilling farewell I trust forever & am wonderfully restored to tranquillity after ten weeks of oppressive suffering – reducing me at intervals almost to despair

I received your letter yesterday – & although this is Sunday I neglect not your request of visiting immediately.

… kind love to your dear Father tell him of our present movements & love to Clara & Ellen.⁴¹ Bourne sends everything kind

Your truly affec^te Old Aunt Bourne. [20.06.[1819]] TdE/H/146/5]

Mary's fondness for her nephew allows her to write on the Sabbath. And in June 1819 George Hildyard's truly affectionate 'Old Aunt Bourne' was forty-two years of age.

Mary was also close to the Somersby children. Alfred's fifteen-year-old brother Frederick tells 'My dear Grandpapa' in April 1822: 'As I passed through London I saw my Uncle and Aunt Bourne, and they were very well but I stay'd very little time as I was going through to Eton, and could not stop' [28.04.1822 4TdE/H/48/7]. Writing to Alfred's sister Emily in December 1832, Arthur

Hallam refers to 'Dalby' as 'the *second home* of your childhood, a spot endeared by numberless early associations'.[42]

Mary's health continued to concern friends and family. In May 1821 John replied to William Cooper, the husband of Sarah, with whom Mary corresponded about 'little Hugh'. His letter is friendly, but more formal than his wife's conversational correspondence:

> We have received your letter and are much obliged to your kind enquiries after Mrs Bourne's health, she has been very unwel[l] for a considerable length of time, & was much reduced by the Effects of the medicines & the regimen which the Phisician thought it right to place her under. I hope she is now returning by degrees to her usual state of health & strength ... Mary begs me to repeat her thanks to your wife & yourself for the trouble you have occasioned yourselves on her accounts ... we do not forget little Bessy who we some time or other hope to see again with us. We are indebted to M[rs] Cooper for a set of shirts making the which we will take the first opportunity of settling, she must tell us what the cloth amounts to, before the conclusion of Summer we shall hope to have her Company at Dalby. [11.05.1821 4TdE/H/55/28]

Mary's recurring headaches worry her mother, who shares her concerns with Samuel:

> I wish I could give you a good account of poor dear Mary, we returned home on Thursday by Dalby purposely to see her and I grieve to add she looks very Meagre ... you know how very painful and alarming the complaint to which she has been subject, the last two or three years ... and her spirits droop with her declining health. [24.06.1822 T2/10/20]

Mary herself remains close to the Turners; their relationship enhanced by shared religious belief. In December 1823 Barbara writes affectionately to 'My ever dear Mrs Bourne':

> your uncle says a visit to Dalby the winter is out of the Question but we are looking forward to Spring with pleasure in the hope of being permitted to see you at Dalby ... I very often regret the distance which divides us I wish the forty miles were four. [22.12.1823 T/2/9/25]

For the first time Mary's faith becomes clearly apparent in a letter to Charles the following March. She writes that 'my Answer to you [is] very late but I have been low spirited & unwell & felt unequal to thinking to purpose'. The Bournes' servant problems continue, 'our establishment at present is all sixes & sevens'; before Mary can visit her sister in Brighton she must arrange 'a proper

Housekeeper in my absence'. She worries about Elizabeth, widowed less than two years ago, who is 'in a drooping state', and the Bournes must also visit Tealby, where her mother's health is deteriorating:

> I hope [Mary continues] this may reach you before you are gone may the Lord of Heaven & Earth prosper your journey to the establishment of your health, as well as to the turning of your mind to the truths which the Scriptures contain 'they are they which testify of Christ' whose spirit alone can direct the Judgement – are these things worth the enquiry of an <u>immortal</u> Soul? may the <u>peradventure</u> my dearest Charles lead you like the [? Bearers] of old to search for <u>yourself</u> – your honest confessions of <u>unbelief</u> – weighs heavy on my Heart
>
> If you would occasionally correspond with me on this most momentous of all subjects I should feel gratified
>
> … Your truly Attached Sister / M. Bourne. [10.03.[1824] 4TdE/H/32/9]

Troubled by her brother's lack of faith, Mary wishes that scepticism may lead Charles to search 'the truths' contained in the Bible, which are evidence for 'Christ whose spirit alone can direct the Judgement'. Mary, perhaps becoming aware of mortality, refers to the 'General Judgement after the Resurrection of the Dead', which, in Christian theology, 'is held to be the occasion of God's final sentence on humanity as a whole, as well as His verdict on each individual'.[43] As a Nonconformist, inclining towards Calvinism, Mary believes she is predestined for salvation; if her brother, whom she loves, were to seek faith he too would be saved. Mary's wish for 'my dearest Charles' counters Martin's belief that Mary became 'almost spitefully Calvinistic, sadly rejoicing that she was one of the elect and trying to regret her own family's certain damnation'.[44]

Mary is mentioned in her mother's letters to Charles in May and July 1824. 'Mary & Bourne are at Brighton' she writes in May: 'I had a letter from her yesterday saying she reach'd B- Thursday last week found her Sister looking better than she expected' [09.05.1824 4TdE/H/32/4]. In July she notes, 'Poor Mary is very ill of her old oppressive Headache & has been ever since & before she left London' [07.07.[1824] TdE/H/92/56], later adding briefly from Leamington: 'I rec'd my dearest Char^s Note with Marys letter, and this is merely to acknowledge the kind remembrance' [[24.07.1824] TdE/H/91/56].

Mary's mother made her final reference to 'the Bournes' in a letter to Samuel in August 1824. In a poignant echo of young Mary's letter to 'my dear Uncles' in February 1805, she describes her recent visit to 'Kennilworth' and asks:

have you seen or heard of the Bournes? I wrote last week to Mary & we feel anxious to know how they both do; both <u>being</u> and have been great invalids ... I hope to hear from you. [20.08.1824 T2/9/3]

'Your heavy and irreparable bereavement': August 1825 to March 1831

Twelve months later Mary Turner Tennyson died aged seventy-two. Charles informed Samuel the following day:

> My Affectionate Mother and your Affectionate Sister is no more. She went without [? ...] about 6 O Clock last night. The distress & occupation immediately consequent, prevented my sending to Caistor last night.
>
> I do not know whether you would desire to attend the Funeral ... My Brother & Mrs Bourne I believe are going. [21.08.1825 T2/10/23]

John's letter of condolence to George, in which he recognizes Mary's empathetic awareness of family suffering, is dated three weeks after his mother-in-law's death:

> Your estimation of Mary's disposition is too correct to think her less to the afflictions of others than to those of her own, and that we should not have delayed in writing so long, could our communicated sympathies have afforded you any alleviation under your heavy and irreparable bereavement. ... we thus lament for what we cannot relieve, and are constrained to fly to the source of all genuine consolation, even to that Sovereign Ruler of all Events, who alone can reconcile to every awful dispensation & support us in every trying calamity – with these feelings of lively interest we would join our hearts with you in mourning departed excellence & shall hope much to hear from you when you can favor us with a line or two.
>
> Mary since her return from Tealby has been very ill in Bed with her old Headache – she is better & unites me in Kind affection to yourself & her Brother Charles. [11.11.1825 TdE/H/159/3]

Mary wrote to 'My dear Charles' two weeks later. She again reflects on the faith that consoles her after her mother's death and that she wishes her father and brother to share:

> I contemplated my poor Fathers letter on reading that he had been to Clea – I hope he may be persuaded to keep moving, & I pray God to bless his every exertion – my own sorrows do not abate my sympathies for those I love & my dear Father especially weigh heavy on my heart but I am sustained by the Joyful

& Scriptural persuasion that our dear departed parent is now one among the thousands spoken of in Revelation – the first verse of the fourteenth Chapter[45] – may the same passage be applied with power to the heart of our Afflicted Father, let him not ungratefully pass by such a Scripture especially recorded for the consolation of those tried like himself in the flesh for this glorious consummation spoken by the God of Truth ... let us her sorrowing relatives lift up our Hearts in praise for the transporting hope that this our beloved Mother is now with her Saviour for whom she longed, to whom in her last days she professes to be entirely devoted, testifying to my devouring ear that she was very very happy in Christ – these her very last words will be a balm to my wounded spirit so long as I grovel & linger here below –

tell me my dear Charles how you are? many a bitter pang of nature has borne you down since I parted with you – May the God of grace shew you himself & comfort you with views beyond this sighing dying world, & God grant that we, & all we love may be led to Journey on the path that leads to everlasting happiness – Search the Scriptures – they are they which testify of Christ without whose blood & righteousness we shall never reach the presence of a God all purity ...

I am going to the Sea perhaps to Clea. [23.09.1825 TdE/H/33e]

From 1825 Mary is mentioned in her nephew Alfred's letters. In October she is again at 'the Sea', as he explains to his grandfather:

I walked over to Dalby early this morning and found that Mr. Bourne, Mr. H. Bourne and my Aunt were all at the sea. It is expected that they will return to-morrow. My *Aunt* perhaps may stay longer if she likes her lodgings.[46]

Henry Bourne of Partney was John's first cousin.

Mary is at Dalby when Alfred writes to Elizabeth from Cambridge in April 1828:

I was at Dalby the other day and thought my Aunt looked remarkably well: she was then however labouring under the effects of a sprain in her leg which was painful but not of any consequence.[47]

Mary's letter to her father, written from Dalby two months earlier, reveals that the relationship has become strained since her mother's death. Biographers argue that she was 'an addict of dramatic quarrels' with 'intimates',[48] but she is clearly distressed by the rift:

I have no Business my dear Father to suppose I shall intrude upon you – to my own knowledge I have given you no offence – when we last parted two years ago I felt you much sympathy & affection evidenced by many tears & on your part apparently <u>kind</u> paternal embraces – this [? farewell] was followed by an affectionate invitation to you from Mr Bourne & myself to come & see us at Dalby where we would do all in our power to soften your sorrows – <u>What</u> & <u>Who</u> has estranged you from your <u>own flesh</u> – from your poor suffering Daughter who has felt & acted towards yourself uniformly & conscientiously for many years past …

You lately conveyed to me an indirect message & offer of my Sister Russell's Coach Horses. I did not tacitly refuse them on the ground of your unkindness, but that owing to the pressures of the times we could not afford to keep them. My Sister has now written begging me to accept of them, & <u>enabling</u> me so to do by an offer to meet the expences of Corn & Hay &c may I now ask <u>you</u> my dear Father to contribute your mite & give me your harness, as we have none to fit the horses in question, & I hope you may <u>otherwise</u> consider the claim I have upon your parental feelings, allowing me to remind you of your unbounded generosity to my Brother at Somersby …

We are straitened as to our circumstances & with difficulty enabled to support our usual Characteristic appearance in the World – a Hundred pound to my private purse would much lighten my Worldly cares & add much balm in a <u>double</u> point of view to my lacerated nerves.

… Mr Bourne knows not of my writing. [02.02.1828 TdE/H/159/4]

Although the Bournes were landowners, their acreage was comparatively small (approximately 227 acres of 'pastures' and 'paddocks' at the time of their marriage in 1811) [3TdE2/1]. Perhaps their income was reduced and they were feeling the effect of rising prices.[49] Mary's requested 'Hundred pound' is equivalent to eleven thousand pounds today.[50]

Relations were restored when Mary writes five months later:

I received you[r] kind answer to my letter from [? …] & had the weather been favourable would have apprized you of our protracted stay at Clea Thorpe in order to have effected your proposed design of seeing us here …

We are going to Hastings, how <u>long</u> to stay there is uncertain as Emma's marriage is again postponed but whenever we do return I shall attend to your invitation of us to Tealby[51] … I feel sorry at any contempt or neglect shown to a <u>parent</u> – why my Brother does not see you or write to you I am totally in the dark, never having seen <u>his</u> face since I last saw <u>yours</u> – I think the greatest part of his kindred are <u>disgusting</u> & <u>abominable</u> even to his recollection, in this remark I do not mean to comprehend yourself I <u>know nothing</u> but from his general conduct …

May God <u>forever</u> bless my dear Father & land us at length on the same happy shore – Mr Bourne joins me in all that is kind. [26.07.1828 TdE/H/159/9]

The relationship between George Clayton and his father has broken down. Mary's rather apocalyptic language reflects her brother's deteriorating mental state and perhaps his intemperate speech. This in turn may have caused relations between the Bournes and Somersby to be severed, as Alfred mentions to his grandfather a year later: 'George [Hildyard] I hear is at Dalby, or going there: but as my Aunt and Uncle have cut us dead there is no communication between them and us'.[52] Mary remained on good terms with George Hildyard and his father and, despite ill health, in October 1830 she writes with humour to 'My dearest Charles':

> Your anticipated summons will be pleasurably answered in person by my Husband next Monday the 11th – weather &c permitting. I am groaning under Mumps & disappointment in being obliged to relinquish the hop[e] of seeing yourself & my dear Father at present. My Face is half enveloped in flannel & though I might travel, I am not viewly for any but the eyes of love, & you might have other optics than your own at Tealby –
>
> I do hope to meet my Father & yourself either at Tealby or Dalby or elsewhere shortly. Your concerns interest the best feelings of my Heart – & we did during your late campaigns especially trudge after you most eagerly –
>
> I shall be curious after particulars on Bourne's return from Tealby. [08.10.1830 TdE/H/159/30]

Mary may be referring to Charles's 1826 election 'campaigns' when he became MP for Bletchingley. She follows his career with interest, writing in December: 'I hear some grand public Situation is offered to you, may God bless you in accepting or refusing every thing the World has to bestow' [20.12.1830 TdE/H/159/29].

Charles was appointed Clerk to the Ordnance on 13 December 1830.[53] Less than three months later the Tennysons suffered a further 'heavy and irreparable bereavement'. Family letters in March 1831 reflect increasing concern as George Clayton's health worsened. The Bournes were constant visitors to Somersby and on 4 March John reported to Charles:

> Your Son George came to us on Wednesday by the Coach, and we with him went yesterday to Somersby. Your Brother was still alive, but without the faintest hope given by Dr Bousfield for recovery. ... Mary is gone again to Somersby.[54]

George Hildyard wrote to his father in London the same day:

> My Aunt Bourne will be here to-day, and I shall return with her to Dalby ... I was pressed to stay here yesterday, and my Aunt Bourne thought it might be as well to do so, as my poor Uncle was thought at one time to be in a dying state.[55]

The following day Charles wrote to 'My dearest Father' from the Ordnance Office:

> I have received your letter of the 3d ... and by the same post 2 letters from my Son George dated Somersby and one from Mr. Bourne giving an account of my Poor Brother up to 11 o'clock yesterday ... The *last* account which my Son gives is somewhat more favourable and on the whole, I cannot give up hope. Our family have weak health, but we have strong constitutions and great tenacity of life.[56]

But as Alfred wrote to his 'dear Uncle' Charles ten days later: 'All shadow of hope with respect to my poor Father's ultimate recovery has vanished. ... It is evident that he cannot last many hours longer. ... We *must* lose him'.[57]

On 16 March George Hildyard confirmed to his father that George Clayton had lost his tenacious hold on life: 'My Aunt Bourne went to Somersby this morning, but her poor brother had departed this life before she arrived'.[58] Six days later 'Mary Bourne came over from Dalby' for the funeral 'and was visibly affected'.[59]

'Fast riding over Life's tempestuous Sea': May 1831 to November 1851

After George Clayton's death the relationship between Elizabeth and her father deteriorated. Writing from Dalby to his 'very dear Father' in May 1831, discussing 'what was to be done with the [Somersby] Children', Charles concludes, 'Nothing has passed here as to any difference between you and my Sister [Elizabeth], except the deep expression of her *sincere regret* at what she was carried away to say'. Relations with the Bournes remained harmonious, as he adds, 'All here unite in most affectionate remembrances. Mr. Bourne is all kindness and hospitality as well as my Sister'.[60]

A month later Mary wrote to 'My dearest Father' in a state of 'agitation'. John is in Skegness and Charles has just fought an election duel:

> This moment I have received your letter conveying your kind intention of coming to Dalby, I feel quite grieved to be obliged to postpone the Visit of yourself & Mrs Vane & I hope only for a <u>short</u> time, the case is that my poor Husband is now at the Sea ordered there by Dr Bousefield he has been there more than a week
>
> Your letter went by mistake with his newspapers to Skegness he is at Enderby's Hotel, I have been once to see him & purpose going again on Friday, he is in a very [? sinking] state but his spirits are tolerable ...

> My agitation I think has followed hard upon yours respecting my dear Brother & his [? persecutor]
>
> I am very unwell – only a few hours ago I <u>suddenly</u> was informed by Major Brackenbury of the close of the Stamford affair. I was driving out in my pony chaise with Mrs George Bourne my eyes are nearly closed with weeping – Bourne & myself would much like to see & converse with you. [22.06.[1831] TdE/H/159/26]

Charles had successfully challenged the Cecil election interests at Stamford. This led to a duel at Wormwood Scrubs on 18 June 1831 between Charles and 'Lord Thomas Cecil, brother of the Marquess of Exeter' at which no one was injured.[61]

Mary is still worried when she writes to Charles from Enderby's Hotel in September:

> My Heart has long been too full for utterance occasion^d chiefly by the House of Exeter – vicious propensities have been excited that I might have died unconscious of, I still feel that I had as much right to point the Tube of Death at Cecil as yourself & if ever I commit murder <u>that is the man</u>
>
> How do you my dear Charles? I should delight to hear from you – poor Bourne has been at this place three months for health he has in some course succeeded but his voice is quite as hoarse as ever but he still threatens to shout his best at Stamford at the next Election …
>
> I understand that my dear Nephew George is at Tealby I do hope to see him before he goes South … How are dear Nieces they are not at all kind to me, & why? <u>I</u> feel interested for <u>them</u>, & should like often to hear of them & <u>from</u> them.
>
> Bourne means to visit my Father so soon as he leaves this place & that will be I think in the course of ten days or a fortnight. [05.09.[1831] TdE/H/14/76]

The Bournes continue to be 'interested for' their nephews and nieces. John reports briefly to Mary:

> I learn that Frederick & Charles after being at Cambridge have both lost the term without taking their degrees – this is expense without profit to a
>
> vengeance – your Father knows it & I fancy it will greatly annoy him …
>
> Pray let me hear from you how your Household goes on. [[1831-32] 4TdE/H/42/[35]]

When Mary replies to her 'dearest Husband' on 'Household' matters, George Hildyard has just returned to Tealby:

> I write in great haste to say that the enclosed flannel is very good for the Money which you sent me the other day with other patterns & without observation if you think it desirable for waistcoats I do for <u>petticoats</u> & therefore a quantity of some magnitude will be wanted ... should silver fall into my lap a <u>new purse</u> will be requisite I should like one <u>nearly like</u> the old one possible ...
>
> George is gone this morning to Tealby
>
> I am gasping for your letter today.
>
> Brant, I believe leaves me next week why particularly just now I know not, but I should be very glad if you can bring a <u>Cook</u> with you – Hugh is my kitchen Maid & a good one
>
> Adieu longing to see <u>you</u> Affec^y thine M Bourne. [[1831–2] 4TdE/H/42/[15]]

John's next letter to 'My dearest Mary' is very different in tone. He is still at Tealby with George, who is preoccupied with 'Somersby concerns' and clearly dependent on his advice. He writes lovingly and with humour, the image of a horse in 'high feather' harnessed to a 'low Carriage' echoing Mary's delight in language:

> I am still playing truant but I know you will forgive me as it is your Fathers wish that I should pass another week with him & he continues pretty well although not free from partial attacks of the Gout, which in my apprehension are attended with some danger – to Day he is tolerably [? stout] & we are going to Rasen ...
>
> The Somersby concerns are always uppermost in your Fathers mind they are a little complicated, & I have been arranging them all – <u>Charles</u> is to have the Curacy of Tealby – in that respect Frederick is yet unprovided for. We hear from your Brother Charles continually he does not expect to be in the country for some weeks – but I doubt much whether your Father will get so far from Home as Harrowgate this summer. He grows old & is much fatigued by the shortest journey. I shall expect when I reach Dalby to see Rosa in high feather & harnessed to your low Carriage – I sincerely hope you are free from domestic troubles, & that you will find in Mrs Willis everything you want for the Summer, and that Squirrel, as your Father calls her behaves well – we expect Mr Barton at Dinner to Day – who we fancy will mention something relating to his Daughter Kitty who your father says is not longer than his little finger
>
> ... write to me in return if you can & make me acquainted with any thing pleasant that may be in your neighbourhood – My best love rests with you
>
> I am Dearest Molly for ever thine Affec^{te} John Bourne. [[1831–2] 4TdE/H/42[35]]

George Hildyard was Mary's favourite nephew. As Arthur Hallam's letters make clear, she was also 'interested for' her Somersby niece, Emily, and supported their frustrated engagement. Hallam found Mary's 'tone' in their correspondence 'extremely kind towards us'. 'I trust this disposition may continue', he adds, 'but in your family there is an unfortunate spell against concord'.[62]

When John observed to Mary that 'your Father … grows old', George was over eighty. He died on 4 July 1835 aged eighty-five, leaving a large fortune. The Somersby Tennysons received 'the land and fortune' he acquired 'through entail or inheritance', while 'Charles was left everything his father had earned or made by purchase and speculation'.[63] Somersby saw this as 'financial disinheritance' and George's will ensured that the family's 'unfortunate spell against concord' continued after his death.

John was informed of the death by Charles and replied in haste:

I have just received your Note conveying the Melancholy news of your Poor Father's Death. Mary went down to Skegness yesterday no time will be lost in making her acquaintance with on the occasion [sic]. I need say no more at present thank you for your kind attention. [04.07.1835 TdE/H/13/13]

Four days later he writes again:

As your letter affectionately dispenses with our presence at the mournful scene on Monday and Mary's health being too indifferent to bear much pressure, we shall I think decline being with you on the occasion –

Mary continues still at the Sea with her neice Cecilia, and we rather plan early in next week to leave home for the South. [08.07.1835 TdE/H/13/14]

Mary's last surviving letter to her 'Dearest Brother' (now Charles Tennyson d'Eyncourt)[64] was written on black-edged paper in November 1851. John had died in Cleethorpes on 15 December 1850 aged eighty-two.[65] His widow is seventy-four, but still 'chang[ing] abode' and writing with undiminished vigour and humour:

How kind of you to acquaint me & how thankful I am for your perilous journeying mercies to a Home apparently calculated for exquisite comforts – I would have written to you on the instant but have been desirous to satisfy your tender anxieties respecting my change of abode –

I have been indefatigable in [? …] but find nothing more eligible than what my smiling old Lady can offer – & she has continued to put a little Bed in the top of the House for my companions …

Miss Cole's countenance is eligible as far as smiles – wide Mouth & wondrous strong teeth can make her but evidently a confirmed toady!

Thank you my dear Brother & Sister for your intended consignment of Christmas <u>missives</u>! Do not load me with loving kindness – you have through Cooper sent to Stainton for Game which I received today – a Hare & Pheasant & braces of partridge which I received with tears of a widowed Heart & <u>bygone</u> recollections – my Shattered Back is fast riding over Life's tempestuous Sea may I & all I love reach [? at length] the desired Haven of <u>everlasting rest</u> & may God be with us to counsel & direct through the <u>Wilderness.</u> [27.11.[1851] TdE/H/146/8]

Mary's 'companions' were her dogs. As the poet's grandson confirms, when Mary changed her lodgings she 'always hired a carriage for their benefit'.[66]

Afterword: 'the desired Haven of <u>everlasting rest</u>': November 1851 to May 1864

Mary outlived her husband by thirteen years. She continued to travel between health resorts and live in lodgings, but she died in Dalby and was buried at the church of St Lawrence on 2 May 1864 at the age of eighty-seven.[67] In her years of widowhood perhaps she turned back to 'the Church'.

Reading the family letters transforms our understanding of Mary Tennyson Bourne. She is not the 'crazy Calvinist'[68] caricatured by Tennyson biographers; she is a compassionate woman of deep faith and with a gift for language. Through her mother's eyes we see her as 'a fine sensible child' and a devoted granddaughter. Her own letters reveal a confident young woman, fond of travel and company. Happily married to John Bourne, she becomes a foster parent to little Hugh and a 'truly affectionate Old Aunt' to many nephews and nieces. For Alfred and his Somersby siblings, Dalby was their second childhood home and, after the event, he felt he 'ought to have gone' to her funeral.[69]

Mary is a vivid and engaging correspondent; even in old age, the 'seat of her wit' continues to be at 'her finger ends'. Her letters suggest a strong will yet, as her mother foresaw, childhood separation from her parents and grandmother made her feel 'anxiety & disappointment more acutely' than other members of the family [22.04.1788 Tenn 2/7/29]. As her husband recognized, Mary was also acutely sensitive to their 'anxiety & disappointment'. These characteristics, together with her independent spirit, perhaps contributed to the discord Arthur Hallam saw as inherent in the Tennysons.

Mary had a Biblical turn of phrase that has been used against her. Her reported observation ('Alfred, when I look at you, I think of the words of Holy

Scripture – "Depart from me, ye cursed, into everlasting fire" ')[70] was recorded by Hallam Tennyson thirty-three years after Mary's death and has been repeated, apparently unquestioningly, by subsequent biographers. As Valerie Purton reminds us, however, the words also have Shakespearean echoes.[71] Perhaps, therefore, the observation is merely a poetic and posthumous embellishment of Mary's Bible-inflected language.

Notes

1 J. Kolb, ed., *The Letters of Arthur Henry Hallam* (Columbus: Ohio State University Press, 1981), p. 700 (12 December [1832]). Italics in the original.

2 Hallam Tennyson, *Alfred Lord Tennyson: A Memoir, by His Son*, 2 vols (London: Macmillan, 1897), I, p. 15.

3 John Batchelor, *Tennyson: To Strive, to Seek, to Find* (London: Chatto & Windus, 2012), p. 12. Calvinism's defining characteristics are 'justification by faith alone' and 'the gratuitous predestination of some to salvation and others to damnation'. Elizabeth A. Livingstone, ed., *The Concise Oxford Dictionary of the Christian Church*, 7th edn (Oxford: Oxford University Press, 1990), p. 84.

4 'Address given by Roger Evans at the Tennyson Memorial Service at Bag Enderby Church 7 August 1994', *Tennyson Research Bulletin*, 6:3 (1994), 183–90. Valerie Purton, 'Travels with an aunt: Mary Bourne revisited', in *Lincolnshire People and Places: Essays in Memory of Terence R. Leach (1937–1994)*, ed. by Christopher Sturman (Lincoln: Society for Lincolnshire History and Archaeology, 1996), 182–4.

5 Robert Bernard Martin, *Tennyson: The Unquiet Heart*, 2nd edn (London: Faber & Faber, 1983), p. 4.

6 Charles Tennyson and Hope Dyson, *The Tennysons: Background to Genius* (London: Macmillan, 1974), p. 32.

7 Purton, 1996, p. 182.

8 See Chapter 3.

9 John Turner (*c.* 1696–1784) was buried at Caistor on 13 April.

10 Amanda Vickery, *The Gentleman's Daughter: Women's Lives in Georgian England* (New Haven, CT: Yale Nota Bene, 2003), p. 239. A local gathering in a small town would be less formal than a grand Assembly in Bath or Harrogate.

11 Although the number of girls' school was increasing, 'polite society did not take girls' minds seriously'; the 'more refined girls' schools aimed to groom girls for their future compliant and decorative role in fashionable society'. Roy Porter, *English Society in the Eighteenth Century* (Harmondsworth: Penguin, 1982), pp. 180–1. See also Chapter 3, p. 6.

12 George Clayton went up to Cambridge on 8 October 1796. Michael Tennyson died two days earlier.
13 John (1749–1812) and Samuel Turner (1755–1835).
14 Queen Anne (1702–14).
15 Charlotte, Princess of Wales (1796–1817), only daughter of the Prince Regent, later George IV.
16 Sydney Smith (1771–1845), English clergyman and wit. With others he started the *Edinburgh Review* (1802). *Chambers Biographical Dictionary*, ed. By Magnus Magnusson, 5th edn (Edinburgh: Chambers, 1990), p. 1364.
17 George Clayton was inducted into the livings of Somersby and Bag Enderby at the end of 1806.
18 The portraits are by John Russell, RA (1745–1806), who also painted Mary Turner Tennyson. The portraits of Elizabeth and her mother are stored in the Usher Gallery, Lincoln (references LCNTE 2016/54 and LCNTE 2016/59, respectively). The portrait of 'young Mary' is owned by the Tennyson d'Eyncourt family.
19 *Tennyson: A Selected Edition*, ed. by Christopher Ricks, 2nd edn (London: Longman, 1989), pp. 124–35.
20 Kolb, p. 675 (30 October 1832).
21 George Clayton and Eliza's first child, George, was born and died in 1806.
22 Matthew's visit to London is discussed in Chapter 3.
23 In 1832 Alfred's recently ordained brother Charles, later Tennyson Turner, became the curate of All Saints Church, Tealby.
24 Charles Tennyson, *Alfred Tennyson* (London: Macmillan, 1950), p. 48.
25 Chris Brooks, 'Introduction', in *The Victorian Church: Architecture and Society*, ed. by Chris Brooks and Andrew Saint (Manchester: Manchester University Press, 1995), pp. 1–29 (4).
26 Jenny Uglow, *In These Times: Living in Britain through Napoleon's Wars, 1793–1815* (London: Faber and Faber, 2014), p. 261.
27 Terence Leach, 'Faces and Places', *Lincolnshire Past & Present*, 8 (1992), 28–9 (28).
28 https://www.findmypast.co.uk/transcript?id=GBPR/D/NB13569665 [accessed 29 June 2019].
29 https://www.findmypast.co.uk/transcript?id=R_876255800 [accessed 9 July 2019].
30 'Mortgage dated 20 Jan, 1847, by which John and Mary Bourne ... devised to John Philips Mather the 130 acres in Dalby and Langton rented by John Stainton ...'. LA 3-DAWSON/2.
31 Martin, 1983, p. 5.
32 Porter, p. 41. See also Malcolm Potts and Martha Campbell, 'History of Contraception', *The Global Library of Women's Medicine* (2009), glowm.com/section-view/heading/history-of-contraception [accessed 23 March 2021].

33 https://www.bankofengland.co.uk/monetary-policy-inflation/inflation-calculator [accessed 23 March 2021].
34 The only Nonconformist chapel in Tealby in 1815 was a Methodist chapel opened in 1780.
35 Approximately equivalent to £780 today, https://www.bankofengland.co.uk/monetary-policy-inflation/inflation-calculator [accessed 23 March 2021].
36 Partney is approximately three miles from Dalby.
37 Levi, p. 16.
38 John Turner died in 1812.
39 Samuel Turner married Barbara, née Bullock, the widow of Robert Haddelsey, in 1808.
40 *The Letters of Alfred Lord Tennyson*, ed. by Cecil Y. Lang and Edgar F. Shannon, Jr, 3 vols (Oxford: Clarendon Press, 1982–90), I, p. 156, n. 1.
41 Clara Maria and Ellen Elizabeth were George Hildyard's younger sisters.
42 Kolb, p. 700 (12 December [1832]). Italics in the original.
43 Livingstone, p. 208.
44 Martin, 1983, p. 4.
45 *Revelation*, 14:1 'And I looked, and lo, a Lamb stood on the mount Sion, and with him an hundred forty *and* four thousand, having his Father's name written on their foreheads'.
46 Lang and Shannon, I, p. 6 ([9 October 1825]). Italics in the original.
47 Lang and Shannon, I, p. 23 (18 April [1828]).
48 Levi, p. 16.
49 M. J. Daunton's *Statistical Appendix* indicates that in 1828 the *Average price of domestic wheat per imperial quarter* had risen to 60s. 5d. *Progress and Poverty: An Economic and Social History of Britain, 1700–1850* (Oxford: Oxford University Press, 1995), p. 578.
50 https://www.bankofengland.co.uk/monetary-policy-inflation/inflation-calculator [accessed 28 March 2021].
51 The marriage between Emma Maria Russell and Gustavus Frederick Hamilton eventually took place on 9 September 1828. Hamilton succeeded his father as seventh Viscount Boyne in 1855.
52 Lang and Shannon, I, p. 41 ([12 July 1829]).
53 'Appointments to this [Tudor] office were made by the crown by letters patent'. Tenure was 'for life until 1690 and during pleasure thereafter'. Charles's appointment was revoked on 16 February 1832; the office was abolished in 1837. https://www.history.ac.uk/publications/office/ordnance [accessed 11 May 2019].
54 Lang and Shannon, I, p. 50 ([4 March 1831]).
55 Lang and Shannon, I, pp. 50–1 (4 March 1831).
56 Lang and Shannon, I, p. 51 (5 March 1831). Italics in the original.

57 Lang and Shannon, I, p. 53 (15 March [1831]). Italics in the original.
58 Lang and Shannon, I, pp. 53–4 (16 March 1831).
59 Tennyson and Dyson, p. 78.
60 Lang and Shannon, I, pp. 59–61 (18 May 1831). Italics in the original.
61 Tennyson and Dyson, p. 83.
62 Kolb, p. 675 ([30 October 1832]).
63 Martin, 1983, p. 206.
64 The royal licence permitting Charles to add d'Eyncourt to his surname was issued on 31 July 1835, four weeks after George's death.
65 John Bourne, 'Gentleman and County Magistrate', died in lodgings in Cleethorpes. His death was witnessed by Susan Appleyard and registered in 'Castor' on 15 January 1851. GRO copy of death entry DYE 366340 issued 24 May 2019.
66 Charles Tennyson, 1950, p. 182.
67 https://www.findmypast.co.uk/transcript?id=GBPR/D/NBI13280838 [accessed 11 June 2019]. John's first wife, Mary Mather Bourne, is buried in the same churchyard.
68 Levi, p. 16.
69 Lang and Shannon, II, p. 363 ([early May] 1864).
70 See note 2.
71 Purton, 1996, p. 184, n. 10. *Henry* IV, I, 3:3, 29–30, Falstaff: 'I never see thy face but I think upon hell-fire'.

Conclusion: 'The noble letters of the dead'

Marion Sherwood

Reading, in memory, Arthur Hallam's letter, Alfred Tennyson was 'touched' by the spirit of his friend and inspiration: 'So word by word, and line by line, | The dead man touched me from the past'.[1] For the poet, Hallam's letters are 'fallen leaves which kept their green, | The noble letters of the dead',[2] they retain their power to bring the past to life. The letters of the Tennyson women have also 'kept their green'. Reading and being touched by their words transform our understanding of the women, allowing us to echo the poet's words to Elizabeth and to 'joy in [their] joy, and grieve with [their] grief'.[3] 'Noble' implies having fine moral qualities, which all the women are shown to possess, but the letters also reflect the flaws that make the women fully human.

Mary Turner Tennyson's letters are particularly important to understanding the women. They connect us with the details of her domestic life and developing family relationships and with the early years of her daughters, Elizabeth and Mary. Mary and George married in June 1775 when she was twenty-two. The progress of their long and eventually happy marriage is related in Mary's prolific correspondence, as no letters from George to Mary survive. In the unsettled early decades, Mary's closest relationship was with her mother. Mary began writing to Mary Turner as a newly married, self-absorbed young woman. The letters continued for almost thirty years and movingly reflect their increasingly close relationship and Mary's deepening feelings for George. Family health became an understandably constant concern, to be inherited by their descendants. Parental preference was soon apparent and shown to continue in the next generation, with the Caenby Hall children of Charles and Frances favoured over the Somersby Rectory children of George Clayton and Eliza. Maturity and faith allowed Mary to accept her mother's eventual death and to acknowledge her love for George and their children.

Biographers correctly refer to Elizabeth's charm, which is clearly apparent in her later letters. She shared her mother and sister's gift for language. But her recurring depression was an inherited element of the Tennysonian 'black blood', perhaps more correctly a Clayton-Tennyson characteristic, as is the litigation Elizabeth instigated soon after her husband's death.[4] Although she remained close to Charles, her husband's most active executor, her relationship with George Clayton and their father deteriorated. Elizabeth's support for Alfred and their affectionate friendship continued until her death.

Nothing is known of Frances's childhood, as no Hutton family letters survive from the period. Her earliest surviving letter was written to Mary, her future mother-in-law, just before her marriage to Charles. Frances was a prolific correspondent. Although her writing lacks the vivid immediacy of the Tennyson sisters' letters, she reveals her devotion to the children and her growing confidence as the manager of a large and wealthy political household. She retained her impartial perspective and throughout her long marriage regarded George Clayton and his sons, particularly Alfred, more kindly than Mary and George.

Reading the family letters transforms our understanding of Mary Tennyson Bourne. Since the late nineteenth century, biographers have continued to misrepresent Mary and her religious faith. Her mother's letters reveal that Mary was a considerate and caring child; young Mary's own words reflect her sociability, wit and enduring love for her maternal grandmother. The Bournes' correspondence confirms their mutual love and understanding. Mary has been caricatured as 'a crazy Calvinist',[5] but her later letters reveal her to be a compassionate woman of firm Nonconformist faith, with a gift for language and a biblical turn of phrase that has been misinterpreted.

Mary and George's marriage lasted until Mary's death in August 1825 at the age of seventy-two. Despite years of poor health, her daughters Elizabeth and Mary lived into their late eighties; Frances died at the age of ninety. Alfred, who had just turned sixteen, marked the death of his 'Grandmamma Tennyson' with an elegy, 'And ask ye why these sad tears stream?', which foreshadows rather than reflects his greatest work, written when, like *Ulysses*, Tennyson has 'become a name'.[6]

The remarkable letters presented in this study confirm that the Tennyson women deserve to be brought out from beneath the shadow of their famous relative. We may truly touch and understand the past by reading the 'noble letters of the dead' that bring the Tennyson women to life.

Notes

1 *In Memoriam A.H.H.* (1850), XCV, 33–4, *Tennyson: A Selected Edition*, ed. by Christopher Ricks (London: Longman, 1989), p. 439.
2 XCV, 23–4, Ricks, 1989, p. 438.
3 *The Letters of Alfred Lord Tennyson*, ed. by Cecil Y. Lang and Edgar F. Shannon, Jr, eds, 3 vols (Oxford: Clarendon Press, 1982–90), II, p. 149 (19 May 1856).
4 Charles Tennyson and Hope Dyson, *The Tennysons: Background to Genius* (London: Macmillan, 1974), pp. 16–17.
5 Peter Levi, *Tennyson* (New York: Scribner, 1993), p. 16.
6 *Ulysses* (1842), 11, Ricks, 1989, p. 141.

Bibliography

Primary sources

[Bellamy, Mrs], *An Apology for the Life of George Anne Bellamy, Late of Covent-Garden Theatre, Written by Herself*, 2 vols (Dublin: Moncrieffe, 1785).

Boucheret, A., *A Description of the New Wet Dock at Grimsby, in the County of Lincoln, 1805* (Grimsby: Morton, 1805).

Bourne family documents (LA 3-Dawson/2).

Bourne, John, copy death entry DYE 366340 (GRO 24 May 2019).

[Bower, Antony], 'A Survey of Several Estates Belonging to Geo. Tennyson Esquire in the County of Lincoln', by Antony Bower (1798).

Brogden, J. Ellett, *Provincial Words and Expressions Current in Lincolnshire* (London: Hardwicke, 1866).

[Burney, Fanny], *Cecilia; or, Memoirs of an Heiress, by the Author of Evelina, in Five Volumes* (Dresden: Walther, 1840).

[Defoe, Daniel], *Roxana; or, The Fortunate Mistress* (London: Warner, 1724).

[Defoe, Daniel], *The Novels and Miscellaneous Works of Daniel Defoe, with Prefaces and Notes Including Those Attributed to Sir Walter Scott – Roxana; or, The Fortunate Mistress and Mrs Christian Davies*, Bohn's Standard Library, De Foe's Works Vol. IV (London: Bell, 1883).

Gainsborough All Saints Parish Register (PAR/1/9, Entry 707).

Gentleman's Magazine, I (1791).

Gentleman's Magazine, I (1795).

[Glasse, Hannah], *The Art of Cookery Made Plain and Easy, by a Lady* (London, 1747).

Glasse, H., *The Servants Directory, Improved; or, House-Keepers Companion*, 4th edn (Dublin: Potts, 1762; repr. Huntingdon, IN: Huntingdon Laboratories, 1971).

Hutton, Arthur Wollaston, *Some Account of the History of the Family of Hutton of Gate Burton, Lincolnshire* (Privately printed, 1898).

Hutton, John, and Mary Stones, Marriage Settlement (LA RED/13/9).

Hutton, Mrs Mary, 'Daily journal: The diary and accounts of Mrs Mary Hutton' (LA 2TdE/H/80 & 81).

'Mrs Hutton's appointment of estates in the county of Lincoln, Leicester and York' (LA RED/1/3/10).

Lincoln, Rutland and Stamford Mercury, 9 July 1835.

Lincolnshire Gazette, 3 August 1861.

Market Rasen Weekly Mail, 3 August 1861.

Miller, Thomas, *Gideon Giles the Roper* (London: Milner, 1841).
Mortgage dated 20 January 1847 [Bourne/Mather] (LA 3-Dawson/2).
New, Melvyn, and W. G. Day, eds, *Laurence Sterne: A Sentimental Journey through France and Italy and Continuation of the Bramine's Journal with Related Texts* (1768) (Indianapolis, IN: Hackett, 2006).
Peacock, Edward, *A Glossary of Words Used in the Wapentakes of Manley and Corringham, Lincolnshire*, 2 vols (London: Trübner, 1889).
[Rundle, Maria Elizabeth], *A New System of Domestic Principles of Economy – And Adapted to the Use of Private Families* (London: Murray, 1807).
Russell, Matthew, will (NA PROB 11/1658/309).
Russell v Russell NA C 13/2791/9; C 13/1739/31.
[Sherwood, Mary Martha], *The History of the Fairchild Family; or, The Child's Manual*, 3 vols (London: Hatchard, 1818–47).
Simpson, Justin, *Obituaries and Records for the Counties of Lincoln, Rutland and Northamptonshire from the Commencement of the Present Century to the End of 1859* (Newcomb, 1861).
Tennyson, Charles, 'Charles Tennyson's Daily Journal, Complete Annual Accompt – Book 1815' (LA 2TdE/H/76).
Tennyson, Charles, 'Diary of his courtship' (TRC/BC/7562).
Tennyson, Hallam, *Alfred Lord Tennyson: A Memoir, by His Son*, 2 vols (London: Macmillan, 1897).
Tennyson, Hallam, ed., *Tennyson and His Friends* (London: Macmillan, 1911).
Turner, Mary, Will, 1784 (LA Tennyson 1/1).
Turner, Mary, Settlement on her son John Turner, 1801 (LA 3 Dixon 1/2/4).
White's Directory of Lincolnshire, 1870 (Sheffield, 1872).
Wright, Joseph, ed., *The English Dialect Dictionary*, 6 vols (Oxford: Oxford University Press, 1898; repr. 1981).

Secondary sources

Adkins, Roy, and Lesley, *Eavesdropping on Jane Austen's England: How Our Ancestors Lived Two Centuries Ago* (London: Abacus, 2013).
Allingham, H., and D. Radford, eds, *William Allingham: A Diary, 1824–89*, 3rd edn (Harmondsworth: Penguin, 1985).
Altick, Richard D., *The English Common Reader: A Social History of the Mass Reading Public, 1800–1900* (Columbus, OH: Ohio State University Press, 1957; repr. 1998).
Arnold, Denis, ed., *The New Oxford Companion to Music*, 2 vols (Oxford: Oxford University Press, 1983; repr. 1984), II, p. 1085.
Bairsto, Rachel, *The British Dentist* (Oxford: Shire, 2015).
Bannet, Eve Tavor, *Empire of Letters: Letter Manuals and Transatlantic Correspondence, 1699–1820* (Cambridge: Cambridge University Press, 2005).

Barker, Hannah, and Elaine Chalus, eds, *Gender in Eighteenth-Century England: Roles, Representations and Responsibilities* (London: Longman, 1997).
Bartholomew's Gazetteer of the British Isles (London: Newnes, 1904).
Barton, David, and Nigel Hall, eds, *Letter Writing as a Social Practice* (Amsterdam: Benjamins, 2000).
Barton, David, and Roz Ivanic, eds, *Writing in the Community* (Newbury Park, CA: Sage, 1991).
Basham, Diana, 'Tennyson and his fathers: The legacy of manhood in Tennyson's poems', *Tennyson Research Bulletin*, 4:4 (1985), 163–78.
Batchelor, John, *Tennyson: To Strive, to Seek, to Find* (London: Chatto & Windus, 2012).
Baylen, Joseph O., and J. Norman Gossman, *Biographical Dictionary of Modern British Radicals*, 3 vols (Hassocks: Harvester, 1979–88).
Bebbington, D. W., *Evangelicalism in Modern Britain: A History from the 1730s to the 1980s* (London: Unwin, 1989).
Boyce, Douglas, *The Tennyson Family in Market Rasen* (Market Rasen: Market Rasen Society, 1992).
Boyce, Douglas, 'The Tennyson family in Market Rasen 1774–1835', *Tennyson Research Bulletin*, 6:2 (1993), 122–9.
Brant, Clare, *Eighteenth-Century Letters and British Culture* (Basingstoke: Palgrave Macmillan, 2006).
Brooks, Chris, and Andrew Saint, *The Victorian Church: Architecture and Society* (Manchester: Manchester University Press, 1995).
Bryson, Bill, *At Home: A Short History of Private Life* (London: Doubleday, 2010).
Buck, Anne, *Clothes and the Child: A Handbook of Children's Dress 1500–1900* (Carlton: Bean, 1996).
Calvocoressi, Peter, *Who's Who in the Bible*, 3rd edn (London: Penguin, 1990).
Campbell, Nancie, ed., *Tennyson in Lincoln: A Catalogue of the Collections in the Research Centre*, 2 vols (Lincoln: Tennyson Society, 1971).
Campbell-Smith, Duncan, *Masters of the Post: The Authorized History of the Royal Mail* (London: Penguin, 2012).
Cash, Arthur H., *Laurence Sterne: The Later Years* (London: Routledge, 1993).
Chisholm, Kate, 'The preserve of women', *Times Literary Supplement*, 6 February 2015, pp. 11–12.
Clery, E. J., 'What Jane saw: Exploring Austen's creative hinterland and recoverable influences', *Times Literary Supplement*, 9 February 2018, p. 28.
'Coffee', *In Our Time*, BBC Radio 4, 12 December 2019.
Colley, Ann A., *Tennyson and Madness* (Athens, GA: University of Georgia Press, 1983).
Concise Oxford English Dictionary, 12th edn (Oxford: Oxford University Press, 2011).
Cook, Daniel, and Amy Culley, *Women's Life Writing, 1700–1850: Gender, Genre and Authorship* (Basingstoke: Palgrave Macmillan, 2012).
Crystal, David, *The Disappearing Dictionary: A Treasury of Lost English Dialect Words* (London: Macmillan, 2015).

Daunton, M. J., *Progress and Poverty: An Economic and Social History of Britain 1700–1850* (Oxford: Oxford University Press, 1995).
Dictionnaire Francais Anglais, nouvelle edition (Paris: Libraire Larousse, 1989).
DiMeo, Michelle, and Sara Pennell, eds, *Reading and Writing Recipe Books, 1550–1800* (Manchester: Manchester University Press, 2013).
Drury, Edward, *The Old Grimsby Story, 1780–1870* (Grimsby: 106 Carr Lane, DN32 8JP, 1984).
Earle, Rebecca, ed., *Epistolary Selves: Letters and Letter-Writers, 1600–1945* (Aldershot: Ashgate, 1999).
'1816, the year without a summer', *In Our Time*, BBC Radio 4, 21 April 2016.
Ellis, Joyce M., *The Georgian Town 1680–1840* (Basingstoke: Palgrave, 2001).
Evans, Roger, 'Address given by Roger Evans at the Tennyson Society Memorial Service at Bag Enderby Church 7 August 1994', *Tennyson Research Bulletin*, 6:3 (1994), 183–90.
Finlay, Michael, *Western Writing Implements in the Age of the Quill Pen* (Carlisle: Plains, 1990).
Garton, Charles, 'Lincoln School Speech Day, 1795: A Tennyson connection?', *Tennyson Research Bulletin*, 5 (1991), 248–58.
Gillett, E., 'Grimsby and the Haven Company, 1787/1825', *Lincolnshire Historian*, 10 (1952), 359–74.
Gillett, Edward, *A History of Grimsby* (Oxford: Oxford University Press, 1970).
Girouard, Mark, *Enthusiasms* (London: Lincoln, 2011).
Golden, Catherine J., *Posting It: The Victorian Revolution in Letter Writing* (Gainesville: University Press of Florida, 2009).
Gomez, Joan, *A Dictionary of Symptoms* (St Albans: Paladin, 1973).
Goulding, Richard, *Notes on Louth Printers and Booksellers of the Eighteenth Century* (Louth: Goulding, 1917).
Goulding, Richard, *Some Louth Grammar School Boys, Part IV, 1799–1814* (Louth: Goulding, 1928).
Gray, Almyra, *Papers and Diaries of a York Family, 1764–1838* (London: Sheldon, 1927).
Hill, Francis, 'The disinheritance tradition reconsidered', *Tennyson Research Bulletin*, 3:2 (1978), 41–54.
In Step with History: 'Alfred and Aunt Elizabeth' Brancepeth & the Tennysons (Brancepeth: Brancepeth Archives & History Group, 2011).
Jackson, Gordon, *Grimsby and the Haven Company, 1796–1846* (Grimsby: Grimsby Public Libraries & Museum, 1971).
Kay, Emma, *Dining with the Georgians: A Delicious History* (Stroud: Amberley, 2014).
King-Hall, Magdalen, *The Story of the Nursery* (London: Routledge, 1958).
Kolb, J., ed., *The Letters of Arthur Henry Hallam* (Columbus, OH: Ohio State University, 1981).
Lang, Cecil Y., and Edgar F. Shannon, Jr, eds, *The Letters of Alfred Lord Tennyson*, 3 vols (Oxford: Clarendon Press, 1982–90).

Leach, Terence, 'Bayons Manor and the Tennyson d'Eyncourt family' (Lincoln: undated typescript).
Leach, Terence, 'Notes for an outing to the trent-side villages of Torksey, Marton, Gate Burton, Knaith and Lea, 18 September 1971' (Lincoln: Lincolnshire Local History Society, 1971).
Leach, Terence, 'Notes for the Tennyson Society Lincolnshire Pilgrimage 1975: Raithby, Partney and Dalby' (Lincoln: typescript, 1975).
Leach, Terence, 'Faces and places', in *Lincolnshire Past & Present*, 8, 1992, pp. 28–9.
Leach, Terence R., and Robert Pacey, *Lost Lincolnshire Country Houses*, 4 vols (Burgh Le Marsh: Old Chapel Lane, 1990–3).
Leader, Zachary, ed., *On Life-Writing* (Oxford: Oxford University Press, 2015).
Lehmann, Gilly, *The British Housewife: Cookery Books, Cooking & Society in Eighteenth-Century Britain* (Totnes: Prospect, 2003).
Levi, Peter, *Tennyson* (New York: Scribners, 1993).
Livingstone, Elizabeth A., *The Concise Oxford Dictionary of the Christian Church*, 7th edn (Oxford: Oxford University Press, 1990).
Magnusson, Magnus, ed., *Chambers Biographical Dictionary*, 5th edn (Edinburgh: Chambers, 1990).
Markham, John, 'The Tennysons in Holderness', *Tennyson Research Bulletin*, 6:2 (1993), 130–7.
Martin, Elizabeth A., *Concise Medical Dictionary*, 3rd edn (Oxford: Oxford University Press, 1991).
Martin, Robert Bernard, *Tennyson: The Unquiet Heart* (Oxford: Clarendon Press, 1980).
Martin, Robert Bernard, *Tennyson: The Unquiet Heart*, 2nd edn (London: Faber & Faber, 1983).
Matthews, Samantha, 'Tennyson and handwriting: "A clean, fair hand" and the "damn pen"', *Tennyson Research Bulletin*, 10:1 (2012), 15–36.
Mead, Rebecca, *The Road to Middlemarch: My Life with George Eliot* (London: Granta, 2014).
Moorman, Mary, *Poets and Historians: A Family Inheritance*, Tennyson Society Occasional Paper Series (Lincoln, 1974).
Murray, Jim, *Tealby Gleanings: Tales of a Lincolnshire Village* (Tealby: Bayons Books, 1995).
Murray, Jim, 'The Tennyson connection', in *Facets of Tealby*, ed. by John Howard (Tealby: Tealby Society, 2002).
Neuman, Victor E., *Popular Education in Eighteenth Century England* (London: Woburn, 1971).
O'Gorman, Frank, *The Long Eighteenth Century: British Political & Social History 1688–1832* (London: Arnold, 1997).
Ottaway, Susannah R., *The Decline of Life: Old Age in Eighteenth-Century England* (Cambridge: Cambridge University Press, 2004).

Parks, Suzan-Lori, *Venus* (New York: Theatre Communications Group, 1997).
Perry, Ruth, *Women, Letters and the Novel* (New York: AMS Press, 1980).
Platizky, Roger S., *A Blueprint of His Dissent: Madness and Method in Tennyson's Poetry* (Lewisburg, PA: Bucknell University Press, 1989).
Plumb, J. H., *England in the Eighteenth Century*, The Pelican History of England, 26th edn (Harmondsworth: Penguin, 1985).
Porter, Roy, *English Society in the Eighteenth Century* (Harmondsworth: Penguin, 1982).
Purton, Valerie, 'Travels with an aunt: Mary Bourne revisited', in *Lincolnshire People and Places: Essays in Memory of Terence R. Leach (1937–1994)*, ed. by Christopher Sturman (Lincoln: Society for Lincolnshire History and Archaeology, 1996), pp. 182–4.
Ricks, Christopher, ed., *The Poems of Tennyson*, 2nd edn, 3 vols (London: Longman, 1987).
Ricks, Christopher, *Tennyson*, 2nd edn (Basingstoke: Macmillan, 1989).
Ricks, Christopher, ed., *Tennyson: A Selected Edition*, 2nd edn (London: Longman, 1989).
Robinson, Edward, *The Early English Coffee House* (Christchurch: Dolphin, 1972).
Robinson, Howard, *Britain's Post Office: A History of Development from the Beginnings to the Present Day* (London: Oxford University Press, 1953).
Rose, Clare, *Children's Clothes since 1750* (London: Batsford, 1989).
Saunders, David, *More Portraits of Caistor, Lincolnshire: A Church, Doctors and Solicitors, Mills and an Inn* (Heighington: Tucann Books, 2007).
Saunders, David, *Caistor Market Place* (Heighington: Tucann Books, 2012).
Sked, Susan, 'Women teachers and the expansion of girls' schooling in England, c. 1760–1820', in *Gender in Eighteenth-Century England: Roles, Representations and Responsibilities*, ed. by Hannah Barker and Elaine Chalus (London: Longman, 1997), pp. 101–25.
St Clair, William, *The Reading Nation in the Romantic Period* (Cambridge: Cambridge University Press, 2004).
Sturman, Christopher, and Valerie Purton, *Poems by Two Brothers: The Lives, Work and Influence of George Clayton Tennyson and Charles Tennyson d'Eyncourt* (Stamford: Watkins, 1993).
Styles, John, and Amanda Vickery, eds, *Gender, Taste, and Material Culture in Britain and North America 1700–1832* (New Haven, CT: Yale University Press, 2006).
Tateson, Tom, *The Tatesons of Market Rasen & Reasby Hall Farm: A 19th Century Family History* (Sheffield: Maud & Tom Tateson, 1996).
Tennyson, Charles, *Alfred Tennyson* (London: Macmillan, 1950).
Tennyson, Charles, and Hope Dyson, *The Tennysons: Background to Genius* (London: Macmillan, 1974).
Terhune, Alfred McKinley, and Annabelle Burdick Terhune, eds, *The Letters of Edward FitzGerald*, 4 vols (Princeton, NJ: Princeton University Press, 1980).

Thorn, Michael, *Tennyson*, 2nd edn (London: Abacus, 1993).
Thwaite, Ann, *Emily Tennyson: The Poet's Wife* (London: Faber & Faber, 1996).
Uglow, Jenny, *In These Times: Living in Britain through Napoleon's Wars, 1793–1815* (London: Faber & Faber, 2014).
Vickery, Amanda, *The Gentleman's Daughter: Women's Lives in Georgian England* (New Haven, CT: Yale Nota Bene, 2003).
Vickery, Amanda, *Behind Closed Doors: At Home in Georgian England* (New Haven, CT: Yale University Press, 2009).
Vogler, Pen, *Scoff: A History of Food and Class in Britain* (London: Atlantic, 2020).
Watt, Ian, *The Rise of the Novel* (Harmondsworth: Penguin, 1970).
Waddington, Patrick, *Tennyson and Russia*, Tennyson Society Occasional Paper Series, 11 (Lincoln: Tennyson Society, 1987).
Whalley, Joyce Irene, *Writing Implements and Accessories: From the Roman Stylus to the Typewriter* (London: David & Charles, 1975).
Wheeler, Michael, *Heaven, Hell, & the Victorians* (Cambridge: Cambridge University Press, 1994).
Willett, Jo, *The Pioneering Life of Mary Wortley Montagu* (Barnsley: Pen & Sword, 2021).
Wilson, Bee, *Swindled: From Poison Sweets to Counterfeit Coffee: The Dark History of the Food Cheats* (London: Murray, 2008).
Wilson, C. Anne, *Food and Drink in Britain: From the Stone Age to Recent Times*, 3rd edn (Harmondsworth: Penguin, 1984).
Wolffe, John, ed., *Religion in History: Conflict, Conversion and Coexistence* (Manchester: Open University, 2004).
Worsley, Lucy, *If Walls Could Talk* (London: Faber & Faber, 2011).

Websites

https://www.ancient.eu/babylon
www.arthurlloyd.co.uk/FindAnyDate.htm
https://www.babycentre.co.uk/a558193/toddler-sleep-concerns-teething
https://www.bankofengland.co.uk/monetary-policy/inflation/inflation-calculator
http://www.bbc.co.uk/history
http://bookhistory.blogspot.com
http://www.brancepeth-parish-council.org.uk/html/history_group.html
https://www.britannica.com
https://www.broughttolife.sciencemuseum.org.uk
https://www.cheltenham.gov.uk
www.clementisociety.com
https://discovery.nationalarchives.gov.uk
http://www.drakesfamily.org

https://www.durhamcountyrecordoffice.org.uk
https://www.18thcenturycommon.org/english-pleasure-gardens
https://www.epilepsy.com
https://www.findmypast.co.uk
https://www.ft.com
https://www.geni.com/people/William-Henry-Scott-Bentinck-Marquis-of-Titchfield
https://www.geriwalton.com
https://glowm.com/section-view/heading/history-of-contraception
https://www.google.co.uk/maps
https://www.gov.uk/general-register-office
https://www.hardysociety.org
https://www.healthline.com
https://hist259.web/unc.edu/marriedwomenspropertyact
https://www.historic-uk.com/History/UK/HistoryofEngland
https://www.history.ac.uk/publications/office/ordnance
https://www.historyireland.com
https://www.historyofparliamentonline.org
https://historyofwomen.org/marriage.html
https://houseofnames.com
https://issuu.com/zerosixdesign/docs/deeping
http://www.italianversereading.ac.uk/liberata/translation/htm
http://www.kyrackramer.com
https://www.learnreligions.com/history-of-babylon
https://www.lincstothepast.com
https://www.livescience.com
https://www.marxists.org/history/france/1802-1838.htm
https://maurerfoundation.org
https://members.pcug.org.au
https://www.merriam-webster.com/dictionary
https://www.memorialhall.mass.edu/activities/dressupo/notflash/1770_girl.html
https://www.mentalfloss.com/article/73575/15-facts-about-year-without-summer
https://www.my.heritage.com
https://www.nationalarchives.gov.uk/currency
https://www.nationalgallery.org.uk/about-us/history/collectors-and-benefactors/john-julius-angerstein
https://www.ncbi.nlm.nih.gov
https://www.news-medical.net
https://www.nhs.uk
https://www.oed.com
https://www.onwar.com/data/francespain1823html
https://www.parksandgardens.org
https://www.poetryfoundation.org/poems/43825/darkness-56d222aeeee1b

https://prezi.com/v2cx1naharo8/gender-roles-in-the-1800s
https://www.royalmailgroup.com
sahistory.org.za/people/sara-saartjie-baartman
https://www.sciencehistory.org/distillations/let-it-bleed
https://www.sellingantiques.co.uk/antique-boxes/antique-snuff-boxes
https://www.stpetersyork.org.uk
http://theclergydatabase.org.uk
https://www.theguardian.com/society/2021/mar/28/how-mary-wortley/montagus/
    bold-experiment-led-to-smallpox-vaccine-75-years-before-jenner
https://www.thornber.net/medicine/html/medgloss.html
https://www.tregeaglefineart.com/en-GB/historical-items/sarah-siddons-as-euphra
    sia-in-the-grecian-daughter
https://wellcomelibrary.org
https://www.westminster-abbey.org/abbey-commemorations/royals/william-iv
https://www.whalefacts.org/spermaceti
https://winemakermag.com/wine-wizard
https://www.worthpoint.com/worthopedia/antique-1800s-handwritten-doctor

Index

Alexander I, Czar of Russia 115
Alington family 61, 126
All Saints church, Tealby 70, 167, 185
Amcotts, Sir Wharton 51
Amcotts-Ingilby, Sir William 73 n.42
Angerstein, John Julius 124
   Anglicanism 5, 171, 188
Apology for the Life of G.A.B., Late of Covent Garden Theatre, An (Bellamy) 36–7
apothecaries 59, 103 n.6
Atkinson, Rev. 71
Austen, Jane 92
   Mansfield Park (1814) 172
   Sense and Sensibility 92

Baartman, Sara (Saartjie, 'Hottentot Venus') 92–3
Bag Enderby 89, 115, 182
Banks, Sir Joseph 50
Barton, Dr Zephaniah 61, 62, 64, 67, 68, 69, 70, 120–1, 126, 127, 151, 152, 155, 158, 187
Barton on Humber 51
Bath 39, 178, 180–2
Bayons Manor 8, 40, 51, 52, 58, 70, 84, 118, 135, 146, 165, 166–7, 182
Beacons Manor, *see* Bayons Manor
Beaufort, Duke of 59
Bellamy George Anne 36–8, 46 n.39
Benniworth 115
Bergen, Battle of 40, 46 n.49
Bickerstaff, Robert 50
Birchall, Robert 146
Blechingley 133, 135, 166
Boswell's Court 123, 140
Boucherett, Ayscoghe 23, 50, 61, 70
Bourne, John 5, 6, 8, 93, 185, 194, 199, 200, 201, 202, 206 n.65
Bourne, Mary, *see also* Tennyson 1, 2, 5–6, 8, 9, 13, 24, 27, 28, 38, 39, 41, 42–43, 48, 55, 69, 93, 113, 120, 123, 171–206, 208
Bourne, Mary (daughter of John Bourne) 185
Bourne, Mary Mather (first wife of John Bourne) 185, 206 n.67
Bourne, Mrs George 199
Bourne, Titus 191
Bousfield, Dr 120–1, 122, 198
Brackenbury, Major 199
Brancepeth Castle 4, 84, 87, 91, 94, 95
Brigg 114
Brighton 103, 193
Bristol 59
Brocklesby 156
Bromhead, Edward 179
Brown, Frances 85
Burney, Fanny 33
Burton, Mr 84, 108 n.15
Burton, Robert 85, 94, 179
Byron, Lord 30, 94

Caenby Hall 2, 7, 124, 147, 148, 157
Caistor 2, 5, 13, 14, 16, 26, 32–3, 39, 41, 47, 53, 54, 55, 77, 88, 172, 178, 179, 180
Caldecot, Mr 135
Calvinism 171, 193, 202, 203 n.3, 205 n.45, 208
Cambridge University St John's College 39, 41, 86, 87, 114, 123, 140, 179
   Trinity college 1
Caroline, Queen 66
Cecil, Lord Thomas 199
Cecilia: or Memoirs of an Heiress (Burney) 33
Chambers, Rev. 62
Chaplin, Charles 124
Charlotte, Queen 118
Cheltenham 5, 59, 97, 106, 118, 130, 163, 165

childbirth 18, 19, 20, 24, 27, 35, 76, 79–80, 148, 150, 161, 163
children 1, 21, 28, 29–30, 174
Cholmely Sir Montague 157
Clarke, Mr A. 70
Clayton, Christopher 40, 52, 86
Clayton House, Grimsby 38, 40, 179
Cleethorpes 186, 195, 196, 201, 206 n.65
Cole, Miss 201
Coltman, Miss 17
Cooper, Sarah 104, 186–9, 190, 192
Cooper, William 104, 159, 192
Court of Chancery, see Russell v. Russell
Cox. Mr 86
Cropper, Mr 16
Cropper, Mrs 20
Cuxwold 47

Dalby 5, 6, 23, 185, 188, 192, 195, 202
Dalton, Henry 142
Dame Betsy Dales's school, Beverley 50
Davis, Ellen 18, 26
Dealtry, George 142–4
Defoe, Daniel 33
Deloraine Court, Lincoln 3, 39, 51, 84
Drewery and Brookes 33
Drummond, Sir Gordon 11 n.20, 101
Duncombe, William 129
Durham 88, 179

Emily Tennyson: The Poet's Wife (Thwaite) 1
enclosure acts 51
Evans, Roger 10 n.7

Ferdinand VII, King of Spain 99
FitzGerald, Edward 24
France 99, 100
Frankish, Mrs 153
Fytche, Elizabeth ('Eliza' *see* Tennyson)
Fytche, Mary Anne (sister of Eliza) 121, 182

Gainsborough 6, 139, 147
Gate Burton 139, 146
George III 59, 60, 92, 96, 97, 118, 129
George IV 50, 66
    Prince Regent 92
Gibney, Dr 67
Gooch, Dr Richard 163

Goodman 16, 20
Gray, William 16, 44 n.7, 50, 65, 71, 84, 93
Grey, Thomas Robinson 101
Grimsby 3, 8, 40, 52, 58, 84, 86, 114, 115, 123, 162
Grimsby Haven Company 52

Hallam, Arthur 1, 171, 191–2, 200, 207
Hardwick Hall 4, 53, 55, 59, 84, 87, 89, 109 n.20, 127, 184–5
Hardwicke's Marriage Act 1753 85
Hardy, William 51
Harrison, Dr 50, 124
Harrogate 59, 66, 94, 179, 200
Hastings 196
health 21, 25–6, 27, 31, 32, 35, 41, 49, 50, 53, 54, 57, 62, 64, 65, 67, 77–8, 80, 117, 123, 134, 155, 164, 172, 187, 200
Heneage, Mr 70, 117
Heneage, Mrs 182
Heaslop, Mrs 96
Hinde, Clara (*née* Tennyson d'Eyncourt) 133, 135, 151, 154
Hinde family 80
Hugh (foster child) 6, 186–90
Hutton, Frances Mary, *see* Tennyson d'Eyncourt, Frances Mary
Hutton, Rev. George 140, 148–9
Hutton, Rev. John 6, 139, 140, 150
Hutton, Mary 149–50, 159
Hutton, Mary (*née* Stones, mother of Frances) 6, 7, 126, 139, 140, 142, 148, 153, 157, 159
Hutton, Thomas 139
Hutton, William 140

Ingilby, Lady 71
Inman, Rev. George 64
Iveson, William 50

Jackson's of Louth 33
Jenner, Edward 32
Johnson, Mary 18, 22, 27
Johnson, Mr 17, 32
Jowett, Benjamin 1, 10, n.2

Kennilworth 181, 193
Kirby, Miss 133

Lackington, James 33
Lambeth 166
Langworth 134
Lawrence, Sir Thomas 57, 59
Leamington 103, 193
Lincoln School 123
Lincolnshire Archives 7, 122, 147, 157
Lincolnshire Wolds 13, 47
London 17, 38, 50, 52, 92, 126, 128, 157, 159–60
Louis XVIII 99
Louis Napoleon 100
Louth 89, 126, 182
Louth Grammar School 86, 123
Ludborough 47

Mablethorpe 77, 115
Main Family 61
Market Rasen 2, 5, 14, 16, 23, 26, 28, 48, 50, 51, 175, 178
Methodism 16, 44 n.7
Middle Rasen 24
militia 40, 46 n.48, 51, 84, 86, 124, 142
Monck, Sir Charles 147
money 127, 143, 165, 187, 189, 196
Montagu, Lady Mary Wortley 32
Morton Hall 6, 140, 147, 152
Mourning customs 89, 97

Napoleonic Wars 59
Neve, Miss 48
Nonconformism 5, 171, 188, 193, 208

Palmer, John Hinde 135
Parks, Suzan-Lori 93
Paterson, John 95
Peacock, Dr 158–9
Perceval, Spencer 92, 93, 109 n.35
Phillips, Catherine Payton 37, 46 n.40
Poor Laws 51
portraits 43, 183
Potter, Sir Brownlow 51
Prisoner of Chillon, The (Byron) 30
Purton, Valerie 203 n.4, 206 n.71

Raines, Ann 17, 50, 53, 54, 147, 148
Raines, Elizabeth 17, 53, 64
Raines, William 17, 53
Rewcastle, Miss 23
Robinson, A. R. 61, 81–3, 126

Robinson, John 39, 114, 178
Roxana (Defoe) 33
Russell, Anne 87, 94–5
Russell, Elizabeth, *see also* Tennyson 1, 2, 3–5, 9, 13, 19–20, 25, 39, 40, 48, 49, 52, 53, 75–111, 127, 130, 163, 178, 179, 184, 185
Russell, Emma Maria 4, 91, 99, 134, 184, 196, 205 n.51
Russell, John, RA 43, 46 n.50
Russell, Mary 87
Russell, Matthew 3, 4, 11 n.20, 40, 75, 86, 90, 92–3, 95, 96, 97–8, 109 n.33, 110 n. 50, 127, 185
Russell v. Russell 11 n.20, 101–2, 110 nn.53, 54, 55
Russell, William 3, 4, 40, 75, 85–6, 87, 99, 179, 185
Russell, William (father of Matthew) 84, 87, 93–4, 106

St Mary Magdalene Church, Lincoln 40, 85
St Michael's church, York 86
St Peter's School, York 38, 39, 79, 108 n.10, 114, 123
Saltfleet 77
Scarborough 59
Scott, Mrs 21
Siddons, Sarah 38, 46 n.44
Simkiss, Mr 70
Skeffling 64
Skegness 198, 201
Sleaford 126
Smith, Sydney 181, 204 n.16
Somersby 6, 89, 115, 118, 180, 184
Somerscales, Mrs 32
South Willingham 115
Spain 99
Spital in the Street 125
Stainton le Vale, Lincolnshire 124
Stainton, Mr 187, 202
Stamford 124, 166, 199
Sterne, Laurence 37
   Sentimental Journey, A 30–1
   Tristram Shandy 31
Stoke Park, Bristol 59
Stones, Francis 139–40
Stones, Mary, *see* Hutton
Stovin, Thomas 13, 177

Swallow 47
Swan, Miss 58

Tasso, Torquato 95, 103, 110 nn.43, 58
Tealby 41, 51, 61, 93, 122, 124, 147, 191, 200
Tealby Lodge, *see* Bayons Manor
Tennyson, Alfred 1, 4, 7, 8, 13, 24, 47, 70–1, 89, 104, 118, 122, 128, 152, 153, 167, 172, 184, 195, 198, 207
  Works:
  'Adeline' 191
  'And ask ye why these sad tears stream?' 3, 4, 13, 43, 106, 108
  In Memoriam AHH 1, 207, 208
  'Margaret' 191
  Maud 8, 106
  'National Songs for Englishmen' 100
  Poems (1842) 1
  Poems by Two Brothers 4, 43, 106
  St Simeon Stylites 183
  Timbuctoo 37
  Ulysses 1, 43, 208
Tennyson, Ann, *see* Raines, Ann
Tennyson, Cecilia 201
Tennyson, Charles, later d'Eyncourt 3, 4, 7–8, 35, 39, 40, 42, 48, 69, 70, 75, 78, 86, 87, 95, 96, 99, 100, 113, 118, 121, 123–33, 135, 136, 140–7, 156, 161, 164, 167, 168 n.13, 185, 193, 197, 199, 200, 205 n.53, 206 n.64, 207, 208
Tennyson, Sir Charles (grandson of Alfred) 7, 139, 167
Tennyson, Clara, later d'Eyncourt, *see* Hinde
Tennyson, Edwin, later Tennyson d'Eyncourt 131, 134, 153, 155, 163, 165
Tennyson, Elizabeth ('Eliza' *née* Fytche) 1, 2, 89, 115, 126, 182, 183, 184
Tennyson, Elizabeth *née* Clayton 76
Tennyson, Elizabeth, *see also* Russell 38, 75–111, 175–6
Tennyson, Ellen Elizabeth, later d'Eyncourt 162
Tennyson, Emily 200–1
Tennyson, Emily (*née* Sellwood) 104
Tennyson, Eustace Alexander, later d'Eyncourt 127, 160, 166

Tennyson, Frances Mary, later d'Eyncourt (*née* Hutton) 6, 7–8, 57, 89, 90, 123, 127, 128, 132, 139–69, 186, 207, 208
Tennyson, Frederick 7, 71, 89, 118, 128, 152, 153, 184, 191, 199, 200
Tennyson, George 2, 13, 14, 17, 18, 29, 38–9, 40, 43, 47–53, 63–4, 65, 67, 68, 71, 98, 135, 141–3, 176–7, 184, 195–60, 201
Tennyson, George Clayton 2, 3, 4, 5, 26, 27, 28, 30, 38, 41, 89, 48, 77, 79, 86, 88, 113–18, 120, 122, 123, 128, 130, 140, 152, 165, 167, 173, 175, 179, 182, 183, 184, 186, 187, 197, 198, 207, 208
Tennyson, George Hildyard, later d'Eyncourt 6, 7, 57, 90, 119, 123, 125–6, 128, 130, 131, 132, 148, 150–1, 155, 157, 160, 163–4, 165, 191, 197–8, 199, 200
Tennyson, Hallam 203
Tennyson, Julia Frances, later d'Eyncourt 131, 133, 149, 156, 161, 164, 165
Tennyson, Louis Charles, later d'Eyncourt 7, 125, 134, 157, 165, 166
Tennyson, Mary, *see also* Bourne 5, 23, 79, 172–5
Tennyson, Mary 116
Tennyson, Mary Turner 1, 2–3, 4, 7, 8, 10, 13–43, 47–73, 77, 78, 96, 103, 104, 105, 113, 123–4, 130–5, 140, 148, 153, 165, 172, 174, 175, 207, 194, 208
Tennyson, Michael (father of George Tennyson) 25, 39, 50, 86, 173
Tennyson Research Centre, Lincoln 122
Tennyson, William Henry 95, 103, 162
Tennyson, William 51
Thornhill, Mary 161
Thorold, Rev. Henry 14, 47
Thwaite, Ann 1
Titchfield, Lord 103, 131, 132
Turner, Charles Tennyson 37, 204 n.23, 208
Turner, Barbara, (*née* Bullock) 90, 95, 100, 190, 192
Turner, John (brother of Mary Turner Tennyson) 14, 47, 49, 85–6, 152–3

Turner, John (father of Mary Turner
    Tennyson) 14, 25, 28, 31, 34, 47,
    76, 175
Turner, Mary 2, 3–4, 5, 13, 25, 34, 35–6,
    37–8, 41, 42, 47, 52, 53, 54, 55, 88,
    113, 172, 175, 179–80, 207
Turner, Samuel 14, 17, 19, 37, 47, 53–4, 62,
    69, 76, 90, 190, 192, 194

Uglow, Jenny 46 n.48, 185
Usselby 70, 71

Vane, John Henry 70
Venus (Suzan-Lori Parks) 92
*Verses Addressed to a Lady on Her
    Departure* (Tennyson, G. C.) 4, 88

Walker, Dr 18, 25
Walker, Mrs 18
Weston, Mrs 23
Wetherby 66
Wheeley Mrs (schoolteacher, Lincoln) 14,
    44 n.44
Will's Coffee House, London 33, 53
Windsor 59
Worthing 165, 191
Wragby 134

Yarborough Lord 156
Yorick's Sentimental Journey Continued 31
York 65, 86
Yorke, Mrs 64, 155
Young, Rev. J. C. 70

www.ingramcontent.com/pod-product-compliance
Lightning Source LLC
Chambersburg PA
CBHW071832300426
44116CB00009B/1514